Expert Bytes

Expert Bytes

Computer Expertise in Forensic Documents

Players, Needs, Resources, and Pitfalls

Vlad Atanasiu

CRC Press
Taylor & Francis Group
Boca Raton   London   New York

CRC Press is an imprint of the
Taylor & Francis Group, an **informa** business

CRC Press
Taylor & Francis Group
6000 Broken Sound Parkway NW, Suite 300
Boca Raton, FL 33487-2742

Printed on acid-free paper
Version Date: 20130808

International Standard Book Number-13: 978-1-4665-9190-5 (Hardback)

Library of Congress Cataloging-in-Publication Data

Atanasiu, Vlad.
   Expert bytes : computer expertise in forensic documents / Vlad Atanasiu.
     pages cm
   Includes bibliographical references and index.
   ISBN 978-1-4665-9190-5 (hardback)
   1. Legal documents--Identification. 2. Evidence, Documentary. 3. Electronic evidence. 4. Forensic sciences. 5. Computer science. I. Title.

   HV8074.A83 2013
   363.25'650285--dc23   2013019918

Visit the Taylor & Francis Web site at
http://www.taylorandfrancis.com

and the CRC Press Web site at
http://www.crcpress.com

Contents

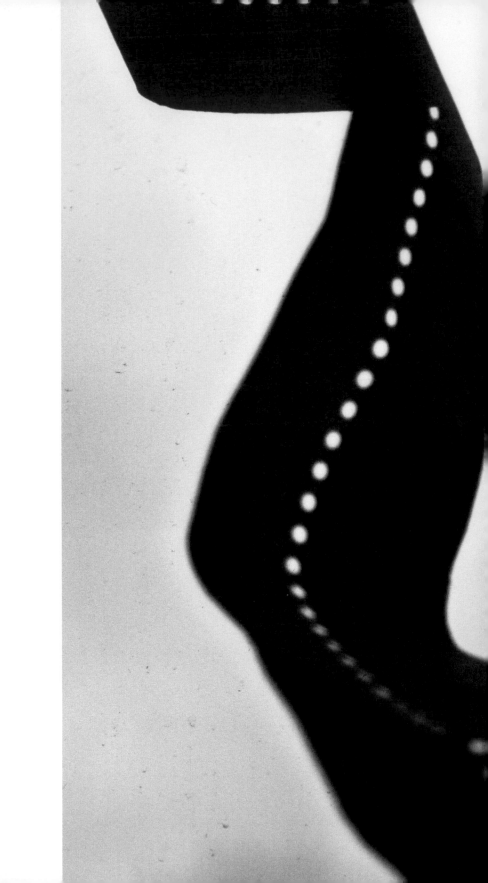

During a radio interview in 1955, Dr Edmond Locard (1877–1966), French pioneer of forensic science and adamant believer in the power of handwriting expertise, lamented in the following terms the pitiable state of the profession, yearning for better days:

"The handwriting expert has been for too long the buffoon in the criminal court!"[1]

More than half a century later, the forensic document examiner equating software for analyzing forensic documents to a hobo's Mulligan stew is not the only voice making a fool out of computational FD,[2] which to the present found indeed very little practical application. There is thus a danger to replace one buffoon with another, bats in the belfry with Golems in the machine.

Yet can we human fools build machines wiser than ourselves? Just how?

1—Locard 1955: 02:38.   **2**—Matley 2008: 6.

Acknowledgments

To the readers of this book, by whom it exists — may it serve them well.

Special thanks to Frank Lebourgeois for impromptu generosity, Wil Fagel for terminological musings, Katrin Franke for talks over meals, Maria Gurrado for proposals to work for free, Elisa van den Heuvel for adventures with the Romans, Marcus Liwicki the scientist-acrobat, the kind suppliers of evaluation software or relevant information: Axel Brink, Marius Bulacu, Tomasz Dziedzic, Angelo Marcelli, Lambert Schomaker; to Rolf Ingold for making extracurricular publications possible, and Denis Lalanne, my independently minded guinea-pig. • To the CRC Press team for the pleasure to work with Becky Masterman and subject her to my typographical fantasies, to Linda Leggio for life after deadlines, to Jonathan Pennell for taking care of bleeding edges, to the anonymous reviewers and copy-editors for a felicitous reading, to David Fausel for everything else. • This research was partially supported by the Laboratoire d'Informatique en Image et Systèmes d'Information, Institut National des Sciences Appliquées, Lyon, France.

Paris, France / Fribourg, Switzerland

Vlad Atanasiu

"COMMON SENSE," that is how Locard, an admirer of Scotland Yard, qualified in a Holmesain manner ("Elementary, my dear Watson!") parts of handwriting expertise.[1] That is also how the profession is usually portrayed in movies: visual inspection—sometimes assisted by the detective's hallmark, the magnifying glass—is sufficient to sartorial gentlemen for recognizing forged documents. Here, in *Charlie Chan in Paris* (1935), the famous Hawaiian detective consults with French bankers over fake bonds.

Today the deceptively simple task of computational recognition and analysis of handwriting is still not solved and it is even not a science-fiction priority. Indeed, some iconic cinema scenes come close to it, being related to pattern analysis (the computer HAL lipreading in *2001: A Space Odyssey* [1968][2]), document visualization (the gestural interface of *Minority Report* [2002]), or computer graphics (a world of character streams in *The Matrix* [1999]). But computers or robots used for document expertise—or forgery for that matter—are filmographic *terra incognita*.

The history of cinema has paralleled in time those of modern forensics and computing and as a major media it is a privileged window into their popular image and envisioned future. The movie frames and quotes acting as cinematic intermezzi in this book are intended as an exploration of some of these aspects.

1—Locard 1955: 02:20, 03:12.   **2**—See p. 51.

Perspective

ACT ONE

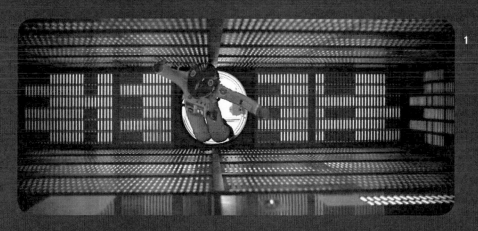

1

[Phone rings 16 times before it is picked up.]

— Hello, IT.
— ...
— Have you tried to turn it off and on again?
— ...
— OK. Well, the button on the side, is it glowing?
— ...
— Yeah, you need to turn it on!
— ...
— The button turns it on?
— ...
— Yeah... You... Yeah...
— ...
— You know how a button works, do you?!

— Hello, IT.
— ...
— Ya-ha...
— ...
— Have you tried forcing an unexpected reboot?
— ...
— See, the driver hooks a function by patching the system call table. So it's not safe to unload it, unless another thread's about to jump in there and do its stuff. ... And you don't want to end up in the middle of invalid memory. ... Hello?

A CURIOUS RELATIONSHIP

Computers fascinate by their information processing capabilities. They can also be very aesthetic artifacts, as perceptible from the astronaut floating inside the memory and logical circuitry of HAL in *2001: A Space Odyssey* (1968) [1], a movie not less memorable for the operatic appeal of spaceships waltzing above earth to the tune of Johann Strauss' *Blue Danube*. The new digital horizons opened by technology are awe inspiring, a sentiment that could be expressed in the words of the astronaut approaching the alien monolith in orbit around Jupiter in *2010: The Year We Make Contact* (1984): "My God, it's full of stars!"

On the reverse side, computers are extremely vexing creatures. With slapstick British humor, *The IT Crowd: Yesterday's Jam* (2006) [2] lays bare the strained relationship between computer experts and users, each—slave to the machine—trying to vent their frustration on one another and earn some social recognition: management relegating the information technology (IT) department to the building's basement and IT delivering offendingly stupid advice or cryptic geek lingo over the hotline.

Book framework

Purpose — The purpose of this book is to introduce computer scientists and forensic document examiners (FDEs) to the computer expertise of forensic documents (FD) and assist them with the design of research projects in this interdisciplinary field. It unveils the sociotechnological landscape were the scientist will evolve: players, needs, resources, pitfalls. It is not a step-by-step recipe on how to examine documents or write expertise software, nor does it teach how to become a good project manager—other books exist for those endeavors. While maintaining a global view on FD, the focus is on a specific topic, writing in all its forms (handwriting, signature, printing, and so forth), where visuality plays a greater role than it has for the expertise of implements (pen, ink, paper). On the computing side the book is rooted in the field of document image analysis.

Readership — It is assumed that the reader has little or no previous exposure to FD. While primarily addressing academic and commercial sector researchers, computing graduate and post-graduate students, the publication is equally useful to forensic practitioners to know what to ask and to expect from computer scientists. Incidentally it is also profitable to paleographers, whose field, close to FD, exhibits similarities in its relationship with computing.[1] Project managers and policy-makers in information technology and forensics will benefit from the description of the sociological landscape shaping the technologies whose birth they are mandated to facilitate. The book can also be seen—by those with such interests—as a snapshot in the history and sociology of science and technology.

Focus — The book is best described as a travel guide to a cultural encounter between scientists. It combines features of a survey, a resource list, an evaluation report, a research agenda, management counsel, a sociological study, and a historical inquiry. The approach is cross-disciplinary and espouses the cultural perspective of computer scientists and FDEs. Currently there is no such publication on the market and this one grew out of the perception that at the present time better mutual understanding between computing and forensics is a key to furthering computational forensics.

This work is a bridge—it does not attempt to explain expertise to FDEs, nor computation to computer scientists, but instigate collaboration. From coordinating and observing projects where technical and nontechnical

---

1—Atanasiu 2011c.

partners interact the author concludes that such mediation can help identify and avoid relational obstacles between professions. This cross-disciplinary exercise sets the book apart from field-specific surveys. It also deliberately indulges in what might be resented as digressions to discuss other aspects than algorithms and software. It shines light on historical, educational, institutional, and other factors shaping the FD computing research, realities that the purely technical literature does not prepare engineers to face (this is the stuff of classes in the sociology of science and technology, and personal mentoring).

Structure — The book is structured as a metaphor of a physical interaction. Once its particular perspective is exposed in this chapter, the inner workings of the object under consideration—FD—are examined in Chapter 2, from its wider context and goals, to the people involved, and their working conditions. What computer scientists can do with FD is suggested in the research agenda outlined in Chapter 3: there are numerous pressing or fancy topics to choose from. How these objectives can be attained rests on the tools at our disposal listed in Chapter 4: datasets, descriptors, methods, software, and hardware. Bearing further on the outcome is the context—expectations should be cast in full knowledge of the expertise performance and the various pitfalls other than technical as exposed in Chapters 5 and 6. The scientist will also need a social map to the world of FD, a gentleman's reading list, and some hard numbers to remember, to be found in the annexes and references. An epitaph on the rationale for computerizing FD concludes the book in Chapter 7.

Related literature — In FD, concise or in-depth surveys of the field exist in the form of encyclopedia entries or handbooks.[1] In computing, there are introductions and surveys on the nature and purpose of computational forensics,[2] computational FD handwriting expertise,[3] handwriting analysis software,[4] writer identification methods,[5] signature processing,[6] and electronic handwriting and signature.[7] Issues of FD quality and policy are treated in the law literature[8] and governmental documents,[9] and management aspects specific to interdisciplinary and international forensic projects have recently been addressed by the law enforcement community.[10]

Credentials — Not unlike an anthropologist, the particular vantage point in observing the phenomena described here is that of a "participating outsider." I am not an FDE: I am a PhD paleographer, art historian, linguist, and Middle East specialist, having collaborated with FDEs on FD projects. I am not a formal computer scientist either—I only recently reenrolled in

---

1—E.g., Huber and Headrick 1999, Found 2009.   **2**—Franke and Srihari 2008.   **3**—Schomaker 2007.   **4**—Srihari 2003.   **5**—Bulacu and Schomaker 2007, Plamondon 1989.   **6**—FD: Liwicki et al. 2012; biometrics: Fiérrez and Ortega-Garcia 2007 [overview, history], Impedovo and Pirlo 2008 [survey], Li and Jain 2009: entries on signature [encyclopedic].   **7**—Harralson 2013.   **8**—E.g., Saks and Faigman 2008.   **9**—E.g., NAS 2009.   **10**—Fleming 2010, Kelty and Julian 2011. See further Kerzner 2009 [4.4 pounds of wisdom on project management], Mendes 2008 [mathematical approaches to cost estimation], and DeMarco 1997 [a humorous perspective, for distressing days].

an academic computer science program, after years of employment in the computing field—and I am certainly not a law scholar—but I enjoy their baroque writing style. However, my desire kindled by coordinating international technology projects to understand why they succeed or fail, and my multidisciplinary interests, provided the necessary motivation and distinctive yet necessary approach to write this book. The opportunity was provided by the request of an academic computing laboratory that wanted to enter the FD market and was seeking a person with project management experience in both computing and forensics.[1]

References — Some of the bibliographical references mentioned here are the only ones pertaining to the topic; others are important contributions. Sometimes an "obscure" Web page was more informative than printed books, and more often than not bits of information had to be collated from various sources, including personal interviews. Many fascinating topics could only be alluded to, or, perhaps, unduly given extended space. The provided references should be understood as pointers toward the wider literature.

Bias — Publications in English and material relative to the United States are heavily relied upon, for various subjective and objective reasons: language barriers; time limitations; American scientific dominance, open discussion culture, and greater use of the Internet, among other. The resulting filtered picture undoubtedly will thus contrast with the actual FD practice in laboratories and courts, variable across and within countries, and sometimes inside the same institution.[2] The strains of the international history of human and computational FD are also intricate: the United States adopts European software (FISH[3]), while the world is influenced by American justice rulings and scientific policies (*Daubert* and the National Academy of Sciences report[4]).

Typologies — The typologies presented in this book are neither the only possible ones, nor could they be exhaustive. The names of classes ("hyperonyms" in lexicology) are one of the problems encountered in building typologies, since their choice is often not obvious and many times such words are nonexistent in one or another language. The intended role of the typologies and terminology is to present a broad spectrum of entities, both common and exotic, and contribute to a shared vocabulary and systematic organization.

Symbols — FD stands for both the professional field and the physical objects under examination; "$" denotes US dollars; monetary values are not adjusted for inflation.

1—Among others, Bernstein [Bernstein 2012] and Nexus [see p. 26].   **2**—Anonymous 2002, Bernstein and Jackson 2004, Champod et al. 2004: 28, Lucena-Molina et al. 2012: 2b, NAS 2009: 6.   **3**—See p. 123.   **4**—See p. 69.

— In Switzerland checks are not accepted—you pay cash!

Object

1

— [Welles] What's new are the experts.
— [Irving] The experts.
— [Elmyr] The so-called experts.
— [Welles] Experts are the new oracles.
— [Elmyr] Who are greatly pretentious.
— [Welles] They speak to us with the
absolute authority of the computer.
— [Elmyr] Pretend to know something,
what they only know very superficially.
— [Welles] And we bow down before
them. They're God's own gift to the faker.
— [Irving] All the world loves to see the
experts and the establishment made a fool of.

— What does that say?
— Can't you read that?
— I can't read this. What's this? "Abt natural?"
— No. It's just "Please put $50,000 into this bag and act natural."
— Does it say "act natural"?
— Eh… Same, "Point a gun at you."
— That looks like "gub," not "gun."
— No, it's "gun."
— It's "gub." That's a "b."
— No. See, that's an "n." "Gun."
— George, would you step over here a moment please? What's this saying?
— "Please put $50,000 into this bag and abt natural." What's "abt"?
— It's "act."
— Does this look like "gub" or "gun"?
— "Gun," see? But what's "abt" mean?
— It's "act." You see? "Act natural." "Please put $50,000 into this bag. Act natural." It's not…
— Oh, I see, this is a holdup.

— [Centurion] What's this, then? "Romanes eunt domus"? "People called Romanes, they go the house"?
— [Brian] It says "Romans, go home."
— [Centurion] No, it doesn't. What's Latin for "Roman"? Come on!

4

— After a long study of this signature, it is my professional opinion that it is definitely in Jefferson Smith's own handwriting. ▼

— As an expert on handwriting, I'd say the name Jefferson Smith on this contract has been forged. ▼

— I would stake my whole twenty-year professional career on the fact that this is not a forgery, but is Mr Smith's own signature.

5

— In the whole appearance of the handwriting there is a hard to prove yet intensively palpable touch of madness.

6

— Even the paper sounds kosher.

EXORCISING THE EXPERTS

Instead of technology and logic (think *CSI* and Sherlock Holmes), the document expertise in cinema relies rather on the senses, all the more the objects are antique and exotic. The auscultation of page flipping of rare books, the caressing of their leather bindings, ink sniffing and ogling small discrepancies in typefaces, even smoking after a particularly intense authentication session, borders an erotic experience for the various art dealers, academics, collectors, and conservators in *The Ninth Gate* (1999) [6] — an FD version of the sensuality of calligraphic tattooing in *The Pillow Book* (1996). Here the expert plays the role of pathfinder, setting apart true and false in man's quest for knowledge in the long list of mystery plots revolving around books, from *The Name of the Rose* (1986) to *The Saragossa Manuscript* (1965). That sometimes the expertise succeeds only with supernatural intervention just brightens its aura.

To undo the morgue of the experts' establishment, so occultly acquired, filmmakers can counter dark magic with artistic wizardry or with laughter. Orson Welles' *F for Fake* (1974) [1] is a whirlwind sleight of hand, perceptually and conceptually, centered on high-quality forgery of paintings, biographies, and documents. An opinion on the ability of experts is provided before running cameras by the forgers themselves: Clifford and Edith Irving, at the origin of the autobiography hoax of the American millionaire, aviator, and filmmaker Howard Hughes, involving faked handwriting (a famous FD case of the 1970s); and Elmyr de Hory, producing Welles' signature on a freshly painted self-portrait of Michelangelo.

In *Take the Money and Run* (1969) [2] Woody Allen questions the very possibility of expertise. The escalating parody of an entire bank arguing about the content of a robbery note, oblivious of the actual robbery supposed to take place, is trumped by reality: unreadable handwriting did made some real robber leave the bank empty-handed after a frustrating attempt at written communication with the teller.[1] In a similar scene from *The Life of Brian* (1979) [3], lousy grammar is used this time to poke fun at policemen — and their "customers" — of all times: instead of arresting the Jew writing anti-Roman graffiti, the centurion scolds him for his bad Latin.

The fictional clash of FDEs in front of the US Senate in *Mr. Smith Goes to Washington* (1939) [4] reflects a closer reality, as reminds us the British FDE John Harrison: "the general and usually well-justified feeling has been that their [the experts'] findings are largely intuitive and that consequently there are often as many opinions as there are experts in the case." [2] It is precisely this hollow "intuition" and the grandiloquent apparatus with which the power of the state is exercised that Fritz Lang's *M* (1931) [5] is indicting as nothing else than institutionalized self-deception of an acquiescing people: not the measurements of the fingerprint expert, nor the speculative gibberish of the psycho-graphological profiler helping to apprehend the murderer, but the perspicacity of a blind beggar.

1—Johnson 2011.   2—Harrison 1966: 1.

Forensic document expertise

This chapter describes common scenarios in the work of forensic document examiners (FDEs), the objects they examine and the goals of the expertise. To calibrate their intended research projects it is important that computer scientists know and understand what the issues are that FDEs have to solve.

Ecosystem: The FD universe

A succinct definition of forensic science is "science used for the purpose of the law."[1] It implies that there are a multitude of nonforensic sciences involved in forensics, as well as there being scientific constructs proper to the forensic field. Forensic documents (FD), also known as questioned documents, is in turn the science of document examination as applied to legal cases. Etymologically "forensic" refers to the Roman-time *fora* where trials were conducted, and "forensics" being—depending on the usage—the act of presenting the evidence, shorthand for "forensic science," or—by suppressing the term "science"—avoidance of debates on the scientific quality of the field.[2]

One among many forensic areas, FD is divided into a number of specialties, and linked to numerous fields outside forensics, not unlike computer science.[3] Some of its branches deal with the material aspects of documents, the hardware, so to speak (instruments, ink, paper), and others with patterns (writing), behavioral traces of human activity characterized by great variability.[4] FD is closely related to biometrics and security documents, despite theoretical and institutional compartmentalization.[5] Among the forensic fields FD is the smallest entity,[6] which means on one hand that it has a sufficient individuality to maintain its independence, and on the other hand that it is of marginal importance, a trend accentuated by the advent of forensic DNA profiling in the 1980s and visible in the proportion of published FD articles.[7] As one FDE put it in his memoirs: "I belong to one of the smallest and least understood professions in the world."[8]

1—Commons 2011: 7, also OED 2012: "forensic."   2—Noctis 2010.   3—"An Ecosystem," p. 93; typology in NAS 2009: 3, 38, NIJ 2006: 10–11, Houck and Siegel 2010: 4–7.   4—Schomaker 2007: 247–249.   5—Dessimoz and Champod 2008, Houck and Siegel 2010: 477, Schomaker 2007. 6—"Basic forensic fields," p. 94.   7—Sauvageau et al. 2009: 44.   8—Doud 2010: xvii.

Inside FD proper, there is slightly more research activity around the material aspects of FD, than for patterns.[1] Overall, handwriting and paints analysis are by far the most important areas, yet the diversity of study topics is clearly visible. We see a predominance of hardware-based analysis for the material aspects and software-based for patterns; digital media analysis is a rising area, with a foothold in both FD and digital media forensics; computing resources are a fairly small portion of the issues debated, of steady interest in time; statistics has a rising trend; demographics is of little concern. The entry and exit of researchers and projects affect the fluctuation in time of various fields: handwriting software and statistics can be clearly traced to research groups at CEDAR (Buffalo, NY), George Mason University (Fairfax, VA), and École des sciences criminelles [School of forensic science] (Lausanne, Switzerland). Although the publications on which this analysis is based are just a fraction of the FD computing research—the majority of work being published in computing and mathematics publications—they are a good indicator of how many software prototypes evolved toward deployment in day-to-day forensic work.

Conspicuously absent from the conferences of the American Academy of Forensic Sciences (AAFS), a major venue for forensics, are other research groups active in computing, biomechanics, and neurocognitive aspects of handwriting (e.g., for identification the University of Groningen [Netherlands]; for biomechanical signal modeling and analysis the École Polytechnique [Montréal, Canada], the University of Arizona [Phoenix, AZ], and the Radboud University [Nijmegen, Netherlands]). For some of them, the International Graphonomics Society (IGS) conferences are the privileged meeting place, where FD and computing converge. Signature computing gyrates around the venues of the biometrics market, where their more substantial applications lie. Finally there is yet another area with fleeting presence at AAFS: security documents, which—heavily commercialized and relying on the precision equipment industry and on governmental procurement programs—evolves in the world of security conventions (such as the World Security Fair, where hundreds of companies show their products each year).

People: Who are the experts?

Before the Second World War FDEs were self-taught individuals involved professionally with handwriting on a daily basis, such as penmanship teachers, bank clerks, and typographers.[2] A few, like Edmond Locard or Archibald Reiss (1875–1929), were polymaths, criminologists officiating in all forensic areas.[3] Later, FDEs were undergoing apprenticeships in government

---

1—"Common Topics," p. 95.   2—A shuddering peroration on this state of affairs in early 20th century France in Guiral 1927: 83–90.   3—Locard was also something of a "gentleman criminologist," true mirror of "gentleman burglars" like Arsène Lupin: a man of independent means, he never received a salary for his forty years of service to the French police, in his own words "nothing being of greater value to me as my liberty." [Locard 1957: 27–28, Mazéret 2006: 85]

forensic laboratories or with established private experts, and since more recently they can take FD specialization courses as part of academic forensic science degrees.[1] Today the duration is two or three years and certifications are issued by professional organizations and universities;[2] laboratories are encouraged to obtain accreditations.[3] The issue of a solid scientific and standardized curriculum has still to be solved.[4] For examples see Fact sheet "Example curricula."[5]

Gender gap — Notice has to be taken about the gender demographics within the profession.[6] FD is currently male dominated and thus contrasts with the overall situation in forensics, where female overrepresentation makes it one of the most popular disciplines among women. The situation is mirrored in the abysmal participation levels of women in computer science compared to that of science and engineering in general, which lately achieved parity. These gender gaps exist both during the educational stage for students and in the professional life. With the present disaffection for scientific careers the trend is likely to deepen. While gender disparity does affect the kind of technologies being produced, what, if any, impact the paradoxical demographics of FD and computing has, is unknown.[7]

In practice collaborative projects are likely to encounter a much greater variety of gender distributions than suggested by the abstracted mean values mentioned above, due to the high variability of demographics across cohorts. Organizational, economical, and political circumstances can drastically and abruptly affect the number of FDEs in laboratories, both public and private. Also, among the computer science students participating in FD projects, percentages of women are different at master and doctorate levels. More fundamentally, gender demographics in computing vary considerably across cultures, making the combined gender composition of a team of FDEs and computer scientists less predictable.

Objects: What is a forensic document?

Although the handwritten message on paper is a popular image of objects examined by FDEs (think threat letters and suicide notes), significant time is devoted to other document types: ▶ identity documents (passports, driver's licenses…); ▶ legal documents (wills, contracts, diplomas…); ▶ legal

---

1—Found 2009: 1447–1448, Huber and Headrick 1999: 4–8, Mnookin 2011: 764–769, list of forensic degree-awarding universities: AAFS 2012a; an FDE autobiography in Doud 2010; on forensic training and issues in general see Siegel 2009, Staufer and Schiffer 2009.   **2**—Huber and Headrick 1999: 341–343, SWGDOC 2012a; on fraudulent diplomas see Bartos 2012, Wolman 2012.   **3**— Standards ISO 17025, "General requirements for the competence of testing and calibration laboratories," and ISO 17020, "General criteria for the operation of various types of bodies performing inspection." Maxwell and Morris 2011; Melson et al. 2009 [laboratories], Schiffer and Stauffer 2009 [organizations].   **4**—NAS 2009, Commons 2005: 44, Edwards 2009, Huber and Headrick 1999: 341–343, 368–372.   **5**—See p. 101.   **6**—Figures and references are provided in "Gender demographics," p. 105.   **7**—But consider the psychology of programmers: e.g., Tognazzini 1992: 93–113 [survey at Apple], Weinberg 1971: 141–159 [caveats on interpreting surveys].

tender (banknotes, checks...); ▸ graffiti and seals; ▸ digital documents (altered PDFs, images...; usually part of digital forensics[1]). In practice virtually any inscription, in any media, is a potential FD.

These documents are characterized by a great diversity of visual shapes; technologies and materials; contexts, contents, and functions; conditions of collection, access, handling, and storage—but they are all inscriptions. All are also part of the work of FDEs and potentially represented as digital images. The main categories as reflected in practical FD work arrangements (personnel expertise, literature classification, financial, and material resource allocation) are optical patterns (handwriting, machine writing, signature, drawings...) and physical traces (ink, printers, paper...). FD typologies can serve to select research project subjects. Note how the forensic document extends beyond the materiality of the written object to include the larger context of its production and origins (its history), as well as the biological and sociocultural characteristics of the writer. For terminology and typology, see Fact sheet "Diverse goals + aspects."[2]

Goals: Why are forensic documents examined?

From a cryptographic perspective, forensic expertise is a process applied to a system of two disentangled parts of a single entity (*agent* and *trace*) and the *link* between them. The goal of this expertise is to question each of these three elements, through: ▸ *identification*: given some traces, answer the question "Who is the authoring agent?" ▸ *verification* (forensics) or *authentication* (biometrics, security documents): given a purported link between agent and trace, is the link genuine?[3] ▸ *recovery*: recover illegible or missing traces (reading of erased writing or charred documents...); ▸ *intelligence*: what can the traces tell us about the behavior driving the agent and about its social network (analysis of the crime phenomenon, respectively criminal intelligence)? ▸ *support*: tasks in support of the aforementioned goals (computerized document management, physical analysis, imaging, establishment of reference datasets, quantification of expert opinion...).

Agent, trace, and link are a terminology that was kept general for a reason: it can be embodied in any of the expertise objects listed in the preceding section. For example, an agent usually refers to an individual, but can equally well signify a typewriter that has to be identified.

Conditions: How does forensic document expertise operate?

It is common to hear FDEs comment that developed forensic software or quantitative methods are irrelevant to their work. For example, many writer identification techniques assume the existence of a substantial amount of

---

1—For a cultural discussion of handwriting in the age of digital media see Neef et al. 2006.   **2**—See p. 97.   **3**—The naming convention might vary with the authors' background. See for example an article titled "Signature Verification" at a conference named "Biometric Authentication" [Yeung 2003].

writing samples from both crime scene and suspects, while in reality many forensic documents are just a couple of lines long, if not just a few words.[1] Knowing the object and goals of FD as described above must be complemented with an intimate understanding of the operating conditions. These physical, technical, organizational, social, and psychological constraints are also issues that FDEs have to address, and ultimately the software and analytical methods too if they are to be of any real use. Operating conditions are indeed part of the forensic document—even if the continuity between the two is materially invisible—because they cannot exist independently.

Expertise circumstances are volatile, varying in time and between cases under consideration, laboratories, and countries. A few of them should be mentioned to show their impact on possible computer science projects and help clarify the expectations of the involved parties.[2] It is noteworthy that they represent a class of computational FD solutions by themselves, on par with those dedicated to the core FD goals.

Software marginality — The logo of the Association of Forensic Document Examiners (AFDE), depicting a microscope, formally reflects what FDEs perceive as their primary tool of trade: "The most important tool for the forensic document examiner has been, is, and probably always will be, the optical stereomicroscope."[3] Hardware-based analyses are preponderant in FD, as the number of publications concerning them suggests.[4] Software use by FDEs is marginal—for handwriting expertise, for example, the active systems that exist (the European and United Stated FISH) are restricted to governments, while the few commercial and academic products are prototypes or not used.[5] The introductory text to the first forensic signature competition, in which the Netherlands Forensic Institute (NFI) explicitly states the goal of its sponsoring to be the acquisition of a signature expertise software for active casework,[6] is one of the signals in recent years signifying the slow turn toward information technologies initiated by the FD profession itself. This is not surprising since the training of human experts consists, after all, in creating a biological pattern recognizer.

Focus on forgeries — Disguised handwriting and signatures are a topic example needing the experience of an FDE to be appreciated as a worthy computer research subject.[7] Disguise cases are not that infrequent to neglect them, but there are very few relevant computational studies. In any case it is an intellectually interesting topic, fusing a number of areas, including psychology and biokinematics (as a historical aside, Alphonse Bertillon (1853–1914), a founding figure of the scientific method in forensics, erroneously conjectured autoforgery in the Dreyfus affair[8]).

1—Brink et al. 2008.   2—On the importance and variability of expectations in interdisciplinary forensic projects see Kelty and Julian 2011; conditions specific to collaborations with the police force in Fleming 2010.   3—Will 2010.   4—"Common topics," p. 95.   5—"Landmark software," p. 75.   6—SigComp09 2009.   7—Closely related to forgeries are anonymous letters: synthetic treatment in Harrison 1966: 469–493, cases in Locard 1935–1937 (6): 501–541.   8—The Dreyfus affair, named after Captain Alfred Deyfus (1859–1935), was a military espionage affair (1894–1906) which   ...

Applications variety — The wide array of forensic document types demands an equally large spectrum of expertise and resources: training, datasets, methods, tools, and so forth. Even when restricted to a single topic such as handwriting, a single software cannot process equally well all possible circumstances where the topic appears. Understanding and explaining to FDEs the conditions under which the software performs optimally is thus necessary. Variety, nevertheless, is also a boon for developers, providing many research and development opportunities.

Topic inconstancy — In addition to the specialization induced by forensic documents, they are also characterized by sometimes fleeting interests born outside the field. Anthrax was a relatively obscure research subject until the 2001 terrorist attacks in the United States—and subsequently faded back to its previous fate.[1] More to the point of FD, research into Arabic handwriting has also—apparently for a longer period—boomed since the same fateful year 2001. Here we talk of a research body matured over the years, but how much time does one have to develop software for a reliable understanding of the conditions of handwriting with a victim's blood on wine cellar doors of the French Riviera?[2] How far can an FDE expect to find computerized help in such rare cases? Time-consuming scientific research also squares badly with a *CSI* TV-series-fed public expecting forensics to be "sexy, fast and remarkably certain."[3] The popular image of forensics is not innocent—one way or the other it does have a bearing on the judicial process.[4]

Time limitations — The issue of FDEs having a limited time to devote to specific document types is compounded by many of these documents not being available for later consultation once the expertise is performed. After examination, forensic laboratories return the documents to courts, lawyers, private persons, or law enforcement agencies, and digital or analog copies are not necessarily made for the lab's own archives. Evidently this influences the expertise range and performance of FDEs (fleeting memories, limited teaching material) and the ability to develop meaningful support software.

Postfactum expertise — Typically FDEs are consulted *after* crimes have been committed (serial murder cases and antiterrorism are some of the exceptions). In this respect their work contrasts with that of signature biometric access control and security documents validation which happen in real time given the speed and volume requirements critical to such transactions. This characteristic has far-reaching implications on the nature of techniques that can be used in an offline setting. For example, code optimization, bandwidth, and detail of analysis, become lesser concerns.

Cultural specificities — Along time, space is also an FD factor: some document types or inquiry topics are culturally specific. Seals have become of interest to the Western FD only for the examination of official documents,

---

degenerated into antisemitism and considerable social dissension in France [Wikipedia 2012a]. On the role of Bertillon see Mansuy and Mazliak 2013, Locard 1937.

1—DoJ 2010.   **2**—Gauthier 2000.   **3**—Roane and Morison 2005.   **4**—Chesen 2008, Podlas 2006.

but metal and stone seals still are the dominant means of personal identification in Japan and Taiwan (former Japanese colony until 1945), as they were throughout Eurasia for most of its history. The contribution of Japan to computational research on Western-style signatures is therefore understandably minimal (less obvious is the disconnection from forensic computational handwriting analysis in general). Also, handwriting written with a brush is common in the Far East, and accordingly, many computer methods for brush synthesis and analysis have been developed in China, which has a vibrant calligraphic culture.

Tailored ergonomics — As a social construct FD is affected by the training of its practitioners and requires adapted software. As the typical FDE educational curriculum is not science oriented, in particular computer science and statistics, forensic technologies developed in these areas must make an effort to be accessible to their final users. Appropriate computer interfaces, terminology, and documentation are some of the topics of concern.

Socioprofessional priorities — Sociologists working with members of police forces have reported being regarded as strangers because it was not clear what they were "doing," the nature and purpose of academic work being alien to the practically oriented culture of the law enforcement.[1] Academic computer scientists too can fall into this trap. Without proper communication it might not be readily understood why it is important to them to concentrate on solving abstract computational issues and publish in specialized journals, rather than delivering a working software.

Organizational considerations — Organizational issues can affect the development of certain FD computational resources. For example, software for detecting forgeries of Euro banknotes can be developed to read the unique serial numbers and check their validity according to a publicly known formula.[2] However, the exhaustive specifications of security features of banknotes and official documents are best known to the issuing institutions. When the development of software methods depends on access to datasets and specifications (e.g., for machine learning purposes), co-opting the goodwill of the relevant institutions is a prerequisite to success. Fortunately, the FD community is quite transparent about its dealings and open to scientific collaborations. Such an attitude might be different in the realms of security documents or cryptography, where nondisclosure is indeed the rule or at least a passionately controversial topic.[3]

Legal constraints — The laws governing FD work also have to be taken into account by researchers since they can affect not only the project's management, but the very nature of the technologies to be developed. Consider for an instant the peculiarities and variety of software that need to be imagined and implemented (anonymization tools, network security…) to build an

---

1—Fleming 2010: 144.   2—Deroche and Prieur 2003.   3—Van Renesse's handbook on optical document security, for example, opens in each new edition with an evolving discussion to the appropriateness of publishing such a book, to which, indeed, some invited experts declined to contribute on moral grounds [Renesse 1998: xxv–xxvii, 2005: xiii–xv].

international networked forensic handwriting database that accommodates the laws pertaining to cross-border dataset sharing. More generally, the evolution of the admissibility of handwriting expertise in courts, especially under the *Daubert* ruling of 1993 in the United States that sets conformance criteria, has initiated a research for a better, scientifically plausible FD. Development of FD practice standards and quantitative methods to evaluate the strength of evidence are two of the more visible results of these efforts.[1]

Judicial use — Finally, computer scientists have to remember that a forensic expert occasionally has to witness in courts. This person therefore needs technologies that can be reasonably well understood and easy to explain.[2] Ultimately FD is about justice and affects the life of individuals — software needs to be ethical.[3]

The neutrality of the expert witness is of particular interest to the adversarial setting of the common law justice systems, mostly Anglo-Saxon. Because experts are hired by the conflicting parties rather than appointed by the judge as in the inquisitorial tradition of continental law of most of Europe, they become more advocates than impartial auxiliaries. Recognizing the issue of a science being bended so as to agree with the desired outcome of a case, the Panel on Statistical Assessments as Evidence in the Courts sponsored by the US National Science Foundation issued in 1989 recommendations for developing standards to preserve the ethical integrity and scientific independence of expert witnesses.[4] Interestingly, the impact of the specificities of a judicial system on the state of forensics resurfaced 20 years later, in the National Science Foundation report of 2009, this time focusing on the too close relation between forensic laboratories and law enforcement agencies.[5]

1—For a glance at the legal aspects of forensics in the United States see Houck and Siegel 2010: 579–611.   2—The confusing explanations and condescending attitude of Bertillon as a handwriting expert during the Dreyfus trials made him a laughing stock of the public. Here is how the *New York Times* correspondent related the court proceedings: "The witness began by saying that only intelligent men could follow his explanations, and the court was half emptied as the audience, after smiling audibly at his extraordinary words and expressions, soon became bored and went out. [...] ¶ The courtroom presented a curious scene while M. Bertillon, whom the Dreyfusards, in their most indulgent moments, describe as a 'dangerous maniac,' spend the remaining hours of the session in explaining, in unintelligible terms, his 'infallible system' of proving Dreyfus was the author of the bordereau. The majority of the public, however, utterly unable to comprehend M. Bertillon's theories, had left the courtroom. Even 'La Dame Blanche' (the white lady) abandoned her post. ¶ In the meanwhile, M. Bertillon, with gestures and in the shrill, pitched voice of a quack at a country fair, continued his monologue, producing every minute some fresh paper covered with wonderful hieroglyphics, copies of which he presented to the Judges, who, with an expression of owllike wisdom, carefully examined them, their heads clustered together, their eyes gazing on the long, wide strips of paper, while M. Bertillon leaned over their table trying to explain his mystifying diagrams, which were afterwards passed to MM. Labori and Demange, who, however, apparently, did not derive much profit from their perusal. ¶ Dreyfus gazed at the scene with a look of stupefaction." [NYT 1899]   3—See the ethics codes of several computing associations in Johnson and Snapper 1985: 14–42, and a philosopher's take on their merits: "the whole notion of an organized professional ethics is an absurdity—intellectual and moral." [Ladd 1985: 8]   4—Fienberg 1989: 11, 13, 148, 156–164, 275–276; NAS 2009: 26, 212–214.   5—NAS 2009: 17–19, 24, 183–184.

Stress — Forensic science is not all science, it is also social performance, as the forensic etymon spells it out. Its judicial use generates psychological stress, fires up egos, and puts reputations at stake. FDEs have to contend with pressure from the laboratory hierarchy or their customers to deliver in time and perhaps in their favor; court appearances can be daunting, adverse parties questioning with inquisitorial fervor every bit of the FDE's qualifications and logic, eloquence and assertiveness being paramount; the media's lights and public opinion can at times attain properly hysterical proportions; and not last, the importance of the case can be a crushing moral burden.[1] In all this the FDE has to maintain professional integrity and defend her or his expertise, maybe shaped by the use of software. Which opens the possibility of the software's creator being summoned in court and subjected to the same grueling experience as just canvassed for the FDE.[2]

1—To internalize this physiological state, readings in history, social science, and history of science and technology, as well as court transcripts are recommended: Moenssens 2009 [description of the expert cross-examination procedure], Zajac and Hayne 2009 [intimidating techniques learned by lawyers, impact of cross-examination on children], Cole 2009 [on the right and duty of scientists to intervene in judicial debates of scientific quality of forensics], Saks 2003b [a scholar's deposition], Fisher 2008: 182–217 [the Ramsey murder case], Wikipedia 2012a [Dreyfus affair], Stone 1984: 96 [how the performance of psychiatrists in court can influence their profession].   2—What happens then see in Lynch and Cole 2005.

1

Agenda

ACT THREE

2

— The famous Bertillon is mad!

— And this cross here?
— It's not me who made it.
— So then why didn't you protest?
— I was forced.
— Who?
— I was threatened to be chased away.
— No, she's lying.
— It's her mark this cross.
— She says the truth! They are capable of everything. They tried to kill me.
— I say it's her mark. I saw her when she did it.
— No, I didn't sign. Because I would have signed with my name.
— How would you have done it? Since you do not know to write.
— I would like a quill and paper.
[She signs her name.]

4

— Shred everything!

— But now the bastards are using sweatshop
kids to reassemble the shreds.

FD HISTORY THROUGH THE LENS

Even if forensic documents (FD) is an obscure and battered profession, people are fascinated by the power of the written document and the power to verify its veracity. It is thus not surprising to see major instances of the history of FD brought to the screen. As early as 1899, motion pictures pioneer Georges Méliès (1861–1938) filmed the *The Dreyfus Affair* (1894–1906) [1], which subsequently saw many incarnations, until not as long ago as 1995 (*L'affaire Dreyfus* [2]), both featuring Bertillon. A more recent event appears in *Argo* (2012) [4]: the hostage crisis at the American embassy in Tehran (1979–1981). In the plot the Iranians learn about the existence of six consular staff in hiding, as children from carpet weaving workshops reconstruct shredded embassy documents with their pictures. →

— This is a mathematical certainty.

— In these computers we store data about approximately 10,000 people.

In both cases the movies are not innocent entertainments, the fiction media are purposely designed to bear on ongoing historical events, rooted, to different extents, in FD. Méliès was a pro-Dreyfusard, his movie triggered street riots between political camps, and it was among the first censored movies;[1] the insisting, and damning, reference to Bertillon in the 1995 version is not only historically accurate,[2] but also reflects a certain disenchantment with science in today's France (represented by the FD examiners (FDEs), as opposed to human abilities (the passion and rhetoric of Zola, the intimate conviction of lieutenant-colonel Picquart in the innocence of Dreyfus); while *Argo* comes at times of heightened tension between the United States and Iran, and features the clash between hi-tech (electric shredders) and low-tech (manual reassembling), a very real issue of modern intelligence and military operations.

The Return of Martin Guerre (1982) [3] resuscitates a resounding FD episode of 16th century France (the philosopher Montaigne is said to have attended the court proceedings).[3] The core idea — identity usurpation — is still viscerally fascinating and, in the era of Internet and biometrics, a topical matter. However, in regard to FD, the movie should be credited with popularizing some aspects of the history of the signature (Princeton historian Natalie Zemon Davis coauthored the screenplay) and fleshing out the remarkably ingrained use that from early on Latin Mediterranean societies made of written documents (as opposed to Northern Europe or Islam). From scene to scene along the movie

the public witness the transformation of the Medieval society where notaries identified themselves by symbolic signs (here a duck) and few could write (they signed with a generic "×"), into the Renaissance world that spread literacy and the signature as we know it (the husband guiding his wife's hand during the writing lesson; the woman later proudly demonstrating in court her new signing skill and status as a modern individual). Along the way, the viewers are also confronted with document expertise in court in times long past and the notions of contested signatures and signing under duress.

Cinema also acts as a public memory about computational FD. *The Baader-Meinhof Complex* (2008) [5] shows how a complex international political and social situation (right-wing terrorism in Germany 1970–1990s, Middle East and Vietnam conflicts, social upheavals of 1968, emancipation of women[4]) creates the opportunity for a technology (computing) to be deployed in the service of state surveillance (police databases, networks, and data processing). Through the prominence given to the German Criminal Office (BKA) the movie lets us witness the intellectual and technological birth of FISH, the most successful handwriting analysis computer system in history. It equally hints at the role played by Germany in the global spread of this and other computational forensic technologies (FISH was exported to the United States), in a scene where foreign officials are given a tour of the BKA hi-tech in Wiesbaden (in the real world the press also noted the visit to the premises of some unsavory characters, such as Lybia's Colonel Qadhdhafi[5]).

1—Bottomore 1984.   2—See note 2, p. 18.   4—Schreiber 1981.
3—Zemon Davis 1983.   5—Spiegel 1979.

Computational research

This chapter reviews possible forensic documents (FD) topics for computer science projects, from some that are central for the advancement of the field, to other major and minor ones, as well as those which are expected to grow in importance in the future. Two typological classes are observed, one revolving around the elements of a forensic document and another dealing with the elements of the expertise workflow. The topics provide a broad yet synthetic panorama of current interests and emerging issues.

Fundamental areas

Resource networking — During the rise of modern systems of law enforcement and criminal justice in the 18th and 19th centuries—in parallel to that of bureaucracy—a lot of effort and exploration went into methods to describe, access and communicate information about people's identity.[1] The same issues are also typical of the networking of FD resources in our days, which harbors great potential for the field's development. The idea this time is to create national and international computer networks to access datasets and software for document management and analysis. These resources are also expected to modify the way FD is practiced and displace its boundaries.

The benefits are multiple: ▸ *access to vaster and richer resources* than any single laboratory currently owns; ▸ some FD scenarios such as finding handwriting samples of a suspect are possible only through a *massive document hunt* (2 million in the case of the Weinberger kidnapping[2]); ▸ building *global expertise* instead of strictly local expertise (FD examiners [FDEs] know well their local and regional archive, less the national ones, and few have international expertise; in an age of easy long-range movement of individuals this is a real issue); ▸ *relieving financial burdens*, another real issue considering, beyond the current economic crisis, that FD work is less well financed than other forensic areas such as DNA evidence or firearms and explosives (in the United States for example, FD expertise was performed in 2002 in 28% of laboratories and 80% of laboratories with more than 100 forensic employees, that is, only organizations with substantial resources have the capability to do FD work[3]); ▸ facilitating and improving

---

1—Denis 2011, About 2011, Kafka 2012.   **2**—FBI 2010b.   **3**—Peterson and Hickman 2005: 4.

the *quality of the training* of new FDEs; ▸ improved insights in *demograph-ic characteristics* of handwriting and documents, which in turn improves the performance of machine learning algorithms that are dependent on the quality of the training datasets; ▸ *improvement and standardization of tools and methods* (an inherent task of such networking projects would be description and encoding of document characteristics, as well as systems interoperability and networking); ▸ foster *collaboration* (acquaintance of computer scientists with the work of FDEs and vice versa); and ▸ a better *acceptance of computerized solutions* in the FD community.

Information systems are harbingers of shifts in the practice of FD and open the possibility of applications beyond the traditional: shifts from ex-pertise to intelligence, from single cases to studies of population behavior, from one-time to long-term analysis, to discovery of crime-to-crime links, to cross-jurisdictional boundary investigations, and many more.[1]

A few FD computer networking projects have taken place, have been devel-oped, or were proposed, but no working system exists yet. ▸ *The European Network of Forensic Handwriting Experts* (ENFHEX), cofinanced by the Eu-ropean Commission running from 1998 to 2002, was an effort to harmonize practices at the European level.[2] Software-wise it collected copybook sam-ples across the continent and the world, and created a semi-public database to store them (IHIS[3]). ▸ *Wanda*, a project by the University of Groningen, Netherlands, funded by the German Federal Criminal Police Office (BKA) from 2002 to 2003, produced a networked software framework for hand-written document management and analysis based on a plug-in philosophy, and a document and handwriting description XML schema.[4] The software is currently not in use. ▸ *Nexus*: European Graphonomics Information Space, a proposal by eight computing and forensic institutions to the European Commission in 2008, coordinated by this author, was targeting the creation of networked forensic handwriting databases, augmented with contextual information and tools for search, visualization, and quantification.

Writer identification and verification — For handwriting and signatures these two tasks are at the core of FD and as such have generated the most com-puter science research and will continue to do so. They are not mentioned at the top of this list, nor will they receive much space here, because we want to draw attention to other important topics and show their dependence on a host of factors that are often underestimated or unknown.

Right away, two connex research subjects can be mentioned. When searching in databases for additional documents written by the same writer of a questioned document, the FDE would need the support of a *writer re-trieval* software. Since on a single document there can be writing belonging to more than one writer, such as annotations, the software would need to perform *writer separation*.[5]

1—Krimsky and Simoncelli 2011, Maltoni et al. 2003: 45–47, Ribaux et al. 2010a, 2010b. **2**—ENFHEX 2002, 2012b. **3**—See p. 67. **4**—See p. 125. **5**—"Writer retrieval" and "writer separa-tion" are terms introduced by this author [Atanasiu et al. 2011].

Datasets, databases, and demographics — Introduced above in the context of resource networking, these are a foundational element of FD, on which rests the identification of suspects, as well as the training of experts.[1] *Datasets* are collections of analog or digitized documents; *databases* are software for managing datasets; *demographics* are the statistics derived from analysis of datasets (such as geographical distribution of handwriting styles). Since forensic documents are more than handwriting, there are accordingly many datasets, databases, and demographics: on signatures, ink (the most extensively documented FD resource), paper, watermarks, printers, and so on. A number of issues are worth mentioning here with respect to datasets.

Functionalities — Basically databases allow users to manually and/or automatically add metadata to describe documents, search for items, and explore datasets. They should allow FDEs to identify to which classes a document belongs, measure the coherence of the class, and visualize similarities; should support statistical descriptions and representations of the topology of characteristics of a dataset (visually, aurally, as physical objects...); and for objects such as handwriting and signatures the measurement of the in-between and with-in writer variability should be possible. Here are some success stories (but for how many failures?) highlighting the importance of a specific database task, of document triage, and of the vast quantities of documents involved: ▸ in 1956 the processing over a period of about one month of nearly 2 million written documents from the "New York State Motor Vehicle Bureau, federal and state probation offices, schools, aircraft plants, and various municipalities" in the New York area led to the identification of an infant's kidnapper;[2] ▸ in 1975 in the United Kingdom a stolen car case was solved after 600,000 handwriting samples were reviewed;[3] ▸ in 1996 it took 12 hours to examine documents from 1,000 US military personnel and successfully conclude a check fraud case.[4]

Text — During the creation stage of handwriting datasets continuing reflection about what constitutes an appropriate text to be copied by subjects is warranted. Such texts are often imported from linguistics, but it is not given that they are also suited to the analysis of handwriting. For example, the semantic dimension of the content affects the writing shape according to factors such as the motivation of the writer,[5] interest for the content, proficiency in the specific language and vocabulary (the graphical equivalent of foreign accents), or the length of the text which induces fatigue. Another example concerns one of the most successful computational writer identification methods, based on allograph statistics,[6] which are largely dependent on the vocabulary used: how is the method's performance affected by word frequencies being highly variable?[7] Linguists have devoted considerable time on developing proper methodologies for the design of corpora,[8] and we should expect the same in graphonomics. Note that contrary to most

1—See Fact sheet "Key datasets + databases," p. 113.   **2**—FBI 2010b.   **3**—Baxendale and Renshaw 1979.   **4**—Shiver 1996.   **5**—Wilkinson et al. 1992b: 10.   **6**—Bensefia 2005, Bulacu and Schomaker 2007, Saunders et al. 2011.   **7**—Baayen 2001.   **8**—E.g., Wynne 2005.

handwriting datasets of computer scientists, some collected by forensic experts are spontaneous samples, the content and length chosen by the subjects, and thus considered to be more realistic to actual FD conditions.[1]

Context — The context in which the samples were produced and collected impacts the relevance of the dataset, the realism of datasets being indeed a substantial problem: handwriting collected in university settings is probably not representative of bank robbery notes, but then such a collection is hard to constitute (the FBI owns one[2]). For ink and other document aspects the problem can be solved by exhaustive collection of samples, but for others such as handwriting, where the variety is much greater, one should collect small but statistically significant datasets. Three datasets, two of them popular with computer scientists and one with FDEs, exemplify the difficulty in understanding what—or who—the data represents.[3] ▶ The CEDAR handwriting dataset developed to train a handwriting identification software has been explicitly designed to address representativeness, randomness, and demographic variation of the entire US population[4]—yet, to account for twins, a special dataset was needed. ▶ The IAM dataset created for handwriting recognition purposes is sampled from private and professional environments in the university, city, and canton of Bern, Switzerland—does it represent "Swiss" handwriting despite including samples from Greek, Chinese, and other international students and expatriates? Yes and no, insofar as it is a biometrical snapshot of the population residing in a specific part of Switzerland at a given time, but not restricted to those having learned to write in Swiss schools. ▶ A Dutch police handwriting archive also used by FDEs was collected from road traffic offenders—are they representative of all Dutch people, or is their handwriting somehow special?

Documentation — Once the data has been collected it is necessary to document both the dataset content and the collection procedure. This will facilitate dataset comparison and aggregation.

Availability — For the exploitation of datasets it is useful to make them digitally available, whenever legally and materially possible. A number of governmental and private organizations exist that manage the distribution and marketing of scientific datasets: the UCI Machine Learning Repository hosts handwriting and documents datasets;[5] the Evaluations and Language resources Distribution Agency (ELDA) and the Linguistic Data Consortium (LDC) are examples of successful enterprises for linguistic datasets;[6] Bernstein is a portal to databases of watermarks and paper structures.[7]

Aging — A further particularity of forensic datasets is their slow aging. For handwriting the factors are a mix between the aging of individuals, generational turnover, changes in writing training and technologies, and population migrations. Datasets used to develop computational expertise methods can become obsolete also by being overused, the algorithms overfitting

---

1—Chaski and Walch 2009: 27.   **2**—See p. 114.   **3**—References: Fact sheet "Key datasets + databases," p. 113.   **4**—Srihari et al. 2002.   **5**—Frank and Asuncion 2010.   **6**—ELDA 2012, LDC 2012.   **7**—Bernstein 2012.

to the particular research data to the detriment of their validity to a wider population.[1] While for handwriting the long-term transformation in style is the most apparent feature, other factors change concurrently, just as for the spoken language: orthography, lexicon, or syntax. The "London Letter," a popular text for taking handwriting samples, dates from the 1920s[2]—how well does it reflect today's grapholinguistic conditions? Moreover, just as some algorithms are trained on individual handwritings, shouldn't there be a different text for each handwriting volunteer?

Privacy and security — Forensic documents can contain personal information in various amounts and of various sensitivity levels, facial pictures and signatures being the most common biometrics. As such, FD data shares with other biometrics their issues of privacy and security which need to be addressed in computational FD projects.

When in 2005 members of the French "Group Against Biometrics" destroyed palm reading devices used for accessing a school's dining hall, it became clear that the proponents of biometric technologies need to invest in social acceptability.[3] And when after September 11, 2001, the United States demanded from the visa-exempt countries to introduce biometric passports and that air carriers share personal passenger information, it also became apparent the kind of political pressure to which data integrity is subjected.[4] Functionality creeping, another calamity, is exemplified in FD by a system that was designed for example for verification of individuals and ended up being used to classify populations in subgroups.[5] Illegal selling of signature datasets amassed by banks, postal companies, and so forth, is not unthinkable considering that this already happens with other biometrical data.[6] Finally, legislation needs to protect the right of biometric donors to information about sampling, data security, rectification mechanisms, and oblivion after an expiration date—aspects that can benefit from partial technological solutions.[7]

Performance evaluation — The last two decades saw the emergence of performance evaluation as a central debate and research topic in FD. Questioned are several elements of the expertise system: ▸ the performance of human *experts* (compared to lay people and regarding particular tasks,

1—See Kermorvant 2012 and Maaten 2009 about overfitting of the MNIST handwritten digits dataset; template update is known in many biometric modalities [for fingerprints see Maltoni et al. 2003: 41].

2—Osborn 1929.   3—Piazza 2011: 383–387. Further on the acceptability of biometrics see Ceyhan 2011 [theoretical framework], Piazza 2011 [French antibiometrics movements], Guchet 2011 [biometrics in schools], Deharo 2011 [biometrics in companies].   4—Ceyhan 2011: 408–409, Didier and Pellegrino 2011: 104–107, Europa 2013.   5—See in this respect the debates on the European information systems (here p. 119) in Preuss-Laussinotte 2011: 314–317, Strugala 2011: 292–295, Europa 2013; similarly for the United States and United Kingdom see Cole 2011.   6—E.g., the arrest of a Belgian policeman in 1998 on suspicion of selling data from the Schengen Information System (SIS 1) to the Mafia [Times 1999], or the involvement of members of the Nigerian government in various international scams with biometric identity cards and banknotes [Breckenridge 2011, Bender 2006: 78–81, 121, 177, similarly for Zaire 200–215].

7—French and European legislation on biometrics: Türk 2011, Preuss-Laussinotte 2011, Strugala 2011; US legislation on DNA and privacy: Cole 2011.

such as identifying writers or detecting disguise); ► the performance of *software* (where the main problem is the difficulty if not impossibility in comparing products because of differences in datasets used and ways to report results — public competitions are doing a great job to improve the situation); ► the nature and appropriateness of quantitative methods for expressing forensic *opinions* about the strength of evidence (statistics, today moving from a frequentist to a probabilistic); ► the quality of the *datasets* used in the case study, to train the software or the human expert (representativeness of the population and crime scene conditions). Computer science projects should be prepared to be challenged on any of these aspects.

User-centered products, as opposed to products made by developers as if they were the end-users, which they are not, is a somewhat neglected dimension of computational FD, albeit an important ingredient of successful projects.[1] FDEs not only operate in particular conditions as mentioned before, but they have a training that is not necessarily that of mathematicians or programmers, they use their own terminology and methodology, and as a result are reluctant to use computational and quantitative tools, or able to apprehend what the outputs of these tools mean. It is often the belief to understand what the tool is doing that makes FDEs prefer microscopes over software.

A few good design principles[2] applied to computational FD can inspire useful research topics.

Concepts meaning — When a software provides a method to measure some writing feature,[3] it has also to explain to an FDE what the measurement is useful for. This is in fact an issue that extends beyond ergonomics, because there are many such features and methods for which we understand little what they mean for writing expertise. To offer an example, the local orientation of the writing trace has been used for writer identification,[4] and further inquiry has revealed that it is related to the roundness of writing, its slant, and a host of other characteristics, but also that many different patterns can create the same orientation profile (probably this is why it is a good, but not the best, biometric marker).[5] Understanding why algorithms behave as they do can lead to better products — and, *pace*, make them look less haphazard creations, as the choice of distance metrics seems to be.

Language affordance — The language of graphical user interfaces (GUIs) and documentation of FD software has to be adapted to nontechnical users, while providing sufficiently clear and detailed technical information.[6] At terminological level a suggested solution is to use intuitive correlates of analytical features, such as "slant" for "mode of the local orientation probability distribution function."[7] Attention has to be paid to the coexistence of three

---

1— Landauer 1997 goes as far as identifying for the period 1970s to 1990s a staggering loss of productivity in the industrialized world due to computerization and he attributes it to poor software usability.
2—Norman 2002. And do not forget to read Tog, still fresh after 20 years on the shelves: Tognazzini 1992.   **3**—Many do: see list in Fact sheet "Landmark software," p. 121.   **4**—Bulacu 2007, Bulacu and Schomaker 2007.   **5**—Atanasiu 2011a, Atanasiu et al. 2011.   **6**—See comments on software on pp. 49–50.   **7**—Atanasiu 2011b.

distinct terminologies, each having various degrees of standardization and dialects, their polysemy and homonymy being potential sources of misunderstandings: the idiom of computer scientists and statisticians, the vernacular of FDEs, and layperson talk (judges, jurors, attorneys, the public).[1]

Interaction affordance — MICS is technologically a simple tool for the three-dimensional (3D) representation of images that elicits very positive reactions from FDEs, who profess to find much insight from playing with the virtual 3D object.[2] This software is an example of success achieved by focusing on the development of the human–computer interface (HCI). The design of HCIs, graphics and navigation, can be laborious[3] and should always be grounded in user evaluations.[4]

Process visibility — Presenting FDEs with expertise software that amounts to a virtual "black box"[5] is making them unable to explain in court how they arrived at their opinions about the forensic evidence.[6] As an example for a step toward a more transparent process is the use of prototypical writing samples from within a dataset when performing writer identification and verification.[7] Quantification of intuitive features — e.g., loops[8] — increases the probability of FDEs adopting computational tools when compared to reliance on even basic mathematical concepts — e.g., Fourier coefficients — or on opaque processes — such as neural networks.

Exploratory discovery — Considerable effort and money have been expended on a computational solution for writer identification and verification, the crux of FD. Considering however the difficulties experienced by this technology in the penetration of the FD market, other subjects, less ambitious, but nevertheless of great practical value to FDEs, are coming to be considered, data navigation and visualization being two of them. Visualization has been pursued in other areas of graphonomics, in particular digital paleography[9] and fonts merchandising.[10] Its underdevelopment in FD might be due to the nature of forensic writing datasets: small, not interconnected, not digitized, and of difficult access.

Basic capabilities — A fundamental issue is the dearth of basic software for FDEs to work with. The few simple tools that exist are the most successful pieces of code yet written for FD judging from the number of citations (Photoshop[11]), number of implementations (Wanda, Graphlog, Color deconvolution[12]), duplication of capabilities (Graphlog and Graphoskop), and training sessions organized by companies (MICS). The most commonly observed needs are: binarization (GIWIS), ruling removal (CEDAR), geometry measurement (supported by most FD software), inks segmentation (Color deconvolution), image visualization (MICS), tabulation of observations

1—McQuiston-Surret and Saks 2008.　　**2**—Anthony 2002.　　**3**—Stone et al. 2005: 387–409. **4**—Nielsen 1993.　　**5**—Van den Heuvel 2008.　　**6**—Mnookin 2008: 344–345; on types of "black boxes" see Bunge 1999: 35.　　**7**—Brink et al. 2007.　　**8**—Blankers et al. 2007.　　**9**—Moalla et al. 2006.　　**10**—FontFont 2012, Identifont 2012, MyFonts 2012.　　**11**—Various citations in AAFS 2011, book-length coverage in Herbertson 2002 and Baron 2008.　　**12**—See Fact sheet "Landmark software," p. 121.

(Write-On), document annotation (FISH, Wanda), and database operations (storage, retrieval, statistics, visualization, and annotations; FISH, Wanda).

Major issues

Global and multicultural FD — Here is an intellectually and technically interesting topic of increasing importance. Although the majority of crimes are committed within a relatively short distance from the perpetrator's residence,[1] which provides the local forensic examiner with a limited and to some degree familiar environment, travel and migration complicate the task. In a recent court case, for example, the testimony of an FDE was excluded for lack of proficiency on Latin script written by Japanese natives.[2] Note also that the mass migrations of the 19th and early 20th centuries, intra- and transcontinental, were the principal factors in the rise of another forensic technique, fingerprinting.[3] The solution consists in creating bigger datasets of reference documents, as observed in the ever increasing and interlinked law enforcement information systems.[4] Document samples of such rich and heterogeneous datasets have to be supplemented with appropriate contextual information. Semantic knowledge is however more difficult to encode for machine processing and a time-consuming process—furthermore, cross-cultural expertise is rare. For writing, present understanding of the relative expertise difficulties of the world's scripts and the impact they have on computing—which might be different from the impact on human experts—is rudimentary, leading to arbitrary distinctions between scripts (are Persian and Arabic signatures indeed different?[5]) and to exaggerate the difficulties of foreign scripts for no other reason than unfamiliarity.[6]

Biological aspects — Of major interest for handwritten and signed forensic documents are their biological production and perception aspects, because handwriting is a trace of some of the suspect's or the victim's biological condition. Biomechanics, motor-sensory control, and visual perception are the most studied aspects, involving the fields of psychology, neurocognitive sciences, clinical medicine, and computing. Most research is done with other applications in mind than FD, but the forensic community has been directly involved in a number of biomedical research projects.[7] There is a substantial body of literature on the subject: biomechanics studies on handwriting production were prominent throughout the 1980s and 1990s in Italy (Genova) and the Netherlands (Nijmegen); medical applications research utilizing handwriting is on the rise since the turn of the millennium in parallel with developments in digital pen computing; neurocognitive research in handwriting flickers across continents driven by mathematical

---

1—E.g., Groff and McEwen, 2006: 1134, Van Patten and Delhauer 2007; geographic criminalistics: Rossmo 2000.   **2**—Fuji 2000; discussion in Huber and Headrick 1999: 327–330.   **3**—Cole 2001.   **4**—Dick 2011.   **5**—Pal et al. 2011.   **6**—Cross-cultural computational writer identification: Louloudis et al. 2011; cultural aspects in FD: Huber and Headrick 1999: 29–32, 175–186, 327–330; Locard 1935–1937 (5): 389–392 [bigraphy].   **7**—E.g., Aşıcıoğlu and Turan 2003, Sciacca et al. 2007.

models and technologies to record brain activity. Three denominators of these intellectual pursuits are cross-pollination between medical science and computing, vivid interdisciplinarity, and the role played by individuals and research groups in crystallizing and sustaining the research effort. The forum of predilection in terms of interdisciplinarity are the conferences of the International Graphonomics Society.[1]

Typical research areas are: ► neural basis of handwriting production and perception;[2] ► mathematical models of handwriting production (for testing neurocognitive hypotheses, helping the handwriting analysis of individuals for medical purposes...[3]); ► pen computing methods for handwriting acquisition and processing;[4] ► biomechanics;[5] ► neurocognitive aspects of reading and writing skill acquisition (for pedagogical purposes...[6]); ► graphopathology: medical diagnosis, monitoring, and rehabilitation (schizophrenia,[7] multiple personality,[8] neurodegenerative diseases [Alzheimer, Parkinson[9]]...[10]); ► psychological state (stress, sleep deprivation...[11]); ► substances intake (alcohol, caffeine, medicine, drugs...; common in civil cases[12]); ► body posture and grip;[13] ► other (twins...[14]).

Preprocessing — Digital image acquisition, content recovery, and preprocessing are topics with which FDEs are continually confronted and where computerized solutions are most readily available or forthcoming to develop. Digital images are important because this is the only document form sometimes available to FDEs (for example, graffiti are not mobile documents which could be taken to a laboratory) and this is the media with which they interact in digital archives. Besides issues relevant to basic technological education (such as photography in RAW format, use of High Dynamic Range techniques for low-light photography, and knowledge about what digital image manipulations are acceptable in the context of court testimony), there are acquisition topics where advanced computing is needed (3D surface scans, image processing of microscope imagery...).

Recovery — Content recovery of text and graphics is often the first and sometimes the only step in a forensic expertise. It is applied to a variety of document types demanding specific solutions: overwritten, erased, charred, soaked, frozen, torn, or shredded. Acquisition and recovery involve hardware (optical microscopes, spectrometers, physical and electrochemical processing of documents...), as well as software components (as part of the hardware or applied subsequently). Often a mix of physical and digital processing takes place during examination of a document. One example is the

---

1—Biannual since 1982; see Fact sheet "Information sources," p. 108.   **2**—Bradberry et al. 2010, Caligiuri and Mohammed 2012, Dehane 2009, Ganagadhar et al. 2007.   **3**—Flash and Hogan 1985, Plamondon 1995.   **4**—Liwicki and Bunke 2008.   **5**—Flash and Hogan 1985.   **6**—Longcamp 2003.   **7**—Caliguri et al. 2007.   **8**—Schwid and Marks 1994.   **9**—Teulings and Stelmach 1991.   **10**—Huber and Headrick 1999: 198–221, Locard 1935–1937 (5): 445–485.   **11**—Conduit 2008.   **12**—Aşıcıoğlu and Turan 2003, Phillips et al. 2007a, 2007b, Huber and Headrick 1999: 232–243.   **13**—Sciacca et al. 2007; samples of writing with the foot or mouth: Pellat 1927.
14—Srihari et al. 2008; Locard 1935–1937 (5): 364–83 [left-hand and mirror writing].

reading entrusted to FDEs of 15 pages from the diary and notes of Ilan Ramon, the Israeli astronaut killed in the Discovery shuttle disintegration of 2003, pages that were subject to the cumulative effects of charring, tearing, freezing, and soaking.[1] On an altogether different volume scale and judicial importance is the ongoing "depuzzling" of 600 million document snippets, or 54 million pages, of the East German secret police Stasi torn shortly before the German unification in 1990. To reconstruct the documents, information was merged on the location within the 16,000 conservation bags, paper geometry, color data, printed patterns, and script style. Apart from the image processing aspect, the challenge of the project was the successful integration of solutions with numerous other technical, organizational, and legal issues.[2] Research in document recovery benefits from having many applications beyond forensics (e.g., MatchMaker, the Federal Bureau of Investigation's [FBI] unshredder software;[3] methods to identify a shredding machine[4]), with evident benefits to the interested parties and attractive to media coverage: business (the shredded Enron papers[5]), intelligence (the Central Intelligence Agency [CIA] documents of the US embassy in Tehran,[6] the 2011 DARPA Shredder Challenge[7]), art (reconstruction of Cambodian temples, Roman mosaics, and Hebrew Genizah manuscripts[8]).

Segmentation — The importance for FDEs of being able to automatically segment handwriting in characters instead of strokes and search for instances of the same character (allographs) in databases cannot be underestimated. Interestingly, much of human handwriting comparison, by experts as well as by laypersons, is made by comparing allographs across different documents, while the best software methods use allographs of parts of the written trace (strokes that can span more than one character).[9]

Classification — The classification of scripts is a major FD topic consisting in the production of classification schemes, frequency tables, and demographic correlations. It helps humans develop mental maps of pattern occurrences in their work environments and serves both the identification of suspects as performed by law enforcement agencies and their trial involving FDEs. In contemporary writing expertise software the classification operated by algorithms is invisible to FDEs, all they see being the result of a database query or a request for identification or verification consisting in a few ranked documents and an opinion. However, so long as FD relies on human expertise, classification is a valid research topic because FDEs still find the ability to classify and visualize collections of scripts very useful. During the last century there were many projects to produce manually or computationally atlases of handwriting, an idea already considered during

1—Brown and Sin-David 2005.   **2**—Nickolay 2010, Weberling and Spitzer 2007.   **3**—FBI 2007a: 12–13.   **4**—Brassil 2002.   **5**—Heingartner 2003.   **6**—Heingartner 2003.
7—DARPA 2011.   **8**—Kleber and Sablatnig 2009, Wolf et al. 2011.   **9**—Humans: Britt and Mensh 1943: 58, Huber and Headrick 1999: 99; software: Bensefia et al. 2005, Bulacu 2007, Bulacu and Schomaker 2007, Vuurpijl and Schomaker 1997.

the 19th century as a *sine qua non* of writing expertise by Bertillon.[1] Yet he himself, scion of a family of statisticians, was just an echo of a wider intellectual and practical interest for script classification as old as antiquity.[2]

Embedded software — Judging by the number of articles presented at the conferences of the American Academy of Forensic Sciences[3] the expertise of inscription instrument, substrate, and—especially—deposit is an FD activity more developed than handwriting and signature expertise. Because of the predominant use of hardware (optical microscope, spectrometers...) and some exhaustive databases (such as the Digital Ink Database[4]), it also functions on firmer theoretical grounds. Among the more preeminent applications of digital image analysis for this type of application are the ink–background and ink–ink separation,[5] paper structure imaging (radiography, thermography, transmitted light, rubbing...), and paper identification (date, location, manufacturer) from optical analysis of constituent materials (image-based fiber analysis) and the internal physical structure of the paper (watermarks, chain and laid lines, sieve pattern, pulp distribution[6]).

Nontext — A study using classical image processing and machine learning methods has shown that it is possible to identify and verify the authorship of forms of the fill-in-the-bubble type—such as election ballots, survey questionnaires, or standardized tests—despite being specifically designed to preserve anonymity.[7] The research is interesting in several ways. It shows that even very small quantities of data—doodles on bubbles—carry enough biometrical information for forensic expertise. It also draws the attention of computer scientists to patterns other than textual useful to FDEs: graffiti, drawings, marks, and scrawls. Last, it shows that computational FD does more than help with *existing* problems. In a quirky autoreflexive twist this research is an example of computing creating its own need for itself, by disclosing the possibility of a hereto unheard-of type of fraud for which it provides at once instructions and countermeasures.

Physicians' handwriting — The writing of physicians is related to FD by providing information about a specific socioprofessional cohort and offers various opportunities for computer science projects. The question is how to make physicians' writing more legible, one considered to be notoriously bad. Difficult handwriting has lead to errors in medication, causing avoidable costs, pain, and loss of life, as well as making medical archives hard to read. As a testimony to the persistent importance of this topic are the number of articles concerning physicians' handwriting which continue to be published to this day and the various kinds of efforts conceived by physicians to correct the problem, be it by taking penmanship classes, using computers for input, or using speech-to-text software devices.[8]

1—Huber and Headrick 1999: 152–164.   **2**—E.g., for the Arabic script: Atanasiu 2004b. **3**—See p. 94.   **4**—See p. 114.   **5**—Berger et al. 2006.   **6**—Atanasiu 2004a, Miyata et al. 2002, Rückert et al. 2009, Van Staalduinen 2010.   **7**—Calandrino et al. 2011.   **8**—Physicians have poor writing: Rodriguez-Vera et al. 2002; physicians do not have poor writing: Berwick and Winickoff 2006, Lyons et al. 1998, Schneider et al. 2006; issue of choosing linguistically and graphically   ...

Special topics

Geographical Information Systems (GIS) — Geographic tools are currently used by many law enforcement agencies, sometimes preeminently advertised (e.g., the Metropolitan London crime map[1]), and they have relevant qualities to become popular with FDEs given that the subject is sufficiently intuitive and already used outside work by most experts through online mapping services like Google Maps. Creating online maps is—up to a point—straightforward and the number of public datasets with spatial information is growing (e.g., mapping paper distribution in the Bernstein Project; crime statistics can be downloaded from the US National Archive of Criminal Justice Data Web site[2]).

Expert systems — A simple approach to the development of expert systems for modeling human expertise consists in integrating various analytical descriptors (for example, macro and micro features of handwriting such as allographs and layout) and weighting their contribution to the final score on the basis of a trained neural network. Another approach is through a set of explicit decision-making rules or ontologies that human experts might (un)consciously use and verbally describe.

Multimodal data fusion — An increasingly common approach (disaster management, intelligence, multimedia data mining, autonomous robots...), it can be expected to also touch FD.[3] A possible application is the integration of information derived from handwriting, documents, speech, fingerprints, GIS, and other trace data to speed up suspect identification.

Electronic handwriting instruments — Handwriting and signatures produced with *electronic* instruments is another topic which FDEs have to deal with.[4] Multiplying yet again the expertise expected from an expert, the new instruments are of three types: *manual* (e-pens, digitizing tablets, and monitors[5]), *robotic*,[6] and *virtual* (computer-synthesized script displayed on monitors or printed[7]). The recording of handwriting dynamics is much richer than the static image, disclosing the 3D trajectory (hence also—to some degree—the movement of the instrument while not in contact with the surface), pen orientation (an information hardly accessible to static expertise), and pressure (highly valuable)—note the absence of pen hold among the acquired signals (how the pen is held by the body limbs). These are tremendous opportunities

appropriate names for drugs: Robinson 1994; financial and judicial impact: Hirshhorn 2000, Mullan 1989; errors in digital prescriptions: Grissinger 2010; improvement techniques: Finegold 1999, Glisson et al. 2011; paleography of medical handwriting: Anonymous 1967; trivia: Anonymous 1929.

1—Met 2012.   **2**—Bernstein 2012, NACJD 2012.   **3**—Biometric fusion: Ross et al. 2006, multibiometrics of identity documents: Dessimoz et al. 2007, multisensory e-pen: Bashir 2011, multimodal writing analysis: Niels et al. 2005.   **4**—Harralson 2012, Huber and Headrick 1999: 285–286.   **5**—Multisensor: Bashir 2011, Bashir et al. 2011, Hook et al. 2003.   **6**—Signature: Franke 2005, Kruger 2008; teaching: Solis et al. 2002; brush: Yao et al. 2004; pen: Gommel et al. 2007.   **7**—Latin script: Lin and Wan 2007; Chinese and Japanese brush writing: Mano et al. 1999, Wang et al. 2004, Yamasaki and Hattori 1996; signature synthesis: Galbally et al. 2012, Wan and Lin 2009; stylistically consistent glyphs: Hofstadter 1996; handwritten captcha synthesis: Rusu et al. 2009; writing texture synthesis: Efros and Leung 1999.

for a finer characterization of handwriting and are ongoing research topics in medicine and biometrics. Of further interest for FD is the impact that the use of dynamic data can have on handwriting identification and verification quality,[1] the availability of dynamic data datasets, and the relatively numerous dynamic handwriting datasets from China and Japan when compared to those from the Western world or to offline datasets. Robotic and virtual writing are useful, *inter alia*, to test the proficiency of FDEs at identifying forgeries.[2] Information shown on various electronic displays is fleeting, not an optimal characteristic for forensics — it has to be seen if e-ink technologies will bring these inscription substrates more within the attention span of FDEs than in the past (see for example the research on remote recovery of text from reflection of monitor contents on objects, human cornea included,[3] or from electromagnetic emissions[4]). At last, mention should be made of the analysis of keystroke patterns as a century-old biometrics method.[5]

Digital media — Digital documents such as camera pictures, scans, text processing, and document files belong to both traditional FD (as documents) and cyberforensics (as digital objects). Common applications are camera identification[6] and verification of the integrity of digital images.[7] Further research is done on digital and physical watermarking of papers, inks, and imaging and printing devices. The watermarks can act as unique identifiers and attest the genuineness of the object[8] and printers can incorporate the serial number, date stamp, and device identity in the pattern of each printed paper.[9] In respect to inks, the US Bureau of Alcohol, Tobacco and Firearms (ATF) has started in the mid-1970s a program in conjunction with manufacturers to include yearly changing identity tracers in inks.[10] Another research studies the impact of the resolution and quality of digital images on forensic expertise and workflows (e.g., imaging with low-resolution devices such as phone cameras, or the quality needed from professional scanners[11]).

Security documents — *Specificity* — Just like biometrics and digital media forensics, the examination of security documents (SD) such as passports and banknotes is a world related to, although different from, FD. It has its own literature, venues, users, and expectations.[12] Most striking is the high degree of SD automation and the industrial quality level of the providers, as visible at international security trade shows (interestingly, there are FD conferences, but no FD fairs). Given the massive amounts of security documents to be processed, which only automated systems can perform reasonably rapidly, the bulk of SD is done without relying on FDEs. There are also socioinstitutional and technological factors involved in the FD/SD separation.

1—Liwicki and Bunke 2008.   **2**—Franke 2005.   **3**—Backes et al. 2008.   **4**—Kuhn 2003.   **5**—Bartlow 2009, Woodward et al. 2003: 106–113.   **6**—Khanna et al. 2009. **7**—Campbell et al. 2004.   **8**—On evidentiary law and cryptographic signatures for digital documents see Blanchette 2012.   **9**—PSAPF 2012.   **10**—Weyermann 2009: 686.   **11**—Mason 2011.   **12**—Bibliographic pointers: on the security documents life-cycle see Ombelli and Knopjes 2008; on optical security features, Renesse 2005; on security printing, Kipphan 2001: 423–433; on US banknotes security, NRC 2007; a no-frills overview of SD paraphernalia is provided by NVVB 2012.

Historically, the production of security documents was a state monopoly, rooted in the printing industry, and SD is either an outgrow of, or tightly integrated in the state–industry relationship.[1] This contrasts with FD, where there is less regulatory pressure and contacts with the document producers.

Purpose — Security documents are portable bearers of symbolic patterns the purpose of which is to authorize their owner to engage in some action.

Security documents are a class of security devices that can be based on many principles, such as physical (keys), electromagnetic (credit cards), biometrical (signature), or logical (cryptographic keys). The symbolic patterns of security documents are writing, symbols, graphics, and pictures, all accessed visually, other media such as sound or touch being unusual.[2] The authorized action can be anything from driving (driving license), traveling (passport), and obtaining goods (banknotes [but not coins], checks), to physical and logical access (badges for accessing buildings and computer systems), to recording events (presence punch cards), and information (birth, marriage, death certificates, academic degrees, receipts for commercial transactions).

Principle — The principle by which the purpose of security documents is achieved is entanglement: of the owner with the document; of the information in the document with physical, logical, and procedural features; and of both owner and document with a set of authorizing entities and conditions.

In traditional cultures where literacy was limited or inexistent (a medieval village, for example), where writing had a legal probatory status inferior to orality (premodern Islam[3]), or simply in common circumstances when no written trace of an action is produced (a spoken promise), in such cases thus, witnesses play the role of security documents. This social entanglement with other individuals, often public and ceremonial, as a way to secure an authorization is often still concurrent with the use of security documents (think of the pomp surrounding the public ceremonies for the signature of international treaties).

Expertise — Security documents expertise is the verification of the integrity, genuineness, and legitimacy of the entanglement and its elements. SD also serves a secondary intelligence purpose, the analysis of the materials, manufacturing processes, and contextual information helping track criminal production sources and networks.

An identity check by the police is a routine of movements covering the entire SD process: the officer turns the identification document around, judging its integrity (verification of the security document), compares the picture with the face of the individual controlled (verification of the entanglement between the document and its owner), and types the information in

---

1—Banknote printers have found it only natural to expand their activities in the development of electronic recognition and authentication systems for security documents [Bundesdruckerei 2013, Giesecke & Devrient 2013, Oberthur 2013; on the cap-and-dagger history of the banknotes industry see Bender 2006].   **2**—Tactile information is not only important for the visually impaired, but the "feel" of security document can be one of its a major features, such as for banknotes [NRC 2007: 73–75, 16].   **3**—Tyan 1945.

a computer that accesses a remote database, or calls a hierarchical superior for advice (verification of the entanglement with third parties).

Requirements — The procedure has to be quick and easy, since it is performed online.

Expertizing security documents is indeed an integral part of their use, contrary to the expertise of forensic documents which are analyzed only after the facts (fraud, crime, their physical damage). In practice, however, just a limited number of security features can be assessed, so it is important to have overt features that exteriorize the genuineness status of a document. Other features are, however, purposely designed to need forensic expertise.

Typology — Security documents can be classified by application area, sensitivity, genuineness status, and status exteriorization. The best known security document types are distinguished by application area: identity documents for access, payment instruments for financial transactions, and official records for the bureaucracy. The security of computer writing (bar codes, QR-codes) is an emerging field overlapping digital and physical forensics. Sensitivity can be low (subway pass) or high (passport), some forged documents can be breeders of genuine documents (a birth certificate entitles one to obtain a passport[1]). The authenticity status of security documents is identical to those of forensic documents (genuine, forged...), except for a higher percent of fraudulently acquired genuine documents (blank passports...) and fictitious documents.[2] Security documents possess overt, covert, and forensic security features,[3] numbering in the hundreds.[4]

Users — There is a broad user pool for SD, both governmental (border agencies, police, intelligence, external affairs, transportation, health, defense, and other departments) and commercial (airport and maritime ports, facilities such as nuclear plants, car rentals, banks, telecoms, shops...).

Capabilities — SD hardware and software come in many sizes and with various capabilities. An example will help frame the typical capabilities of a SD system.[5] iA-thenticate of MorphoTrust, United States, part of Safran Group, France,[6] is a desktop printer-sized authentication device for passports, driving licenses, and other identity documents. It performs a checksum test (on the number sequence in the Machine Readable Zone [MRZ]), maturity test (expiration date check), B900 ink test (checks the type of ink), visible light, UV and IR pattern test (checks for patterns visible only in specific light spectrum bands), UV brightness test (checks for specific light properties), seal pattern test (checks seal integrity and authenticity), laminate tamper test (checks for damage to the laminated document), and database check (control on stolen, missing, and invalid documents).[7] A great deal of effort is put by organizations such as the International Civil Aviation Organization (ICAO) in standardizing SD processes in order to make infor-

1—Bicknell and Laporte 2009: 1256b.   **2**—EU 2012.   **3**—Bicknell and Laporte 2009: 1256b.   **4**—EU 2012, NRC 2007: 64–77, 90–95, 124–128.   **5**—For an overview of the capabilities and features checked by currency authentication machines see NRC 2007: 18–20, 36–39, 61.   **6**—MorphoTrust 2012.   **7**—NVVB 2012.

mation secure and interchangeable, leading to developments throughout the SD industry.[1] The existence of online commercial SD services is proof of the branch's success and modernity.

Computing research — The implications for digital image analysis projects of the current state of SD are positive. The market is dynamic, of high quality, and computerized. Much expertise is done through imaging, leaving ample room for image processing developments, applied to a wide spectrum of features beyond signatures or seals, typical of FD: complex drawing examination, nonvertical indentations, face recognition, fingerprinting, and hologram analysis, to name just a few. Optimizing for speed, portability, and networking are some of the research avenues with strong interest. Low-end users (shops) are a vast market, for which quick processing, simple instruments and interfaces able to be handled by virtually untrained operators have to be developed.

1—ICAO 2006: I-1, 2007: 6–7.

Technology

— If you don't mind, you fill in the names.
That will make it even more official

2

3

4

— Badges? We ain't got no badges! We don't need no badges!
I don't have to show you any stinking badges!

5

— What is it?
— The stuff that dreams are made of.

— Is this your husband's passport?

— And this?

— And this?

— And this?

— Yes.

— I don't understand.

— ...

— ...

— Until two days ago the only thing I really knew about Charles was his name. Now it seems I didn't even know that.

SECURE IDENTITIES, STAGED

Security documents are ubiquitous in movies, emphasizing their alluring power as magic wands of modern times. The identity control theme appears already very early, in *The Fake Amputee* (1896) [2], a short by the Lumière brothers, where the police control scene doubles with that of presumably fake documents (as it does in *M* (1931) [3], by way of watermark examination). Identification through documents is however a cultural construct and as such not universally shared, an incongruity made colorfully clear by the Mexican pistolero in *The Treasure of the Sierra Madre* (1948) [4]. As for the subversion of security documents, it is part of some iconic plots: *Casablanca* (1942) [1] (getting hold of passports to escape from the Nazis) and *The Maltese Falcon* (1941) [5] (where the character played by Humphrey Bogart finds one of his many aggressors to carry passports of several countries). Employing bewilderment to create paradoxes, and comedy to solve them, as in *Charade* (1963) [6], cinema reveals itself as an effective medium to make us question what identity means. ...

— [Biometric software] Identification please.
— [General Perez exhales into the breath sensor]
— Boo! Please try again!

In biometrics, which challenges if not displaces security documents, more exotic-looking types than handwriting are preferred: voice, already in *2001: A Space Odyssey* (1968); blood from the black market to gain physical access rights in *Gattacca* (1997); breath (spoofed) in *Alien: Resurrection* (1997) [7]; and in *A.I. Artificial Intelligence* (2001) identity devices embedded in the android's flesh.

Know-how + Tools

This chapter presents common technical aspects on how computational expertise of forensic documents (FD) is performed: definition, typology, and examples of FD datasets, demographic cohorts, and criteria for quality datasets; terminology and typology of the description of writing by FD examiners (FDEs) and computer scientists; human and computational expertise methods; and a survey of FD software and hardware.

Datasets

What is a forensic dataset? — Forensic datasets exist for all document aspects previously identified, such as handwriting, signature, pens, ink, or paper. One can distinguish between operational documents and research datasets.

Operational documents are used to identify individuals. They are collected for this specific purpose by law enforcement agencies (police files), are part of public records (judicial system, government), or private and public archives (companies, individuals, libraries, archives, museums). Some particularly laborious investigations used dozens of repositories and millions of documents. See Fact sheet "Key datasets + databases" for a compilation.[1]

Research datasets are for research, training, and evaluation purposes. ▶ *Demographic* studies undertaken by FDEs produce datasets — very few, however, are accessible, which makes verification and reuse difficult. A commendable exception is the International Handwriting Information System (IHIS) created by the European Network of Forensic Handwriting Experts (ENFHEX), comprising copybook models and handwriting samples from across the world.[2] Forensic laboratories used to collect print and typewriter fonts catalogs, but since the advent of the Internet the quantity of fonts has exploded and the catalogs are accessible online.[3] Note the commercial availability of some FD datasets, such as the font catalogs and the security documents datasets. ▶ Datasets created by computer scientists to train and evaluate *software* is a second research dataset category.[4] Only some are specifically designed for FD (most having a dual role of recognition

---

1—See p. 113.   2—ENFHEX 2002: 9–10, 2012a.   3—11 typewriter catalogs described in Levinson 2001: 191–203, see also Kelly and Lindblom 2006: 186–188; on the font epidemic see Cahalan 2008.   4—See Fact sheet "Key datasets + databases," Computing, p. 113.

and identification) and they are criticized, as mentioned before, for their usefulness in real FD conditions. ▸ Datasets for evaluating the proficiency of *FDEs* are generally smaller; designed for specific tasks such as establishing whether a document is genuine, forged, or disguised; the documents are ranked according to task difficulty (disguised signatures are harder to identify[1]); and can be drawn from real cases, such as graffiti.[2]

Interesting demographic cohorts — Research on handwriting datasets is intended to establish differences and similarities between groups of people sharing some characteristics so that starting from features observed in a document the identity of a suspect can be narrowed to a specific population or excluded. Studies have focused on many cohorts, which are also part of the metadata in the better documented datasets: age, gender, handedness (right, left, ambidextrous), education, social groups such as cultural and racial groups (e.g., Chinese, Malay, and Indian in Singapore;[3] physicians,[4] military personnel[5]) geographical peregrinations during one's lifetime (especially where one has learned to write),[6] twins,[7] polyglots and polygraphs, medical conditions, psychological states, and substance intake.[8]

What makes a good handwriting FD dataset? — *Representativeness* of the target population (sample randomness, sample population size, demographic representativeness[9]). ▸ *Relevance* to FD conditions (writing implements, body posture, psychical state...). ▸ *Diversity* and *length* of the recorded writing (mix of free style, constrains (forms), digits, symbols). ▸ *Extensiveness* of metadata gathered on the subjects. ▸ *Protection* of personal privacy and sensitive information.[10] ▸ *Documentation* of the collection process (absence of proper documentation can make the reuse of the dataset impossible, both by the originating producers and other potential users). ▸ *Accessibility* of the dataset; ideally published, free, without prohibitive legal hurdles, and permanently archived.

In the pursuit of attaining the above criteria one quickly discovers a supplement, which is that the seminal quality of a good FD dataset is a properly designed production process. The magnitude and potential implications of what appears *de prima facie* a simple undertaking are apparent from the example of the 1990s handwriting datasets of the US National Institute of Standards and Technology (NIST), outstanding in scale (tapping into the millions of national census forms[11]), temporal length (4 years), methodological complexity (especially this being a first in the handwriting field), fastidiousness (painfully recalled[12]), quasiphilosophical insights (on the ambiguity of writing and impossibility to achieve perfect reading: "it is possible to create four ambiguous characters to represent all ten digits"[13]), organizational involvement (harnessing major institutions), human

---

1—Found 2009: 1444.   **2**—Rowles et al. 2006.   **3**—Cheng 2005.   **4**—See p. 35.
5—Nguyen et al. 2011.   **6**—BKA-AT, see p. 114.   **7**—Srihari et al. 2008.   **8**—See p. 33.   **9**—Srihari et al. 2002 [handwriting], Aitken 2009b [forensics], Lohr 2010 [techniques].
10—Woodward et al. 2003: 197–279, 307–328.   **11**—Geist et al. 1994: 29–31.   **12**—Garris 1994: 203, Geist et al. 1994: 23, Wilkinson et al. 1992a: 2.   **13**—Wilkinson et al. 1992a: 1, Geist et al. 1994: 22.

resources (dozens of people at NIST relying on the vast network of Census employees and interviewed citizens[1]), and symbolic dimension (the Census Bureau was instrumental in the development of the first American commercial computer in the 1950s, UNIVAC[2]).

A few words about sampling. Sampling of handwriting cannot be restricted like in an opinion poll to a representative collection of individuals from the entire population of a country (the United States in one study)—apart from the fact that we do not know what the sample size appropriate for studying handwriting should be.[3] It must be carried out individually for various sociocultural groups and perhaps even for the many factors that affect handwriting. This approach provides the different error rates for the specific combinations of cohorts and contexts under consideration. It sheds light on the individuation power for, say, Latin script compared to Arabic or Chinese, the similarity of calligraphers' writing or that of people suffering from Alzheimer's, the intriguing peculiarities of Basque terrorist handwriting,[4] the impact of using tactile screens on the ability to distinguish signatures (notoriously bad for anyone having had to sign a FedEx receipt).[5] In the past 15 years, research has already shown the importance of considering the production conditions when assessing writing individuality. For example, its value is lower for simulated writing collections when compared to purely genuine samples[6] or twins' handwriting compared to that of nontwins', an astute experiment long since favored by psychologists and FDEs.[7]

Sources of datasets — Excellent datasets exist for some FD aspects: ▸ online access to images and descriptions of major security documents such as passports from virtually all countries, comprising multispectral reproductions, and supported by automated expertise software and hardware; ▸ a comprehensive and international ink library, dating back to the 1920s. For handwriting, signature, and machine writing, however, researchers can use for all practical purposes only a limited amount of datasets produced by computer scientists, which suffer from issues of representativeness. Fortunately, vast quantities of data exist in analog form in governmental, public, and private archives, but—unfortunately—digitizing is only slowly progressing and beyond the financial reach of individual research laboratories. The sensitive nature of forensic documents and copyright issues add further hurdles to the open access of document samples so fundamental to computational FD.

The typology of FD datasets overlaps that of FD documents.[8] Since any aspect combination is possible, the possible number of datasets increases

---

1—Map in Garris 1994: 194.   **2**—Wilkinson et al. 1992b: 1.   **3**—Srihari et al. 2002: 858–859 propose to adopt the size of opinion polls, around 1,100 subjects, but Sacks 2003a: 916–917 points to medical experiments commonly with as few as 10–20 patients and epidemiological studies carried out on tens of thousands of individuals.   **4**—Bisotti 2011.   **5**—Harralson 2013: 62–64.   **6**—E.g., Found and Rogers 2007.   **7**—References in Harrison and Seiger 2003, Huber and Headrick 1999: 196–198, study in, e.g., Srihari et al. 2008, critique in Page et al. 2011: 15; for comparison see sampling issues in the FBI mtDNA database in Kaestle et al. 2006.   **8**—See p. 13.

substantially. Two implications are that for each combination there are few available datasets and that the datasets are difficult to compare.

Descriptors

The terminology used by FDEs to describe writing is rich—2,224 items in one case[1]—but terms and definitions vary across sources (a typical example is the typology of script styles[2]) and they are not convincingly systematized, described exhaustively, or generalized across script systems.[3] Therefore, the list presented here integrates the main descriptors according to the author's personal vision.[4]

Computational handwriting descriptors largely differ from those of FDEs, and are mostly not intuitive without mathematical knowledge, hence with implications for their use in the FD context. No clear systematic approach to writing description is apparent. Cross-pollinating between computing, FD, and paleography can make useful descriptive structures appear.[5] In striking contrast to offline writing description, as much as 78 descriptors of the dynamic recording of handwriting have been systematized and defined mathematically, or algorithmically,[6] and 100 others ranked by discriminative power.[7] Pen grip and body posture have been studied in FD, occasionally in computing and paleography, but mostly in psychology and education.[8] Fact sheet "Main descriptors" details the better known and performing descriptors.[9] Interestingly, the top positions are held by the allographs, which are also a central FD criterion, and by stroke curvature and orientation, which are determinant in paleography for script style classification and in human vision for shape identification. Texture and fractal dimension are other descriptors with perceptual correlates and good performance, but have been less successful in attaining development stage in FD software.[10]

Physical and chemical analysis can be more conclusive than digital image processing for examining inscription instrument, deposit, and substrate. Paper is the richest of the three in visual attributes, the principal descriptors being laid lines density, chain lines pattern, watermark shape, and paper pulp distribution.[11] In instruments one may look for any peculiarities of the model or individual item (created by manufacturing variability or through natural wear), for shape of fonts (typewriters), and pattern of printing raster (offset printers).

1—Huber and Headrick 1999: 163. **2**—On that of line quality see Huber and Headrick 1999: 120–121. **3**—Discussion: Huber and Headrick 1999: 89–141, list on 91; standard: ASTM 2012: E 2290 Standard Guide for Examination of Handwritten Items; additional lists: Sedeyn 1998, Locard 1935–1937 (5): 183–200, 274–343; useful descriptors for FD are found in graphology books, such as Branston 1989. **4**—See Fact sheet "Main descriptors," p. 128. **5**—Brink 2011: 7. **6**—Niels 2010: 40–51, Willems and Niels 2008. **7**—Fiérrez and Ortega-Garcia 2007: 200, Impedovo and Pirlo 2008: 612–615, Martinez-Diaz and Hangai 2009: 1185–1192. **8**—Doermann et al. 1994, Huber and Headrick 1999: 127–130, 302–312, Sciacca et al. 2007, Selin 2003, Sirat et al. 1990]. **9**—See p. 128. **10**—Hanusiak et al. 2012, Séropian et al. 2003. **11**—Rückert et al. 2009.

Methods

Human FD can be cast from a computing perspective as being essentially a quest for outliers in the description spaces of samples from different origins (identification) or the same origin (verification).[1] This process is based on unconsciously acquired models of in-between and with-in writer variability,[2] and the integration of probabilities of individual descriptors into a single output opinion.[3] It can involve contextual knowledge about the document.[4] The process is for most parts not explicit, written or quantified, is taught informally, and learned by experience.[5] An example is a British murder case from 1975, where investigators were looking for documents containing letters "F" similar to those of the questioned letters, then triaging the selection based on the letter "G," and finally the letter "C" and figure "9." After half a million documents were processed, a suspect was identified and the man confessed.[6] Human FD does however involve a number of explicit rule-based decisions, such as inferring writing direction and sequence from ridge pattern of ball-point pens or from the variation of ink along strokes.[7]

Current computational FD is similar to the human one, except for the use of quantitative models,[8] of different descriptors, little if any integration between descriptors,[9] no contextual factors, and no use of rule-based decisions.[10] Note that the quantitative models can derive from artificial learning (usually) and statistical analysis (less often). As part of the method, the metrics for valuing distances are also a research topic.[11]

Soft- and hardware [12]

Overview — Visual inspection by the expert remains the dominant tool for the expertise of writing. For other document aspects some sort of hardware is overwhelmingly employed. Computational analysis is marginal to nonexistent, with a few exceptions for tasks such as image processing or simple data tabulation. Forensic documents archives, as pointed out before, have rudimentary software support and are used locally (i.e., not networked); reproductions datasets of security documents are, however, numerous, extensive and commercially available, even online. This chapter reviews handwriting analysis software beyond research stage available for use by FDEs and makes cursory reference to tools for the other FD aspects.

1—Huber and Headrick 1999: 73–85.   **2**—Huber and Headrick 1999: 64–66.   **3**—Huber and Headrick 1999: 47–51, 61–63.   **4**—Huber and Headrick 1999: 63–64.   **5**—Huber and Headrick 1999: 38–42.   **6**—Baxendale and Renshaw 1979.   **7**—Atanasiu 2000, Doermann and Rosenfeld 1995, Gerke 2010.   **8**—Exhaustive list in Impedovo and Pirlo 2008: 612–615.   **9**—But see the inroads in in Bulacu 2007, Bulacu and Schomaker 2007.   **10**—The computational modeling of FDEs' expert reasoning is an open research topic. For inspiration see for example how logic is used in the adjacent field of computational law [Prakken and Sartor 1997].   **11**—Bulacu and Schomaker 2007, Cha 2007, Deza and Deza 2009 [encyclopedia of distances].   **12**— The FD software list in Fact sheet "Landmark software" (p. 121) is a companion to this section, pertaining mostly to handwriting.

Script processing — One handwriting expertise system, FISH, has been used by two government agencies for more than 20 years. Another, Write-On, is a simple image database software optimized for FDEs. Other tools might be used on an occasional basis (Graphlog) or have been discontinued (Script). As experienced while preparing the present survey, the software has irritatingly poor accessibility, sparse product information, shrill commercial claims, few maintained Web sites, unsuccessful installations, insufficient documentation, and user-enraging interfaces. When compared to the number of forensic laboratories, the insignificance of computer support for operational handwriting expertise is thus striking. Noteworthy also is that state-of-the-art solutions have received the greatest acceptance among FDEs, but technologically simple tools, often developed in-house by FDEs, suggest that the problem has strong cultural, organizational, and marketing roots.

Preprocessing — Many FD and—more often—non-FD software offer preprocessing capabilities, some rich and sophisticated, especially in the professional photography field (for example, Photoshop [all-rounder], DxO [camera-specific corrections], NoiseNinja [noise reduction], Photomatix [High Dynamic Range rendering]). Yet, a toolbox derived from the myriad of methods described in the image processing literature would still be extremely useful to FDEs. The basic needs should cover: ▸ *measurement* (size, orientation, surface…);[1] ▸ *comparison* (juxtaposition, superposition…); ▸ *segmentation* (ink–ink, ink–background, text–nontext, bleeding-through…); ▸ *enhancement* (of regions of interest, in various color spaces, in the frequency domain, dynamic range…); ▸ *correction* (deblurring, geometry correction…).

Signature — Only sporadic mention to commercial signature analysis software has been encountered in the forensic literature.[2] However, such automated software has been in field use in biometric applications for several decades.[3] Two possible explanations are that the software is embedded in complex systems (e.g., banking), and the biometric and forensic markets are disjointed.

Hardware — Hardware for document examination may be combined with image processing software, depending on its nature, for two-dimensional (2D) and stereo image acquisition, enhancement, segmentation, 2D-to-3D image transformation, geometry measurement, visualization, and so on. Within the goals of identification and verification the principal applications are detection of indentation, separation of multiple inks, establishment of writing strokes sequence, and recovery of inscription content. A short typology of techniques is given in Fact sheet "Noticeable hardware,"[4] with further details being provided in dedicated publications.[5]

1—Locard designates by "graphoscopy" and "graphometry" the verbal description of script shapes, respectively their quantitative measurements [Locard 1935–1937 (5): 182–200, 274–343].   **2**—Huber and Headrick 1999: 360.   **3**—Fiérrez and Ortega-Garcia 2007: 192, Woodward et al. 2003: 106–113.   **4**—See p. 129.   **5**—UNODC 2010, 2011.

Context

— [Computer HAL] I'm not questioning your word Dave, but it's just not possible. I'm not capable of being wrong.

— The whole darn building's been fired! That crazy fool machine of yours in Payroll went berserk this morning and gave everybody a pink slip!

— I think "Frankenstein" ought to be required reading for all scientists.

— [The detective] Go screw yourself with your logic!
— [The computer scientist] My judgment is just and I work for the universal good.

— [The Evil One] And when I have understanding of computers, I shall be the Supreme Being. God isn't interested in technology. He knows nothing of the potential of the microchip or the silicon revolution. Look how He spends His time. Forty-three species of parrots!

— All I wanted was a better world. A world where men were men, and women were cherished and lovely. [...] A world of romance and beauty. Of tuxedos and chiffon. A perfect world.
— But you were married to a robot.
— The perfect man.

— Burn the witch! On the stake with her!

— No power in this universe can stop the Daleks!

IMPACT OF COMPUTERIZATION

Even in comedies computers are diabolical and the engineers Satan's minions—no wonder FDEs should have concerns about the impact of computing (*Time Bandits* [1981] [5]). In cinema the theme is a substantial and often negative one, used both for its thrilling effect and for countering the uncritical embrace of technology in the real world. In this context movies clearly play the role of modern fairy tales. The dictatorial Colossus (*Colossus: The Forbin Project* [1970] [4]) and the evil Daleks (from the *Dr Who* BBC TV series, here in a video for *The Trial of Davros* stage play [2005] [8]) are just two more memorable instances of computers and robots attempting to take over the world. As for

their neurotic cousin HAL (*2001: A Space Odyssey* [1968] [1]), he threatens to derail the first encounter with an extraterrestrial race. In a reinterpretation of Pygmalion's myth, unfulfilled love is what drives scientists to build androids in both *The Stepford Wives* (2004) [6] and *Metropolis* (1927) [7], where these end up burned on the stake by modern-day Luddites!

The jobs lost by humans to computers, artfully played by Spencer Tracy and Katharine Hepburn in *Desk Set* (1957) [2], and the hubris of replacing intuition and emotion by rationality, exposed in Jean-Luc Godard's *Alphaville* (1965) [3], are also issues repeatedly voiced by the FD community. ...

9

10

11

Nonetheless positive feelings about technology are also animating experts of both documents and computing. One specific area of fascination is that of data representation and manipulation, ever since the gestural human–computer interface of *Minority Report* (2002) became a hit (here one of its numerous avatars, from *Eva* [2011] [**10**]). That the police of year 2054 is using it to visualize future crimes, only reinforces the parallel with the seer's crystal ball. So much so as spherical projection surfaces for massive data visualization—not unlike what is seen in *Star Wars: Episode VI, Return of the Jedi* (1983) [**11**]—have been built, for example, for the US Department of Homeland Security (DHS), or, for scientific research, at the University of California Santa Barbara: building-sized, immersive-reality environments.[1]

In *Brazil* (1985) [**9**], the omnipotent Information Retrieval government department employs for its dark endeavors chimerical machines that fuse antiquated typewriters and bulbous television displays, a playful revival of the copper-clad technologies of yore, the same ones as those with which tinker—on the reality side of the cinema screen—steampunk technoartists.

1—PNNL 2013, UCSB 2013.

Expertise performance

How good is a forensic documents (FD) opinion? To this question there are many possible answers depending on whether we look at the human or software performance, quality of datasets, public perception, or legal and scientific value. If FD is not scientific what are its usefulness and its future?

FD performance evaluation is part of the research agenda and a resource. It is also a hotly debated topic of forensic policies. Its importance is ethical—people's lives are affected by the quality of FD opinions—and existential—the livelihood of FD examiners (FDEs) depends on the profession's reputation. These considerations call for a thorough examination of the issue.

Expertise performance is fundamentally constrained by the limits imposed by the expertized artifact: a biometric such as handwriting yields greater variability between samples than fingerprints. The quality of an opinion is further degraded by the empirical expertise apparatus: human or software expert, datasets, opinion quantification method, and handling of physical samples. At times in contradiction with the objective evidence, is the FD performance as perceived by various social groups: FDEs, courts, nonforensic scientists, and the public.

Theoretical limits

Individuality of handwriting — In order to identify two documents as originating from the same source, a core goal of FD, there has to be some amount of distinguishability between sources and homogeneity within signals of the same source. This defines the resolution power, to use an image processing term, of a given forensic technology. DNA profiling yields literally astronomical figures, while earprint identification is notoriously unreliable. For handwriting and the various expertises carried out in FD, there are only a handful of empirical studies approaching this issue, mostly on unsound philosophical and statistical grounds. Yet forensics with the exception of DNA operate as if, *ipse dixit*, one bullet or fingerprint could be distinguished from all others in the world with zero error, which indeed surprises, to say the least, the scientific mind.[1]

1—On the individuation fallacy debate see Saks and Koehler 2008 [initiator], Kaye 2010 [comment], . . .

Fingerprints are a good example to think about individuality: anybody can see the difference between one's own and those of others, and they are physical, sort of rubber stamps, which makes it easy to conceive their stability over time. But this simplicity is treacherous.

Source — First, the epidermic surface has an elastic topology due to biological metabolism, environmental conditions, and pressure exerted by the finger on surfaces. "The" fingerprint is thus a constantly morphing entity—is it still singular as invariably predicated in language or more like plural but not quite? For handwriting the question is far more difficult, because the source is a living neural tissue with a much greater plasticity, of which we have far less understanding. It is tempting to even drop the idea of the individuality of the emitter and concentrate on the individuality of the signal emitted by a specific writer.[1]

Context — Second, fingerprints and handwriting never exist *in* the source, where at best we find cognitive prototypes and motor-control programs. Signals are signals only once emitted by a source and then they are consubstantial with their propagation medium. Thus, skin ridges acquired by a piezoelectric scanner will look different from a manually inked fingerprint in a police record or from the smudgy fingermark found on a bloody knife.[2] Handwriting is subject to further, more complex contextual variability.

Observer — The third aspect to consider is the observer who evaluates the a signal's individuality. From common experience it is apparent how—like twins' faces—unfamiliar writing styles appear indistinguishable, be it because they belong to other cultures or other times. Remoteness is even not necessary for confusion to happen: an FDE studying homographs[3] in registers of Los Angeles voters once remarked that "so many of these [signatures] lacked individuality and looked alike that they were not worth photographing."[4] The individuality of handwriting is thus indeed in the eye of the beholder, fluctuating whether this or that expert or software is consulted.

Sampling — Fourth, the receiver has access to only a sampling of the emitted signal to consider its individuality. For handwriting expertise, as for the Oriental elephant and dervishes of the parable describing it each his own way, depending on which body part they grasped, a certain amount of

---

Koehler and Saks 2010 [refinements], Page et al. 2011 [summary], Champod 2009 [encyclopedic entry]; on the experts' assertions about uniqueness and zero error Saks and Koehler 2008: 206, Cole 2005: 987, 990; the mathematics of fingerprint individuality in Maltoni et al. 2003; historical perspective in Cole 2001; two famous fingerprint misidentification cases in DoJ 2006 [FBI and the 2004 Madrid bombings] and Inquiry 2011 [Scottish policewoman]; individuation studies for the United States in Srihari et al. 2002, 2008, critically reviewed in Risinger 2007: 493–494 and Saks 2003a, author's response in Srihari 2005; for niche demographics see Anand 2011 [urbanites vs. ruralites], Cheng et al. 2005 [Singapore], Li et al. 2005 [Hong Kong], Horton 1996 and Nguyen et al. 2011 [US military]; further discussion in Huber and Headrick 1999: 74–77.
1—See Van der Ploeg 2011 and Lyon 2011: 358–361 on how human variability is a discrimination factor in biometrics and how this seemingly purely physical fact is predicated by cultural stereotypes and perpetuated by their implementation in technologies.   **2**—Maltoni et al. 2003: 28, Champod et al. 2004: 181–183 [terminology].   **3**—Identically written words of different meaning.   **4**—Harris 1958: 647b.

text is needed, meaning that "identity" does not start from the beginning. What then, if we look at larger scales: is the elephant—or handwriting—under the tree the same as the elephant in the jungle or the elephant on a distant planet? Possibly its IP address, but not its cosmic importance.

Conclusion — To cut short a sufi excursion, it appears that the system defining individuality, even for fingerprints and handwriting, is not that much well defined and static. Rather we should contemplate the concept of a *dynamic identity*. The shifting shape of flowing water and the question "Am I still I?" are metaphors that can help explore the issue. In practical computational terms this paradigm amounts in the current state of knowledge to adopt a probabilistic approach toward the discriminative power of various FD identifying markers. It suggests the evaluation of specific combinations in pattern–population–observer–context systems.

Empirical performance

Human experts — The 1993 *Daubert* ruling in the United States on expert testimony admissibility in court served as a wake-up call for the forensic community regarding the importance of performance evaluation. The US Forensic Sciences Foundation conducted during the 1970s and 1980s seven unpublished FDE performance evaluations, which were deemed incomplete and of dubious quality, and ceased altogether by the time of *Daubert*.[1] In 1989 jurists Michael Risinger, Mark Denbeaux, and Michael Saks initiated a series of articles that turned out to be highly inflammable page-turners revealing not only the absence of serious evaluations of the experts, but also that the quality of their expertise was not much better than what chance would produce.[2] The quantitatively very limited test by computer scientist Moshe Kam (seven experts, all from the Federal Bureau of Investigation [FBI][3]) is still cited by some as establishing the expertise power of FDEs.[4] FDEs Bryan Found, Douglas Rogers, and collaborators in Australia have been devoted since the late 1990s to designing and conducting large-scale proficiency tests of experts in handwriting and signatures (during the period 2002–2005 alone, 121 FDEs expressed 19,361 opinions on 599 signatures[5]). A consulting firm is now pursuing worldwide their methodology, started as a collaboration between academia and the police.[6]

1—Risinger et al. 1989.　　**2**—Details on the controversy in Risinger et al. 1989 [initial paper, detailed history of admissibility in the United States, role of Osborn], 1998 [response to critics], Risinger and Saks 1996 [international history, newer studies], Risinger 2007 [review of Found et al. and Srihari et al.], Saks and Faigman 2008 [sociohistorical perspective, role of courts and scientists], Galbraith et al. 1995 [criticism], Risinger 2010: 539–540 [reflection on reaction], Mnookin et al. 2011 [scientific culture], Cole 2009 [role of social scientists], Bernstein and Jackson 2004 [heterogeneous application of *Daubert* in US courts], Flores et al. 2010 [impact of *Daubert* on US courts], SWGDOC 2012b [repertoire of 1,600 cases], Nordberg 2012 [*Daubert* portal].　　**3**—Kam et al. 1994, Risinger 2007: 486–492, Risinger and Saks 1996: 59–63.　　**4**—Kelly et al. 2006: 39, Prime 2005.　　**5**—Bird et al. 2010: 104.　　**6**—Found et al. 1999 [project description], Risinger 2007: 492–493 [review], SHF 2012, ST2AR 2012 [companies].

Their conclusions are nuanced. FDEs are marginally better than laypersons at expressing correct opinions and far better at not making errors;[1] they are better at judging genuine writing, but fail on disguised and simulated samples.[2] Furthermore, the proficiency of laypersons depends on motivation, task difficulty, and time spent on a case;[3] and there is no demonstrated relationship between the length of an expert's career and performance.[4] The authors underline that the conclusions must be tempered by the fact that only a small fraction of FDEs willed to participate and only a very limited range of writing behaviors and conditions could be tested, thus paralleling the same sampling issue encountered with FD dataset representativeness.[5] Shedding additional light on human expertise besides that of professionals and laypersons is the recognition of one's own handwriting and signature, of which there is a much more intimate acquaintance. Experiments undertaken by psychologists (yet again outside FD) found low performances (59.8% errors) coupled with high confidence in one's capabilities (79.0%), results consistent with other self-recognition tasks such as face recognition (and the beliefs of handwriting experts in their discriminative powers).[6]

The juxtaposition of psychological and forensic experiments in identification leads to intriguing questions about the personal, social, legal, and technological construction of identity: given unreliable selves and others, we delegate identification power to machines, which in many respects have already surpassed human performance.

System performance — Another way to evaluate expert performance than by proficiency tests is to look at the success of FD in the real world. Running the entire gamut between forgeries of checks and last wills to bank robbery and kidnapping notes, the examination of documents is ubiquitous in civil and criminal litigations and intelligence work. A number of high-profile cases have grabbed the public's imagination about the power of FD to trace down suspects (the millions of documents searched in the 1956 Weinberger kidnapping),[7] authenticate documents (testimony of Albert Osborn [1858–1946], doyen of North American handwriting analysis, in the 1932 Lindbergh kidnapping),[8] or recover lost information (documents from the 2003 *Discovery* shuttle disaster).[9] The annals of FD also contain such dismaying performances as the 19th century Dreyfus affair which threw France in social turmoil,[10] and many examples of sideline roles, such as one of the most complex investigations in history, carried out on the 2001 anthrax letters.[11] Beyond such anecdotal evidence, there is little quantitative and detailed study on the operative and judicial impact of FD. Research on other expertise types revealed that the use of forensic evidence in court has less

1—Sita et al. 2002.   **2**—Bird et al. 2007, Found 2009: 1444, 1447, Found and Rogers 2007.
3—Found 2009: 1437b, Risinger and Saks 1996: 59–63.   **4**—Found 2009: 1448a, Sita et al. 2002.
5—Found 2009: 1437b; on sampling bias in FDE tests see Park 2008: 1123–1124 and Risinger et al. 1989: 749; other remarks in Huber and Headrick 1999: 69–70.   **6**—Britt and Mensh 1943, Mensh 1942, Saks and VanderHaar 2005, Tresselta 1946.   **7**—FBI 2010b.   **8**—FBI 2010a, Risinger et al. 1989: 764–771.   **9**—Brown and Sin-David 2005.   **10**—Wikipedia 2012a.   **11**—DoJ 2010.

impact on conviction than on sentencing, leading to more imprisonments and longer sentences,[1] and that erroneous forensic expertise is the second most common cause for wrongful sentencing, next to eyewitness errors (57% and 79%, respectively, of 200 exoneration cases analyzed[2]). Studies from France (1987–1996) and Canada (1990–2001) — countries with strong forensic technologies — found that human sources rather than technological expertise are the primary means for solving crimes such as homicides in about 80% of cases.[3] Overall, an ongoing Australian project on the forensic value for criminal justice considers that "the policing and forensic services community has been 'flying blind' in terms of the true impact of its works."[4]

At system level there is a striking contrast between the dynamism of FD and that of other biometric fields like fingerprinting and DNA profiling. From an FBI commemorative monograph come images with a cinematographic power equal to the utopian *Metropolis* movie, of a World War II football-sized hall where clerks are busy manually checking millions of fingerprints, of a 2002 robotic retrieval system for fingerprint files on magnetic tapes fit for the infinite library of Borges' novel, of past century rows of dactyloscopes at which experts check on computer screens matches detected by the Automated Fingerprint Information System (AFIS), a network that spans the nation and greets every visitor to the United States at major entry ports.[5] The scale is equally staggering for DNA profiling: in the United Kingdom alone close to 6 million citizens, or 10% of the population, have DNA information stored in a governmental database.[6] Yet even these numbers pale in the face of suggestions made for universal DNA profiling of newborns, in a replay of the voluntary fingerprinting campaigns of the 1930s advocated by director of the FBI J. Edgar Hoover (1985–1972) and others in the United States, in which many tens of thousands willingly participated.[7] The utility of such Molochs is justified by authorities by the number of matches between crime scene and reference profiles: almost half a million for DNA reported in the last decade in the United Kingdom and an average of 23,000 monthly for fingerprints in the United States at the present time.[8]

In comparison, typical FD computing datasets are comprised of less than 1,000 writers, and the largest law enforcement databases attain 100,000 individuals at best. Physical governmental FD archives are substantially larger, but one would need to look at a busy public library, that is outside FD, to find the same hectic scene as that surrounding the fingerprint and DNA information hives. As noted before, the impact of FD is not quantified.

1—Peterson et al. 2010: 1.　　**2**—Garrett 2008: 76, 81–86.　　**3**—Ocqueteau and Pichon: 224–226.　　**4**—Julian et al. 2011: 220.　　**5**—FBI 2008: 40, 102–103, Wikipedia 2013d, Borges 2000. With their round scopes reminiscent of radars and those used in the Cold War SAGE air defense system, the sight of which has permeated the popular imagination as props in many TV series and movies, the older AFIS analyzers exude an image of power and ominous surveillance with little equal in the FD world [BKA 2013, CHM 2013, Loewen 2013, Wikipedia 2013c].　　**6**—NPIA 2012; for the rest of the world see FBI 2012a, Walsh 2009: 677–680, Walsh and Buckleton 2009: 831.　　**7**—Cole 2001: 197–199, 245–250, 295, Krimsky and Simoncelli 2011: 134-166.　　**8**—FBI 2012b, NPIA 2012.

So where might the roots of the difference be? The quality of identification based on writing is clearly inferior, fingerprinting being precisely the result of the search for a more reliable biometric during the late 19th and early 20th centuries. Yet personal commitment (Sir Francis Galton [1822–1911] to name a personality) and historical opportunities (British imperialism, every nation's nationalism, universal exhibitions) made fingerprinting possible, not its scientific value. A crucial aspect in forensic successes and failures seems to be their ability to serve as tools of surveillance—a striking example is the world-wide boom of the biometrics industry after the terrorist attacks of September 11, 2001.[1] While FDEs are active principally during the trial phase to verify identities, fingerprints and DNA are also used to identify suspects and survey populations. These tasks demand a scaling up of resources and reinforce the field's dynamics. Technical advances have made possible the use of signatures as an identifier in a number of civilian biometric applications (signing for receipts on electronic screens, future inclusion in e-passports...), leading to new know-how and potentially vast pools of written data that could positively affect FD. However, the fact that signature biometrics evolved outside FD despite its close topical relation, and that operational security document expertise is largely disentangled from forensics, leaves open the possibility of a gradual attrition of FD to the profit of new players. Furthermore, signature biometrics and security documents validation is performed nowadays in real time by largely automated systems, which is not the case for traditional FD approaches.

Software evaluation — For the pattern recognition community a major driving force was a series of competitions organized by the US National Institute of Standards and Technology (NIST) starting in the 1980s on speech recognition and then on Optical Character Recognition in the early 1990s.[2] Despite a growing number of computing publications on FD themes, forensics-oriented competitions were lacking until very recently. The biometrics community organized in 2004 the first International Signature Verification Competition,[3] followed in 2010 by a forensics–computing joint effort, the first challenge pitting computers against human FDEs in signature expertise tasks,[4] and last, in 2011, took place the first Writer Identification Contests for Latin and Arabic scripts.[5]

There are several families of evaluation metrics typically in usage for writing expertise, according to the targeted applications and historical influences at work. Popularized by document retrieval systems, the percent of hits in the top-1, top-10, or top-k retrieved documents are simple and practical metrics.[6] Extended to include all documents of the same source, a retrieval task is transformed into a classification problem.[7] Imported from the speech processing literature, and more broadly from industrial quality control, the current standard performance indicators revolve around

1—Cole 2001: 305; Didier and Pellegrino 2011: 101, 104 –107.   **2**—NIST 2012a.   **3**—Fiérrez and Ortega-Garcia 2007: 190.   **4**—Blumenstein et al. 2010, Liwicki et al. 2010.   **5**—Hassaïne et al. 2011, Louloudis et al. 2011.   **6**—Brink 2011: 95–99.   **7**—Louloudis et al. 2011: 1476b.

aspects of the confusion matrix and the Receiver Operating Curve (ROC).[1] As the metrics for biometric systems evolved,[2] thus the latest computational forensic competitions shifted from the previously mentioned decisional results toward evidential values, that is, likelihood ratios, which are better suited to forensic realities.[3]

Some of the commercial or governmental handwriting expertise systems report a 100% identification performance, and similar high rates are found for the nonforensic research software of the computing literature.[4] There are, however, a number of issues with these figures. ▶ *Benchmarking*. It is hardly possible to confirm, compare, or understand the published data since it is based sometimes on different evaluation methodologies and usually on different datasets, so that it measures performances of different numbers of writers (from 1 to over 10,000!), text quantity (single words to whole books), script systems, writing styles, contents, native/nonnative language proficiencies, forgery skills, or writing implements. ▶ *Applications*. The figures are derived from laboratory tests, not resulting form field trials. We do not know what their performance will be in the many different conditions in which the software is supposed to be used. For example, in the case of one signature competition the sample contributors were, for legal reasons, asked not to use their habitual signatures but invent new ones[5]—as for the "skilled forgeries" no professional forger was hired, obviously also for legal reasons[6] (however collections of forged documents do exist[7]). ▶ *Thresholds*. Any statistic over 90% looks great, but there is little research to give threshold brackets for how much is good enough in which conditions, so that we can make sense of the evaluation figures. ▶ In conclusion the results are "encouraging," to use a beloved fig leaf word of scientific publications, but more work is needed. For one observer looking from the standpoint of biometrics, the venerable MITRE Corporation, the performances of writing expertise software are "inconsistent with published international standards for biometric testing and reporting."[8]

Datasets representativeness — Among the evaluation domains this is the one in which the least progress has been achieved. As mentioned before, there is only one major handwriting study explicitly designing a statistically representative dataset, for the contemporary US population (modeling census data on age, gender, and ethnicity for 1,568 writers, initially targeting to achieve stratification also on education, origin country, handedness, and geographic spread [5 out of 50 states][9]), and one signature dataset modeling Spain's population (based on age and gender distribution; 400 subjects[10]). (A subset of the NIST SD19 datasets containing the writing of about 1,099

1—Davis 2006, Fawcett 2006, Zweig and Campbell 1993.   **2**—Dunstone and Yager 2008. **3**—Liwicki et al. 2011.   **4**—Brink et al. 2007: 95–98, Impedovo and Pirlo 2008: 621–625, Liwicki et al. 2011.   **5**—Martinez-Diaz and Fiérrez 2009: 1180, 1182.   **6**—Yeung et al. 2004: 18– 19.   **7**—See p. 114, "FBI." Discussion of professional forgers and skilled impersonators in [Huber and Headrick 1999: 272–275.   **8**—Wayman and Orlans 2008: 5-8–5-9.   **9**—Srihari et al. 2002: 858–857.   **10**—Fiérrez et al. 2010: 237–238.

citizens reporting on the Census forms might also be statistically representative, but was never to this author's knowledge used to study writer demographics.[1]) For an example of how twisted, bonsai-like, FD datasets can be, in the case of the first signature verification competition, of 2004, just mentioned, signature donors were asked for privacy reasons not to use their real signatures. One can only muse what kind of signature this dataset best represents—probably it is an excellent collection to study the genesis of signatures. Further interesting questions on representativeness arise from a comparison of handwriting and signature datasets: usually the former are collected in a single session, the latter in more than one session, sometimes spaced months apart, to combat the "boredom" factor arising from repetitious signing.[2] Handwriting and signature datasets thus clearly exhibit their nonequivalence in terms of temporality and emphasize the drawbacks of not always knowing in how many sessions, at what intervals, and when during the day the writing was performed, all important biometric factors.[3] Also at the core of representativeness is a datasets gap that has long been apparent, one between authentic forensic documents (e.g., threat notes[4]), realistic, elicited writing samples (e.g., free instrument and text length choice[5]), samples taken under controlled conditions (e.g., a set content copied by all subjects with the same type of instrument on ruled paper[6]), and synthetic samples.[7] Overlaps on this topic exist between FD and writing recognition.[8] In conclusion it can be noted that many forensic fields are plagued by low dataset representativeness, as sample collection is expensive and time-consuming, but it is essential for producing software that is marketable and does not harbor the risk of justice miscarriages.

Opinion quantification — Expert opinion is currently expressed on ordinal scales using natural language,[9] for example: Identification, Highly Probably Did Write, Probably Did Write, Indications Did Write, No Conclusion, Indications Did Not Write, Probably Did Not Write, Highly Probably Did Not Write, Elimination;[10] or, shorter: Identification, May Have, No Conclusion, May Not Have, Elimination.[11]

In parallel, a desire to use quantitative values has existed since the formative period of FD. Indeed, one of the earliest usages of statistics in court (the 1868 *Howland* will case, United States) involved signature comparison, a practice that later, Albert Osborn would commend.[12] Statistical reasoning in the context of law can be traced back to antiquity and cultures as diverse as Greek, Christian, Judaic, and Chinese; but it is only since the 1960s that statistics had produced an actual impact in the courts.[13] The British, who gave the world Sir Conan Doyle and Agatha Christie, produced

1—Geist et al. 1994: 18–19.   2—Munich and Perona 2003: 200–202.   3—On the related subject of writing synchronicity see Huber and Headrick 1999: 164–169.   4—NARA 2007.
5—Chaski and Walch 2009.   6—Schomaker and Vuurpijl 2000.   7—Bunke 2003: 453–456.
8—Chen et al. 2011.   9—Critique in Champod 2009: 1510, McQuiston-Surrett and Saks 2008.
10—ASTM 2012: E1658 Standard Terminology for Expressing Conclusions of Forensic Document Examiners.   11—FBI 2007b.   12— Fienberg 1989: 214–216.   13— Fienberg 1989: 212–218.

another legendary logician, Thomas Bayes (c. 1701–1761), whose Age of Enlightenment theorem has become the staple of modern computing and suffused scientific practice.[1] Using the likelihood ratio to evaluate evidence was arguably suggested in handwriting expertise since 1934 and used in court since 1965.[2] Under influence of other forensic areas, notably DNA analysis, and biometrics, and due to the efforts of individuals and research groups originating from the mathematical statistics community in Europe and the United States, the probabilistic approach has gained acceptance, if not widespread usage, among FDEs due to various practical and theoretical issues.[3]

Perceptual performance

Public perception — Independent of the objective performance of a technology, its public image often plays a crucial role in its acceptance and development, making a glance into it worthwhile in a review of the state of the art. Public perception on human and computational FD is shaped by different information channels, in different ways. *Firsthand experience* of the technology is the most direct, although not neutral channel, being tainted by expectations (about biometrics, for example). *Secondhand knowledge*, the most common mediation channel, is important because its shear omnipresence (news media), instructional value (documentaries, exhibitions, museums, scientific material), or accessibility (works of fiction, mainly literature and visual arts). I will succinctly address some of these for exemplification.

Experience — An opinion survey for signature verification shows that this biometric modality is the least trusted among users in the United States and the third least trusted after keystroke and gait recognition for nonusers.[4] This negative social disposition with regard to the quality of writing expertise is compounded by a quantitative factor, there being an entrenched belief that graphology, the unfashionable relative of FD, is widely employed in the job hiring process, at least in some countries such as France.[5]

A perverse impact of the ever-increasing role of FD software on its public image could very well develop in the near future, with repercussions in court: "numerical obscurantism" as a pendant to technophobia, consists in overvaluing the results of computational expertise. And indeed, cases have long been known where the use of science, such as statistics and DNA tests,

---

1—Fienberg 2003 [links to the actual role of Bayes in Bayesianism, and the history of the term], Bertsch McGrayne 2011 [a popular history of Bayesianism, featuring famous FD cases], Risinger 2010: 535–539 [on Sherlock Holmes and forensics].   **2**—Huber and Headrick 1999: 65.   **3**—Lawless 2010: 6–8, and Lawless and Williams 2010: 733–736 [history in a nutshell of probabilities in forensics], Aitken 2009a [evolution of approaches], Taroni et al. 1999 [more background], Champod and Evett 2009 [encyclopedic entry], Fienberg 1989: 191–210 [comparison on the use of frequentist and Bayesian approaches in law], Lawless and Williams 2010: 745–748 [issues example], Royall 1997 [probabilistic fundamentals], Taroni et al. 2010 [a Bayesian framework for forensics], Taroni et al. 2006 [Bayesian networks], Neumann et al. 2011, 2012 [fingerprints], Curran 2009 [glass, DNA], handwriting specific: Davis et al. 2012, Day 2009, Hepler et al. 2012, Saunders et al. 2011, wording of probabilistic opinions: Evett 1998.   **4**—Nelson 2011: 50.   **5**—Which is a myth: Bangerter et al. 2009.

as well as the image of science, informed a judge's attitude and had an intimidating effect on the members of the jury.[1]

Cinema — How does cinema portray FD? The answer seems straightforward in one respect: modern technologies are practically absent FD props—at best, silver screen experts use magnifying glasses.[2] As witnessed in courts, studies have found, movie FDEs fare better than badly reputed lawyers, but they are never far from ironic takes on their abilities.[3] As for computer engineers and computers, they are mostly "mad, bad, and dangerous," in line with the stereotype of the scientist in popular culture.[4] From bikini vamps and bespectacled lab assistants in supporting roles, women scientists have slowly moved center stage, a trend particularly visible in criminal investigation TV series.[5]

Why are the portraits as they are? Although there is a heavy zest of reality to the cinematic image of FD beyond the filmmakers' urge to meet public expectations, "all professions look bad in movies," argues scientist, filmmaker, and writer Michael Crichton.[6] Indeed, the very format of the movie favors the dramatic, while the ambivalent image of science, technology, and knowledge in general has deep historical roots.[7] Movies are furthermore complex constructions, many factors impacting the final product: budget, marketing, studio policies, ideology, aesthetics, technical feasibility, and last but not least, people—producers, directors, cameramen, actors, props suppliers, scientific consultants, and many more.

Does it matter? There is a mutually reinforcing interplay between the cult(ure) of image—still and moving, silent, then in color, lately three-dimensional—in which we live and the technologies of image which we develop. Their impact on science is apparent from the growing acceptance of visual representation and visual thinking in even reluctant fields to these approaches, like mathematics (remember the success of fractals in the popular culture of the 1980s) and statistics (through the contemporary fascination with data visualization)—and as we saw it, visuality is equally popular in FD. So it does not come as a surprise that the public image of science as conveyed by the cinema appears to have the capability of conditioning court proceedings. However, empirical studies are missing so as to know more on how fiction about science impacts actual science, in particular FD, and consequently opinions diverge between "real-world consequences" and "none at

---

1—Caudill 2008: 929–931, Fienberg 1989: 150–151, 215, Reichman 2007: 923–931.   **2**—Own research, largely based on Western films, as most studies on science in cinema.   **3**—Caudill 2008: 927–928, 931, based on US movies. The image of lawyers has reversed since the 1960s. Portrayals of real and fictitious experts on pp. 6–10, 20, 90, 132.   **4**— A formula used as book title [Frayling 2006]. Studies of the scientists' public image in Frayling 2006 [cinema], Skal 1998 [cinema], Pansegrau 2008 [cinema, typology], idem p. 264 [computers displacing scientists], Flicker 2008 [cinema, women], LaFollette 1990 [magazines], 2008 [radio, TV], 2013 [TV], Haynes 1994 [literature], Carter 2013 [computers], Dirk 2013 [robots], Mainguet 2013 [biometrics], MRC 2013 [bibliography]. On forensics in American popular culture see Steenberg 2013 and on the modern culture of violence Seltzer 2007.   **5**—Flicker 2008, Weingart 2008: 273.   **6**—Crichton 1999: 1461b.   **7**—Weingart 2008: 269–271, 277, 280; Pansegrau 2008: 264.

all."[1] As scientists and their employing organizations become aware of the benefits of participating in movie productions the situation can be expected to change.[2]

Of course movies are fiction, but for most people they are the sole context to experience FD in action. Cinema is therefore a powerful public relations instrument, that famous organizations seek to instrumentalize—to paraphrase a National Aeronautics and Space Administration (NASA) scientist, "Hollywood speaks better about FD than FD can do."[3] Fiction acts as a strong motivational factor, especially in the formative stage of life—without Sherlock Holmes there would be no Edmond Locard according to a letter of his to Arthur Conan Doyle, and many an FDE could find similar fictitious characters at the root of his or her career.[4]

Imagination defines each of the words forensic and science, an indispensable tool for research and persuasion, and alas, sometimes wrongdoing. Among FDEs the Frenchman Edmond Locard was as nobody else better aware of the seamless semantic drifts between the flows of imagination, fantasy and confabulation. He was an inventor, administrator, novelist and comedian. This picture is from the film shooting of *Docteur Locard : l'heure du crime* [Doctor Locard: The Crime Hour] (1964), a biopic in which Locard awakens in dream as Dr. Watson, Sherlock Holmes' right hand [Frangin 1964]. In other terms a nested back and forth between reality and fiction and multiple layers of self-awareness— "he had a knack for paradoxes," as his nephew once put it [Larriaga 1988: 23:38].

Creating model roles for female computer scientist in cinema—think of Lara Croft anointed ambassador of British science and technology by the UK government[5]—is seen as a way to improve the gender gap in computer science, just as forensics-focused TV series boosted enrollment in forensic curricula.[6] Cinema continues to also play a role in professional education, with many universities offering classes on law and cinema, conferences being organized on the topic, and papers published.[7] An analogue interest for learning from fictional representations is nascent in computer science.[8] The human–computer gesture interface of *Minority Report* (2002) is a case

1—Complex issue, studies are missing: Steinke 2003: 4, Weingart 2008: 267; has impact: Caudill 2008: 932, Flicker 2008: 242, 251, Pansegrau 2008: 258–259, Steinke 2003: 4, 2005: 34–36, Kirby 2011: 223–226, 235; no impact: Crichton 1999: 1461c.   **2**—See the rationales in the interaction between filmmakers and science consultants in Kirby 2011.   **3**—FBI 2008: 89, Kirby 2011: 53, 55.   **4**—Steinke 2003, 2005: 31–36 [motivator]; Crauser 2010: 31 [Locard's letter to Doyle, similitudes between the two]; Locard 1924: 12–13, 25, 89–91, 96–97, 123 [utilities of fiction].   **5**—Flicker 2008: 250.   **6**—Smallwood 2002.   **7**—Reichman 2007: 1–2.   **8**—Shedroff and Noessel 2012 [interface design], Dourish and Bell 2013 [ubiquitous computing], Johnson 2010a, 2010b [science-fiction design].

in point on cinema's potential for FD: the consultants build the movie props in such detail—an entire dictionary of gestures materialized—as if developing functional consumer products; later the success of the movie helped them obtain the funding to do exactly this.[1] Even more important is the acculturation of the public to a specific technology or theory, a sensitive issue in many aspects of computational FD such as large-scale database networking or software performance. Cinema also has the capacity to address issues that other media deal with less successfully, to initiate public debates on controversial topics, stimulate political action, and promote specific research agenda.[2] The long-standing bashing of FDEs and computer scientists in cinema cannot but contribute, one hopes, to put computational FD on a better footing.

Architecture — France's first forensic laboratory established in 1910 "was located in the attic of the courthouse of Lyon, in some rooms from which the spiders had to be chased away. You got there after climbing five floors on a staircase that looked like a ladder."[3] Today, the public can enjoy a positively more glorious image of FD materialized in architecture from around the world. Driving between the picturesque city of Delft and the cruel shibboleth Scheveningen, the Netherlands Forensic Institute appears from the highway as a translucent ship of glass and steel floating among clouds on the green Dutch prairie.[4] Hidden like a gem in Virginia's woods, the FBI's forensic laboratory is no less a monumental hymn to high-tech proudly advertised in the Bureau's publications.[5]

Toponymy — Edmond Locard, the pet FDE of this book,[6] expected nobody to remember him six weeks after his death—he was utterly wrong: a street in his hometown, Lyon, bears his name.[7] There is also an Alphonse Bertillon street and a Mabillon subway station, both in Paris.[8] In Eldersburg, MA, one gets from Conan Doyle Way directly to Sherlock Holmes Street and then can wander at lust in Watson and Moriarty Courts or Baskerville and Elementary Drives. A more geeky spirit and some detours in the outback are needed to appreciate the Forensic Circle in Melbourne (location of the Victoria Police Forensic Service), the Investigation Parkway in Quantico, VA (at the FBI's forensic facilities), Document Road (Otis Air Force Base, MA), Calligraphy Court (Oceanside, CA), or Signature Boulevards, Streets, Drives, Courts, and other lofty Circles sprouting in the English-speaking world. Place names such as these create an imaginary landscape that secures FD its own space

1—Kirby 2011: 199–201.   **2**—Kirby 2011: 6–7, 12–18, 48–63, 96–117, 169–172, 293–218 [extensive analysis], Caudill 2008: 921–926, Weingart 2008: 280–281.   **3**—Locard 1957.   **4**—NFI 2013, McNamara 2006.   **5**—Waggoner 2007.   **6**—Not without reason: towering figure in the history of forensics (the location of the Interpol headquarters in his hometown Lyon is a tribute to Locard), he is equally "a character out of a novel," wrote one biographer [Artières et al. 2010: 8].   **7**—Archives municipales de Lyon 2010: Biographie, 6.   **8**—After Jean Mabillon (1632–1707), historian and founder of paleography and diplomatics. Compared to strictly FD, much more figures of the history of forensics, many with broad scientific interests, are honored in street names, for example fingerprinting pioneer Sir Francis Galton (1822–1911) or medical criminologist Cesare Lombroso (1835–1909), quite popular in North Italian cities.

in the public mind.[1] Which celestial bodies will be named after the pioneers of computational graphonomics?

Admissibility in court — *Premises* — While the archeology of FD is hardly touched upon, the existence of forged documents and thus a modicum of authentication know-how is evident from the presence of various security features since the oldest antiquity in many cultures. Where literacy was scarce, the ability to write was itself a protection; the threat of punishment (banishment, crucifixion, perpetual imprisonment, the modalities varied) acted as a virtual security device against forgery and was inscribed on many paper money still of living memory; "laws carved in stone" is not just a Biblical metaphor, but the immanence of legal instruments wished by the likes of Hammurabi, the Ur-legislator, and, much later and for another medium, Islamic and European rulers preferring paper and papyri to the easier to alter parchment; issuing documents in double exemplary or entrusting them to a *manus publica*, the notary, as practiced in Ptolemaic Egypt and by the Romans; appending heavy seals to graphically and linguistically elaborate medieval charts; the invention of watermarks, watermark counterfeits, and admonitions against such deceits in 13th century Italy; the long evolution of signatures; the calligraphy forgery market of Renaissance Persia; all are random picks from a cornucopia of indices revealing a pervasive preoccupation with securing the integrity of documents throughout history.[2]

Formative past — The legal formalization of document expertise is, however, a development scattered across time and space, made of reoccurrences and cultural specificities.[3] During antiquity and medieval times legislations in the Western world deal at length with issues of document authentication. The primary means is through the probatory strength (documents kept in public repositories, issued by notaries, or written by private persons) and use of oral witness testimony, while the physical expertise of documents and writing is quasi absent from legal texts. The explanation advanced in the 6th century Justinian compendium of Roman laws containing some of the oldest documented legislation pertaining to FD and a historical fundament of modern law, is the expressly stated unreliability of such an expertise.[4]

The shift toward a physical approach to document expertise is due to the rise of notaries from the 12th century onward initiated in Northern and Central Italy. It released a flurry of document-related practices that spread across continental Europe— the birth of diplomatics, paleography,

---

1—On toponymy see encyclopedic Kadmon 2000, or—for its deep role in the existence of a people—Basso 1996.   **2**—Gacek 2000 [parchment, calligraphy], Johnson 1987: 144 [Egyptian notary], Haighton 2010 [Roman notary, punishment], Bedos-Rezak 2008 [seals], Rückert et al. 2009: 29 [watermarks], Fraenkel 1992 [signatures].   **3**—Why the term forgery as understood today might not be appropriate for the medieval period: MacNeil 2000: 8–9, Clanchy 1993: 318–327.   **4**—Blume and Kearley 2012: C4.21.6, C4.21.20, C8.17.11, N49.2, N73. The existence of dedicated FD experts in Justinian Rome cannot be assumed on the basis of the Code, the Latin original [Schöll and Kroll 2009] using—in Blume's English rendering—the terms "those who make the [handwriting] comparisons," but not "experts" as translated by Scott 1932: 49.2.2 and perpetuated by a number of forensic publications.

graphology, and modern history starting with the Renaissance are to be read as epiphenomena of this legalistic culture.[1] The Italian seeds are perceptible in the French royal deed of 1554 by Francis I, stipulating that contracts have to be signed, as well as the abolishment during the subsequent century of the use of seals and notary signs (personal marks made of a standardized drawing and the written, but not stylized, name), which made the manual gesture into a preeminent means of authentication.[2] Two other legal examples concern the notaries' protocols and their matriculation. Stipulated *inter alia* by the 1231 Sicilian legal code of King Frederick II and the 1446 notarial statutes of Rome, notaries had to present to officials a bound volume of all protocols prepared by them during the year, with handwriting and signature samples affixed, to be used for document authentication in case of litigations. As part of the matriculation process with the authorities, notaries were furthermore required to deposit with supervisory administrations the same samples of their handwriting, signs, signatures, or seals. This practice, spectacularly illustrated in the notary registers of Toulouse containing 11,000 notary signs from the 13th to the 16th centuries, was also stipulated in 16th century Rome as in other peninsular cities and has been perpetuated into modern use through the Napoleonic Code.[3]

In 1570 was created in Paris under royal auspices the proto-FDE corporation of "sworn masters and expert verifier writers for writing and signatures, accounts and computations contested in court."[4] Together with a number of books on FD matters published throughout the late Renaissance (in Italy first, then in France) and laws (such as that of 1737, again in France, that made provisions for the use of handwriting expertise in court[5]), these various strands set in motion the admissibility of FD in modern legislation. The United Kingdom followed suit in 1792 and the United States in 1835.[6] For comparison, the use of fingerprints for individuation is attested in judicial contexts in Mesopotamia in the 18th century BC and was common in China from maybe the 3rd century BC onward, from where it spread to Japan, Persia, and India, where Europeans adopted the idea in the 19th century.[7]

Present evolution — Today, handwriting expertise is admitted in many courts worldwide,[8] under specific provisions for evidence admissibility. The key rulings for the United States are *Frye v. United States* (1923), Federal Rule of Evidence 702 (1975), and what is known as the *Daubert* Trilogy: *Daubert v. Merrell Dow Pharmaceuticals* (1991), *General Electric Co. v. Joiner*

1—Byrne 2004 [overview of notary's historical role], Amelotti and Costamagna 1975 [the 12th century expansion], Nussdorfer 2009: 1–3, 10 [scholarly impact].   **2**—Fraenkel 1992: 12, 24–25, 158.
3—Caravale 1982: 161–162 [Sicily], Nussdorfer 2009: 39, 41–42 [Rome], Roschach 1866–7 [Toulouse], Archives départementales du Tarn 2012 [Southern France and Italy], Darmé 1909: 97 [Napoleon].   **4**—"Maîtres jurés écrivains experts vérificateurs en écritures et signatures, comptes et calculs contestés en Justice" [Guiral 1927: 10–11].   **5**—Risinger and Saks 1996: 22–35.   **6**—Risinger et al. 1989: 751–771, containing a description of Albert Osborn's role in the American FD history.   **7**—Ashbaugh 1999; Cole 2001: 60–96, 125; Barnes 2011: 1-8–1-9. For the history of the measurement of bodies for identification purposes in France see Denis 2011.   **8**—Found 2009: 1437a.

(1997), and *Kumho Tire Co. v. Carmichael* (1999).[1] During the 1990s, the validity of handwriting expertise came under increased questioning, leading to a refinement of judicial reasoning and a swing between successful (*United States v. Starzecpyzel*, 1995) and rejected challenges (*Pettus v. United States*, 2012).[2] Our times seem like a mix between the period straddling the turn of the 19th century when FD was much derided in courts—"As a class, such experts ought not to have influence enough to hang a cat"[3]—and the greater part of the 20th century which accepted FD unquestioningly—"Handwriting never lies. Handwriting analysis is an amazingly accurate tool."[4]

Differences between legal systems might also have an impact on the admissibility of scientific evidence, but there is difference of opinion whether the adversarial or inquisitorial tradition is more inductive of setting forensics on firmer ground and thus having an impact on computational forensic research.[5] In conjunction with the advent of DNA expertise, the *Daubert* ruling had a profound impact on the admissibility of expert testimony in forensic areas far beyond its initial FD scope.[6] At least due to its visibility on the Internet, in publications, at conferences, during collaborations, the United States plays a pioneering role in globally shaping forensic admissibility standards,[7] the implications of which are already apparent in the direction taken by FD-oriented projects in computing and mathematics. One such development gaining acceptance is that experts should use a probabilistic approach to explain the evidence instead of giving an opinion on authorship, which would be the responsibility of the jury.[8] Hence we witnessed a move for software performance being expressed in terms of Receiver Operating Curve (ROC) typical of industrial quality control and biometrics (e.g., GRAWIS[9]), toward the use of likelihood ratios (e.g., CEDAR-FOX[10]).

Scientific value — A question that has plagued the history of FD for a long time is whether FD, and in particular handwriting expertise, is a science. What sounds like a theoretical musing has very practical implications for those intending to do computational research in the field, since their projects will have to address a number of questions that might otherwise have

---

1—Discussed in, e.g., Risinger and Saks 1996; impact in Flores et al. 2010.   2— Risinger and Saks 1996: 31 n 68 , Pettus 2012.   3—Banker 1883.   4—Dresbold and Kwalwasser 2006: 3. On the evolution of the acceptance of FD see Risinger 2010: 538–539, Guiral 1927: 83–90. Remarks from FDEs suggest that Europe might have been more skeptical on FD well into the 20th century. Bertilon's quip that "[handwriting] expertise has not progressed since Raveneau [i.e., anno gratie 1666]"was a quite popular book opening [Guiral 1927: 9, Locard 1935–1937 (5): 11]. Here is another: "This is not a glorious history." [Guiral 1927: 9] Or, 40 years later: "In the past, not only in this [United Kingdom], but in other countries as well, 'handwriting experts' and 'graphologists' in general have enjoyed a very low status in the courts." — a British understatement of what Locard called "a reputation at the same time atrocious and farcical." [Harrison 1966: 1, Locard 1935–1937 (6): 825]   5—Fienberg 1989: 11, 13, 148, 156–164, 275–276 [American praising Europeans], Champod and Vuille 2011 [Europeans praising Americans]; Turner 2009.   6—Giannelli 2003.   7—Champod and Vuille 2011 [Europe], Commons 2005: 75–76 [United Kingdom], Lucena-Molina et al. 2012 [Spain], Edmond and Roberts 2011: 359–361 [Australia], Meintjes-Van der Walt 2003: 101 [South Africa], Wikipedia 2012b [Canada, United Kingdom].   8—Day 2009: 1453a.   9—See p. 124.   10—See p. 122.

been neglected and because of the need to know the theoretical and practical limitations in which they will operate. Let us clarify first what the criteria are for an endeavor to be considered scientific, see if FD meets them, listen to what FDEs have to say about it, and then consider the path forward.

Definition — There exists a number of varying, although essentially consistent, criteria sets defining what can be considered as science, spanning logical, empirical, sociological, historical, and legal aspects.[1] For FD, the *Daubert* ruling has set forth conditions for the US legal system: the methods should be tested, peer reviewed, the rates of error known, enshrined in standards, and accepted by the scientific community. Additional criteria are reproducibility of expertise results between laboratories and within the same laboratory, estimation of accuracy and bias, method selectivity, limits of reliability, and robustness (as defined for ink analysis[2]).

History — FD had a long and stagnant history. Writing in the 1930s, Edmond Locard qualifies an FD manual of 1666 (!) as "the capital work, the one that until the last years, and until the advent of laboratory methods, remained the most complete, the most informed and the model."[3]

The only academic subject concerned with authorship expertise of handwriting and signatures is paleography and its cousin branches diplomatics, epigraphy, and a couple more, to which FD entertains few historical links. Well into the 20th century, FD was influenced by graphology[4] and evolved in judicial and law enforcement environments with little sensitivity for scientific considerations. Furthermore, looked upon by academia,[5] FD has created its own, extra-academical body of knowledge, contrary to DNA profiling or textual style expertise, for example. Unfortunately, FD (or paleography and graphology for that matter) has not been able to develop the same empirical proofs and theoretical soundness that characterize genetics or linguistics. Such qualities suffused FD only marginally, in those areas where machines and materials are employed (analysis of writing instruments, deposits, and substrates) or where sciences found an interest (biomechanics and neurocognition, at the origins of the International Graphonomics Society).

Evaluation — As various court rulings, studies of the relevant literature, and evaluations of the working and training conditions have shown, FD fails to meet the criteria that would make it a science. More particularly, FD lacks reproducible, tested, universal analysis procedures; it lacks empirical data on variability distributions given complex, interrelated conditions; it is prone to contextual and sociological bias;[6] it has to deal with an broad range of factors, little understood (for example, the near impossibility of evaluating

---

1—Formal criteria: Black et al. 1994, Goodstein 2000, Root-Bernstein 1984, Lance 2012; collateral characteristics: Yaffe 2013.   2—Weyermann 2009: 688b.   3—Locard 1935–1937 (5): 12, apud Guiral 1927: 12, alluding to Raveneau 1666.   4—Risinger et al. 1989: 751–771, Thornton 1998, Wilkins 2011 [United States], Locard 1935–1937 (5): 14–16, 272–273 [France].   5—Palenik and Palenik 2004.   6—E.g., Busey and Dror 2011 [fingerprints], Dror and Rosenthal 2008, Dror et al. 2005 [experiments], Krane et al. 2008 [sequential unmasking], Risinger and Saks 1996: 64 [handwriting], Risinger et al. 2002 [typology of psychological biases], Thompson 1997 [sociological bias].

the age of ink traces[1]). Additionally, due to no standard technical vocabulary, training curriculum, and laboratory accreditation programs ("forensic handwriting examination is essentially a deregulated discipline"[2]), there is an "absence of a strong scientific culture" within the FD community to test underlying beliefs and performance (in the words of an FDE who has carried out extensive proficiency tests[3]). Its strength comes from historical acceptance (FD was "admissible for eons" spoke a trial court[4]), official status, and mutual self-reassurance, rather than empirical studies, underline scholars of the field's history.[5] More abruptly, handwriting expertise was compared to hunting witches and to folk medicine by Risinger, Denbeaux, and Saks, the jurists at the origin of the recent FDE's performance controversy,[6] and called by the risibly ponderous oxymoron "nonscience forensic science,"[7] thus ironically equating the field to graphology, from which a majority of FDEs take pains to stay clear.[8] Perhaps reflecting the confidence of FDEs in their own art, the 19th century abbot Jean Hippolyte Michon (1806–1881), father of graphology, was genuinely convinced of the scientific nature of his brainchild— "the fortune-teller of the past transforms himself into the psychologist, a man of reflection"—and the idea that graphology might be debased to the level of astrology, divination, necromancy, and chiromancy was to him anathema.[9] To historians of computer science these tribulations are reminiscent of the troubles their field had to defend its "science" accolade.[10]

In conclusion, the limited fashion in which FD addresses criteria of scientific quality rather than entirely discrediting FD casts it as a craft instead of a science[11]—like a harbor pilot whose knowledge is good only in his own port, was the metaphor used by a judge.[12] In this respect, Roy Huber and Alfred Headrick, authors of a leading handwriting expertise handbook, have this to say: "So handwriting identification as presently practiced is not a science. So what?"[13] Indeed, there are still sufficient ways in which FD is useful.

First, FD can play with better confidence its role at guiding an investigation to a suspect (investigative role), than serve evidences in courts (testimonial role; this is sometimes the rationale of the exclusion of handwriting expertise in trials). Second, FD becomes more proficient as the evidence is difficult to contest (anachronistic features are a good example—e.g., ballpoint

---

1—Weyermann 2009: 684–692. 2—Found 2009: 1448a. 3—Found 2009: 1448b, also Mnookin et al. 2011. 4—Florence 2003: 3. 5—Found 2009: 1448b, Lucena-Molina et al. 2012: 2a, Mnookin 2010: 1209–1211, Saks and Faigman 2008: 157a. 6—Risinger et al., 1989: 731, 734. A similar link to irrationality has already been expressed in 1929: "[The scientific expertise of handwritten documents] is one of the means to liberate the individual from ritual bonds and sacred gestures" [Locard 1935–1937 (5): 22]. 7—Saks and Faigman 2008: 150a. 8—Huber and Headrick 1999: 389–392. 9—Panchasi 1996: 11–12, a cultural reading of French graphology; Gladwell 2007: 43-44 discusses how tricks used by astrologers mirror techniques from forensic psychological profiling—they could as well apply to graphology. 10—Ensmenger 2010 and ongoing debate among computer scientists in Cerf 2013, Abrahams 2013, Denning 2013 [symposium]. 11—Huber and Headrick 1999: 372–373. 12—Risinger and Saks 1996: 31. 13—Huber and Headrick 1999: 372.

pens did not exist before 1944[1]). Third, the use of hardware has benefited
FD quality (mostly those areas geared toward ink and printer analysis, such
as in document alterations[2]). All these considerations are susceptible to
shape the computing research in FD.

Extent — The state of handwriting expertise is anything but singular in
forensics: fingerprints, firearms, and toolmarks—to point only to the tip of
the iceberg—are all challenged.[3] Apart from DNA profiling (not without its
own problems[4]) the issue is general, as stated by a recent report of the US
National Academy of Sciences on forensic science mandated by the Congress:
"With the exception of nuclear DNA analysis, however, no forensic method
has been rigorously shown to have the capacity to consistently, and with a
high degree of certainty, demonstrate a connection between evidence and a
specific individual or source."[5]

Reactions — "Handwriting is even more precise than DNA evidence for
identification purposes."[6] As this rather extreme claim of an FDE suggests,
and despite the shortfalls in FD practice laid bare in the last two decades, it
was found that the issues were acknowledged, but ignored by the FD community at large and the judicial process.[7] One longs, in these circumstances,
to see more statements such as "I believe that what cannot be demonstrated
is not evidence," written in 1958 and opening the FD manual of Harrison, a
trained chemist.[8] Regarding handwriting and signature analysis software,
it is often heard that "the machine cannot replace the human" to pretext
away from computational methods.[9]

On a positive note one can reveal proposed or enacted legislation to improve forensics (e.g., a proposed National Institute for Forensic Science in
the United States, uniform expression of evidence opinion across all forensic
areas within the Swedish National Laboratory of Forensic Science, clarify-
ing regulations for court experts in the Netherlands[10]), scattered efforts to
address the bias issues (e.g., at the Netherlands Forensic Institute[11]), the
increasing number of recently published basic standards regulating FD expertise (no fewer than 31[12]), the eager participation of some FDEs in the interdisciplinary conferences of the International Graphonomics Society, and
too few collaborative forensic computing research projects.[13]

Reformability — A subsequent question whether handwriting expertise
is scientific is whether it can become scientific at all. Obviously, being a

---

1—Weyermann 2009: 686.   **2**—Mohammed 2009.   **3**—General references in Gianelli 2003:
1096–1098, Mnookin 2010: 1209–1211, NAS 2009; for a glance at the lively debates on fingerprints, the
infallible triple-crown of forensic identification for a hundred years, see the historical perspective in Cole 2001,
the particular issues in Haber 2009, or the media coverage splashed in such highbrow publications as *Nature*
[Spinney 2010] and *The New Yorker* [Specter 2002].   **4**—Kaestle et al. 2006, Walsh and Buckleton
2009.   **5**—NAS 2009: 7, summarized in Edwards 2009, reviewed in Bohan 2010 and Mnookin 2011,
predecessors: NIJ 2006: 2–3.   **6**—Risinger 2010: 519.   **7**—Edmond and Roberts 2011: 361, Lucena-Molina et al. 2012: 1–2, Mnookin 2010: 1209–1211, Saks and Faigman 2008.   **8**—Harrison 1966:
1.   **9**—E.g., FBI 2007a: 30, Goudreault 2010: 5.   **10**—NAS 2009, Edwards 2009; Lucena-Molina
et al. 2012: 2a; Fagel 2011.   **11**—Stoel 2011.   **12**—See p. 111; on forensic standards history
and use see Lentini 2009.   **13**—See p. 82.

behavioral biometrics its variability and complexity are greater than for other forensic domains, such as DNA analysis. Extrinsic factors like the will of the involved parties to change how FD is practiced are probably even more important; the capacity of the society to invest sufficient financial, material, and intellectual resources; and sociotechnological developments that push areas of traditional FD into irrelevance—a trend seen in genetics and digital media, with nanotechnology on the horizon.[1]

In light of the developments in FD and computing for FD in the last decade, what is their likely future? In one scenario—already in motion—FD becomes a forensic backwater, supplanted by other evidence taking full benefit from modern technologies (the discontinuation by the FBI in 2005 of bullet lead examination is a recent example of the complete disappearance of a forensic method[2]). Or, electronic text input devices—keyboards, e-pens, voice recognition, and so forth—become so ubiquitous as to either sideline the analysis of analog writing altogether (also to some extent an existing trend), or make computational forensics unavoidable. It took 10 years to develop in a past computing era, from 1966 to 1976, the first Automated Fingerprint Identification Systems (AFIS),[3] spawning thereby a small revolution in terms of the forensic technology market, intelligence capabilities, and controversies on forensic quality and individual freedoms. The future will tell if the computerization of handwriting and signature expertise will meet with the same success. In the mean time, addressing the forensic community, Micheal Saks preaches "honesty and humility"![4]

1—On solutions to scientificization of forensics see Cole 2010 [separation in forensic researchers, diagnosticians and technicians], Jamieson 2008 [match], Risinger 2010 [error]; on need for generational turnovers to effect change Risinger 2010: 538–539; Paradise et al. 2009 [nanotechnology].   2—FBI 2005, Gabel and Wilkinson 2008: 1004–1006.   3—Cole 2001: 250–258, Moses 2011: 6-4-6-6, Woodward et al. 2003: 50–56, 60–62.   4—Saks 2010: 16.

Policy landscape

Discussion on integrating computing and forensic documents (FD). Presentation of the actual state and probable trend. Identification of obstacles.

The preceding chapters canvassed a state of the art in human and computational FD and proposed a research agenda. Its successful implementation depends on a policy for, or at least an awareness of, the role of computing and the nature of obstacles likely to be encountered. Symptomatic for the need of a high-level perspective are the inquiries on the state of forensics sponsored by lawmakers in a number of countries, the baptism of a new discipline of forensic science administration,[1] the creation of an eponymous institute in the United States,[2] and the launching in 2009 on a new journal devoted to the very subject—*Forensic Science Policy & Management: An International Journal*—in which computer scientists can read about how to make collaborative forensic projects succeed.[3]

Role of computing

Artificial expertise — The review of the ongoing controversy on forensics shows that it focuses on the human expert. However, there is a new player, the software expert, which has escaped scrutiny, perhaps because computer-assisted FD did not yet show up in court (the incomprehension on what FD software is about is apparent in the exchange between law and psychology Prof. Saks and computing Prof. Srihari[4]). Computing is already permeating FD in peripheral roles—imaging, databases, measurements, or visualization—and scholars of science and technology could certainly point out how this alters the practice and quality of FD.[5] Nevertheless, computing is poised to become the primary player in the surveillance and investigative phase of activities involving FD (national systems like FISH are the precursors), and expected to play a central role in shaping the expert opinion (all today's advanced commercial handwriting analysis software deliver automated opinions). In an era when autonomous vehicles land on asteroids far out in space, drive our cities, and conduct financial transactions on our behalf, it

---

1—Koppl and Kobilinsky 2005.   **2**—IFSA 2012.   **3**—Kelty and Julian 2011.   **4**—Saks 2003a, Srihari 2005.   **5**—For the impact of computing on the legal profession see Marcus 2008.

is a denial of reality not to see that computing will be as much protagonist in court as the human expert. Once "computational law"[1] will come about, a whole host of new, Asimovian issues will arise. For example, when considering an expert error, who's error is it? of the human user who did not master the computer? of the computer that acted in unpredictable ways? of the computer's producer? or the science behind it? Automated justice should hopefully remain a scarecrow, but the critical role computers will play in forensics should make Human 1.0 reflect.[2]

Silent revolution — Behind computers there are computer scientists and they are the true new players in modern FD and forensics. Let's look at their role. The transformations we witness in forensics were set in motion during the 1990s by law scholars with their challenges to the admissibility of forensic experts in court, the judges through their rulings defining scientific criteria, and the DNA technology shifting expert testimonies toward opinions expressed as probability likelihoods. During the 2000s, the impetus came from lawmakers commissioning official inquiries on forensic capabilities, and the efforts of scientists — for FD a nucleus of FD examiners (FDEs)-*cum*-academics dedicated to human expert proficiency testing — and statisticians working for sound mathematical foundations. The present decade could see private companies and governments stepping in.

By and large computing was not a fellow of these sometimes vocal challengers, but silently was working on its own revolution. Electromechanical machines for the recording of handwriting — the precursors of modern tablets and e-pens — are documented way back into the 19th century and involved inventors like Elisha Gray and Vannevar Bush.[3] Computational handwriting and signature expertise appeared thus quite naturally during the early days of computing in the 1950s and 1960s in all of the private, governmental, and academic sectors.[4] A sustained academic interest in forensic-specific writing expertise — as opposed to paleographic, banking, and other authentication applications — is however young, about two decades old. Among the computer scientists who are also entrepreneurs one was a member of the influential National Academy of Sciences 2009 report (Sargur Srihari, at the origin of CEDAR-FOX[5]) and another was president of the interdisciplinary International Graphonomics Society (Angelo Marcelli, of HG4FDE). Part of the academic research was funded in the framework of computing–forensics collaborations which acquainted computer scientists and FDEs with one another (FLASH ID, Wanda, GRAWIS, and GIWIS), and some software was the own initiative and in-house development of FDEs (FISH, Graphlog), which lowered the cross-disciplinary acceptance thresholds. Thus software is silently creeping into the house of forensics.

1—Love and Genesereth 2005.   **2**—Kizza 2007 [reference material on computers and ethics], Friedman 1997 [implicit and explicit human values in computers], Wallach and Allen 2009 [practicals of designing moral machines], Anderson and Anderson 2011 [the need for collaboration between computer scientists and ethics scholars], Lin et al. 2012 [ethics in robotics], Epstein 1997 [fictionalized approach to computing ethics].   **3**—Renard Ward 2006.   **4**—Huber and Headrick 1999: 154–155.   **5**—NAS 2009: v.

The amazing thing about the phenomenon is that even the very ones to en-gineer it seem not to notice it. There is indeed a naïveté bordering on autism from computer scientists in regard to the controversies and stakes around forensics that could be interpreted at will as frightening or blessing. Lis-tening to the discussions between computing students, the ones doing much of the computational FD research, and skimming through the references in their published papers, there are, barring a few exceptions, no references to the implications on computing opened up by the expert admissibility debate. The issue is not only an idealistic wish for the academia to sculpt enlightened engineers, but also a very practical one, because awareness of the forensic ecosystem is necessary to successful scientific and technologi-cal advances, as shall an enumeration of obstacles in the way of computing FD make clear over the next paragraphs. A report on technological education commissioned by the US National Academy of Engineering and National Research Council starts with a strong-worded observation about the fore-most economical, military, and technological power in the world: "Although the United States is increasingly defined by and dependent on technology and is adopting new technologies at a breathtaking pace, its citizens are not equipped to make well-considered decisions or to think critically about technology. As a society, we are not even fully aware of or conversant with the technologies we use every day. In short, we are not 'technologically lit-erate.'"[1] The emphasis is here not on understanding the inner workings of innumerable technologies, but on critical thinking on the role played by technologies in human life.

Factors

Computing — With obvious drawbacks, much academic research in com-putational FD and handwriting in particular is not picked up by companies to be developed into end-products. On the one hand basic FD needs are not addressed since researchers want to work on challenging topics, not product development or trivia. It is indeed not their job to man technical support hotlines. On the other hand critical topics like handwriting segmentation are still not solved after their first formulation half a century ago, blocking breakthroughs in handwriting expertise. Research software is notoriously and understandably full of bugs and limitations, has bad user interfaces, and often comes as not compiled code—in other words useless for operation-al deployment. The continuity of research is a structural problem to address, rooted in a high turnover of students and projects, preventing knowledge evolution and strategic thinking, and an issue equally affecting forensics.[2] From the frequency distribution of the references mentioned throughout this book it becomes clear that some of the most important contributions were made by scientists having committed themselves to this field for long periods—sometimes for their entire career.

1—Pearson and Young 2002: 1.   **2**—Kelty and Julian 2011: 143, similar remarks in Fleming 2010: 141.

On the mind-set side, acculturation is necessary when two such different fields as FD and computing meet. Cross-education in the scientific, forensic, and law communities is a recurrent recommendation of reports on forensics and expert testimony.[1] Computer scientists should behave like anthropologists: read the FD literature, assimilate the language, participate in forensic venues, and spend time with FDEs in their field, laboratory, and court work.[2] The practical experience and mutual esteem thus gained are seminal ingredients of successful research ideas.[3] It begins by avoiding such barbarisms abounding in the computing literature as saying "written in such and such language" when one means "script" or calling Chinese ideograms "letters" (these are "characters"; "letters" [or—oh sweet sacrilege!—"alphabets"] are elements of alphabetic writing systems; for basic graphonomic literacy consult the references in Fact sheet "Information sources"[4]).[5]

Industrial engineering — Computational FD in its most complex form is about building systems. There is more to it than image processing: it involves mathematics, logic, databases, networks, human–computer interfaces, visualization, project management, law, and marketing—it is software in symbiosis with its environment. In all these areas there is need for research, but no academic laboratory on its own can master the entire workflow. The complexities of real life deployments imply interacting with other players: developer companies, users, regulators, markets. The Wanda FD software is an example of a beautiful idea sunk on nontechnical rocks, while Methuselahic FISH (it runs on VAX computers!) is technologically inferior but institutionally viable.[6]

Market — Most FD technology suppliers produce analysis hardware, a few do security documents databases, but just a couple offer handwriting analysis software. Because of its close relationship to forensics,[7] the biometrics market can be used as proxy to FD market analysis, knowing that the wider customer basis of biometrics will give the forecast an optimistic tint.

1—E.g., Fienberg 1989: 139–154, NAS 2009: 26–28, 234–237; see also on lawyers and policy makers Faigman 1999: ix–xiv.　　**2**—The sociologist H.M. Collins, to take an example from artificial intelligence, relates how for the study of expert systems he underwent apprenticeship in a crystal growing laboratory and actually wrote the code of such a system [Collins 1990: 135–178]. In forensics, Rodolphe Archibald Reiss, first director of the criminalistics institute of Lausanne, recommended to mingle with the mob—"Apaches" as their more flamboyant members were known in the early 20th century French-speaking world—to become an accomplished forensic expert [Quinche 2011: 245].　　**3**—At times engineers can be a bit rough, after all the profession is still mostly a male's club. But things change and such questions as "Do we have a nastiness problem in computer science?" start to be asked in the pages of the flagship publication of the Association of Computing Machinery rather than in the seclusion of the couch [Meyer 2013: 9].　　**4**—See p. 64.
5—An echo from the related field of digital forensics to this state of affairs is the divide between the theory and practice communities in cryptography, detrimental to the widespread social use of electronic signatures for digital documents. "In the end," notes perplexed the historian, "even when confronted with technologies claimed to possess extraordinary powers of conviction, judges continued to enjoy significant latitude in considering the evidence presented to them." [Blanchette 2012: 118; for the divide see p. 164].　　**6**—There is an entire literature on brilliant, but failed technologies. French-speaking readers can refer to the excellent book by Catherine Bertho [1981] on French telecom history.　　**7**—Comparison in Dessimoz and Champod 2008.

Between 1999, 2003, and 2006 the share for signature biometrics de-
creased from 3.0% to 2.4% to 1.7% ▬ıı, compared to an increase for fingerprints from 38% to 52% to 43.6% ▬▬▬▬▬ ▬▬▬▬▬ ▬▬▬▬▬.
The entire market was valued at $0.2 billion (B) in 1995, $0.9B in 2003, $3.4B
in 2009, and expected to attain $9.3B by 2014 ı▬ ▬▬▬ ▬▬▬▬▬▬,
with a geographic spread shift between 2001 and 2006 from 75% to 33.5%
▬▬▬▬▬▬ for North America, 12% to 16.5% ▬▬ for Europe, 9% to
23.8% ▬▬ for Asia–Pacific, and 4% to 26.2% ı▬▬ for the other regions. In
2006 the top two applications were 33.9% civil and 26.1% criminal identification ▬▪, and the top two sectors 36.7% government and 25.4% law enforcement ▬▪. Only about 5 in 200 companies are profitable, and those deal in
strong technologies such as iris biometrics. In sum, signatures is an increasingly marginalized biometrics in an unprofitable market, despite increasing
revenues and globalization.[1] As a comparison token the forensic expenditure
of the police force in England and Wales in 2004, all types of services confounded, was estimated at £400 million, for a market expected to shrink
throughout the near future.[2] While the bulk of forensic services providers
are governmental (70 FD-performing laboratories in the United States in
2005[3]), there are numerous private practices, especially in the United States
(up to 200 in 1996[4]), and various FD professional forensics associations
(four major ones in the United States for approximately 5,000 experts[5]). The
ongoing economical downturn has already impacted the growth ability of
the market, with less research investment in forensics and downright clos-
ing of laboratories. The paradoxical growing number of graduates with forensic degrees have very limited employment opportunities (500 applicants
for 30 posts in the United Kingdom in 2004;[6] the number of core forensic
programs proposed in US universities increased by 1.3% per year for the
period 1977–2002 and 110% [sic] ı▬▬▬▬▬▬
for 2003–2007;[7] in 1975 there were 21 higher education institutions where
one could study forensics and 120 in year 2010[8]). Technologically too, the
present times are not favorable to a dynamic FD market, giving the receding
role of documents as investigation material. Looking at the share of FD in
forensic research or at the number of expertise requests made to laboratories, its small and declining importance readily contrasts with that of
other methods.[9] That Interpol has no handwriting database can be seen as
another troubling symptom, just as the focus on cybercrime of its futuristic
research and development complex to open in Singapore in 2014.[10] The bleak
market prospects canvassed here are reflected in (or do they reflect?) the
moribund state of many FD online discussion fora consulted by this author:
they are practically empty.

1—IBG 2005, 2008, Thot 2004: 28–35, Lalam and Nadaud 2011.   **2**—Commons 2005: 12, 2011:
12–17.   **3**—Peterson and Hickman 2005.   **4**—Risinger and Saks 1996: 46.   **5**—Risinger
2007: 478; Fact sheet "Foremost organizations," p. 103.   **6**—Commons 2005: 43.   **7**—Jackson
2009: 3–4.   **8**—Tregar and Proni 2010: 1488.   **9**—See Fact sheets "Basic forensics fields," p.
94, and "Health trends," p. 107.   **10**—Interpol 2012.

Technology — From the many computational solutions needed by FD, one will be cited in this section because its nature is only partially technological. Datasets on various aspects of an FD, such as handwriting, ink, and paper samples, are fundamental for developing forensic software. Yet, few are published and the advertised hyperlinks kept alive. The disclosure of datasets and software by researchers is culturally conditioned within the scientific community, and constrained by financial, time load, and legal considerations, but this situation has begun to be challenged in a number of sciences and accepted by publishers. When viewed in terms of organization of science, the solution is, however, not by burdening scientists and publishers, but by creating new entities specifically geared for the archival, maintenance, and distribution of scientific datasets and software permanence.

Politics — Technology, even more than science, is coupled to the social environment in terms of developed areas, target applications, and ultimate success.[1] A case in point, the rise of Bayesianism in the practice of forensics in the United Kingdom is the direct response of scientists to the prevailing culture of rationalization and marketability underlying neoliberal politics.[2] Opening up for scrutiny the black box of the experts' cognitive processes, the likelihood ratio formula "is just so perfect for forensic science" marvels a statistician, which in the eyes of the management translates to "enhancing long-term shareholder value."[3] It has to be seen what role in the current and coming political and economical contexts will computational FD play in respect to its own sustainability (the *tools*), its impact on the future of traditional FDEs (the *humans*), and its shaping of FD expertise (the *know-how*) and legal performance (the *product*).

Education — The National Academy of Sciences report on forensics sciences has found "a gross shortage of adequate training and continuing education of practitioners; the absence of rigorous, mandatory certification requirements for practitioners; [...] the absence of solid scientific and applied research focused on new technology and innovation,"[4] while a report by the UK House of Commons mentions a majority of forensic academic degrees to be "a savage waste of young people's time and parents' money"[5] (in the United States in the late 1990s only 3% of crime laboratory personnel had an MA[6]). Such a state of affairs can only lead to incomprehension about what computing has to offer, what its current limitations are, what the scientific method is, and how it impacts FDEs' work. It adversely affects the ability to use software and quantitative methods effectively, and communicate results; it encourages antiquated approaches and no computer-supported expertise, if not outright rejection.[7] Educational unpreparedness and the perceived cavalier stance of computer scientists corners some FDEs to resent software and proficiency tests as threats to their careers, jobs, and the field's

1—MacKenzie and Wajcman 1999 [cases compendium], Hughes 2004 [historical overview].   **2**—Lawless and Williams 2010: 748–749.   **3**—Lawless and Williams 2010: 735, 737.   **4**—Edwards 2009: 2–3.   **5**—Commons 2005: 44.   **6**—Saks and Faigman 2008: 167b.   **7**—Matley 2008.

existence,[1] despite the ritual reassurances that "automated writer recognition cannot replace Forensic Document Examiners."[2] The introduction of a Bayesian approach to frame caseworks in the United Kingdom generated a feeling of insecurity among forensic experts and the police force: "we were challenging conventional wisdom, and we were almost challenging the basis of their expertise."[3] Note that the firmer grounds on which forensic DNA expertise rests is due in part to being a technology developed in a scientific, not a forensic, environment.[4]

Government — Governments have a role to play when the link between academic research and industrial development is wanting, as it appears to be the case for FD. Some remarkable results in computational processing of written language have been achieved through just such governmental involvement. ▶ In the early 1990s, the US National Institute of Standards and Technology (NIST) was instrumental via two public competitions in spurring the handwriting recognition market, establishing software evaluation procedures, and creating datasets still in use. The success came from NIST being an influential governmental organization and having access to the vast resources of other organizations, in occurrence 17 million Census handwritten files on which the datasets were based.[5] ▶ Two decades later, a military research organization this time, the US Defense Advanced Research Projects Agency (DARPA), funded as part of a $220 million automatic language translation program (Gale and Madcat, 2007–2011[6]) the largest ever handwriting research dataset: more than 46,000 documents from all over the Arab world.[7] As a token of comparison, popular handwriting datasets have about a thousand items (Firemaker, IAM, or RIMES[8]).

Failures are equally worth mentioning. ▶ The disparaging scientific state of FD can be imputed at least in part to suboptimal support of governments for scientific education. A decade before the National Academy of Sciences 2009 state of forensics, itself initially obstructed by the Departments of Defense and Justice before being sponsored by the Congress,[9] another report by the same organization chastised the role played by politics: "Neither the educational system nor the policy-making apparatus in the United States

---

1—Risinger and Saks 1996: various locations, e.g., 65.   2—Wayman and Orlans 2008: 5-15. Even in the visions conjured by Nathan Myhrvold, former Chief Technology Officer of Microsoft, software will not replace FDEs, although for the entirely different reason of humans becoming themselves software! "Ultimately, I think we will be able to treat humans as application programs […] I hope I am software." [Myhrvold 1999: 52–53]. At the same 50-year anniversary conference of the Association for Computing Machinery where Myhrvold spoke in 1997, Pattie Maes, from MIT's MediaLab, proposed her own alternative: "we should try to work toward a future where we don't try to build these stand-alone machines, because there are far more pleasant and easier ways of reproducing human intelligence. Instead, we should be focusing on building combined forms of human and machine that are superintelligent and where both complement each other" [Maes 1999: 39].
3—Lawless and Williams 2010: 747.   4—Giannelli 2003: 1160–1161.   5—Garris 1992 [sample pictures], Geist et al. 1994 [second conference report], Grother 1995 [final SD19 dataset, ground-truthing method], NIST 2012c [Web site], Wilkinson et al. 1992a [ambiguities, laborious ground-truthing], 1992b [first conference report, history, software performance].   6—DoD 2007, Olive 2007.   7—NIST 2012b, Strassel 2009.   8—See Fact sheet "Key datasets + databases," p. 113.   9—Kennedy 2003, NAS 2009: xix.

has recognized the importance of technological literacy."[1] Indeed, observers of the history of forensics put a heavy blame for its lack of scientific culture on poor staffing decisions and disinterest within the police forces and the relevant ministries. With outright lyricism, the director of the world's oldest institute of criminalistics, established in 1909 in Lausanne, Switzerland, remarks that "forensic science is like a hospital serviced by clerics and nurses for most of the activities."[2] Add to this the chronic underfunding already decried by the founding fathers of forensics,[3] and the implication for the judicial system is that often judges and jurors take uninformed decisions based on evidence presented as "scientific," when in fact it is what has come to be known as "junk science," a problem of credulity compounded by financial greed.[4] The proper education of the parties involved in courtroom proceedings is surely a right step.[5] ▶ In another example, in the profit and efficiency post-Cold War world, the UK government desired to create an open forensic market and thus chose to privatize its forensic services agency, the Forensic Science Service (FSS).[6] It was the FSS who pioneered DNA profiling and set up the first national DNA database, and was reputed for delivering world class expertise and training far beyond the country's borders. In 2004 the FSS employed 2,500, and had 80% of the forensic market share in England and Wales; by 2010 the share dropped to 60% and the workforce to 1,600 and it was losing at times £2 million a month. Its closure was decided and the last furniture auctioned in May 2012. The United Kingdom lost in the process a top scientific and operational asset, with no assurance that the private sector will fill the gap and do better. Obviously, the House of Commons Science and Technology Committee concluded that "forensic science R&D in the United Kingdom is not healthy."[7] Apart from the immediate and long-term human costs and damage to the judiciary system resulting from a like mismanagement, this story serves to show the role not always beneficial played by governments and ideologies in shaping forensic sciences.

A few words on large-scale FD projects and funding opportunities will give an idea of what computer scientists can expect in this respect. Most computing FD projects are ad hoc collaborations between the academia and forensic laboratories (Groningen University and the Netherlands Forensic Institute; National Center for Scientific Research [CNRS] and the Marseille Police), sometimes with governmental funding (CEDAR from the Department of Justice; Purdue Sensor and Printer Forensics Project from the National Science Foundation; EFHEX from the European Union; Fraunhofer Institute and University of Groningen from the German Federal Criminal Police Office [BKA]) and more rarely industry funding (George Mason University, Gannon Technologies, and the FBI). In the United States, the National Institute of Justice, a research, development, and evaluation agency of the Department

---

1—Pearson and Young 2002: 1.   2—Margot 2011: 799–800. On the institute history and its founder, R.A. Reiss, see Quinche 2011.   3—E.g., Locard and Reiss [Quinche 20012: 37; 2011: 259].
4—Vivid examples in Huber 1993.   5—E.g., Saks and Faigman 2008: 161–162.   6—Commons 2005, 2011, Lawless 2011.   7—Commons 2011: 3.

of Justice, offers substantial funding for forensics (up to \$1 million for FD). FD projects were awarded on such topics as individuality of handwriting and datasets creation,[1] demographics (twins,[2] descriptor frequencies), software (CEDAR-FOX[3]), performance (dataset size and sample quality[4]), signature expertise, or human factors[5] However, in an international perspective, forensic research is chronically underfunded in the United States.[6] In Europe, the European Commission cofinanced between 1998 and 2002 a project that established the European Network of Forensic Handwriting Experts (ENFHEX),[7] part of the European Network of Forensic Science Institutes (ENFSI). ENFHEX continued to flourish to this day: among its activities are coordination and harmonization actions, a series of annual conferences, and development of resources. As an example of a computing project with explicit FD applicative potential having received worldwide media coverage and inquires for possible use abroad, is the already mentioned reconstruction of the millions of torn Stasi documents spanning its last 20 years of existence. The pilot project, which began in 2007, was undertaken by the Fraunhofer-Institute, Berlin, in collaboration with Vienna Technical University, arvato services, and SAP Germany.[8]

1—Srihari et al. 2002.   **2**—Srihari et al. 2008.   **3**—Shin 2009, Srihari 2010.   **4**—NIJ 2011: 50–51.   **5**—NIJ 2012.   **6**—Bridgemon 2007, Palenik and Palenik 2004.   **7**—ENF-HEX 2002, 2012b.   **8**—BStU 2012, Nickolay 2010, Weberling and Spitzer 2007: 24, 26.

1

2

— It may possibly recur to your memory that when I examined the paper upon which the printed words were fastened I made a close inspection for the watermark. In doing so I held it within a few inches of my eyes, and was conscious of a faint smell of the scent known as white jessamine. There are seventy-five perfumes, which it is very necessary that a criminal expert should be able to distinguish from each other, and cases have more than once within my own experience depended upon their prompt recognition. The scent suggested the presence of a lady.

— Well, what do you make of it?

— That it was written in a train; the good writing represents stations, the bad writing movement, and the very bad writing passing over points. A scientific expert would pronounce at once that this was drawn up on a suburban line, since nowhere save in the immediate vicinity of a great city could there be so quick a succession of points. Granting that his whole journey was occupied in drawing up the will, then the train was an express, only stopping once between Norwood and London Bridge.

Closure

ACT SIX

— Now just one more thing.

4

— [Hubot to human] We are your creation.
You must accept to live with us.

FUTURISTIC FD

While the prospect of malevolent androids remains off in the future
(but already a successful theme of the early cinema exemplified
among others by *Metropolis* [1927], *Frankenstein* [1931], *Golem*
[1915], or, indeed, *R.U.R.* [1935 movie, 1920 novel], which gave us
the word "robot"), present day FD software and robotics look clum-
sy, like Robby the Robot of *Forbidden Planet* (1956), resurfaced
in *Columbo: Mind Over Mayhem* (1974) [3], of which Richard
Epstein asked in his novel *The Case of the Killer Robot*, "But
are you replicating intelligence or stupidity?" [1] The presence side
by side of the down-to-earth, harmless looking detective character
and a clunky robot (somehow reminding us of *Star Wars'* [1977]
verbose antics of cute R2-D2 and C-3PO), marks the trivialization
of modern technology, the subversion of the machine by humans,
and an accommodation process in their relationship. It seems that
"resistance is futile."

In *Real Humans* (2011) [4] the police investigator is not a human
Colombo anymore, but a humanoid robot: a "hubot." For sure this
is still fiction (very good at that), but already FDEs have to contend
with the need to examine robotic and computer synthesized handwriting — a fantastically sounding reality.

We can get a far longer glimpse of the future of computational
FD if we travel back to the times of Sherlock Holmes' exploits. But
before, a word from Edmond Locard: "I do not consider at all the
study of [Edgar Allan Poe's] *Tales of Mystery* to be for the detective
a simple entertainment and only a pleasure, I see a necessary study
and an education for the mind." [2] Fiction is a vision into possible
futures that can be taken, like Locard did, as a literal source of
inspiration in forensics. *The Hound of the Baskervilles* (1983)
[1] and *The Adventures of Sherlock Holmes: The Norwood
Builder* (1985) [2; quotes from the respective novels] present document expertise based on olfactive and body posture factors, and
complex logical inferences fed on rich contextual knowledge. This
holistic approach is the hallmark of human experts — under Conan
Doyle's pen supremely flattering for the ability of FDEs, to the point
of extravagance — and the Grail toward which software is headed.

1— Epstein 1997: 134.   **2**— Locard 1924: 25.

Why computerize?

This book is about the use of computers in forensic documents (FD) expertise. From the beginning, the reader might have waited for an overdue answer to a primordial question: What is the rationale to computerize FD?

The question is perplexing in our digital era and to the ears of those software creators entrusted with this very task: the gain in processing quantity, speed, and more recently novel applications for FD, are obvious. The previous chapters describing the FD digital agenda should have made it clear.

There are nevertheless a number of additional factors driving the computerization of FD, originating in society, that are easily overlooked despite their influence on what FD will mean in the future and to what ends it will be employed. Digital automation, for example, is nothing less that the continuation with modern means of the mechanization brought about by the industrial revolution of the 19th century. True to its historical roots (the profusion of century-old mechanical antecedents to computing and robotics is fascinating), digital automation not only makes the human redundant, but dehumanizes what is left of it: the project management charts and standards resembling microchip specifications which I mention in this publication, are, at times, indeed designed to make human activity more amenable to computers and as compliant as that of robots.[1] Mark Seltzer summed up the inevitable confluence of science and forensics in a much quoted aphorism on the modern disenchantment of the world: "The death of God leaves us with mathematics and the death of Satan leaves us with forensics."[2]

The ideology of rationalization and efficiency that sweeps over forensic laboratories can also be read as a form of social control and capital maximization. The automated networks for the verification of security documents such as biometric passports imposed on citizen would have delighted Jeremy Bentham and Michel Foucault as examples of panoptic societies.[3] As for the companies producing FD software, their *raison d'être* is profit, however the employees might emotionally invest in the products.

The issues listed here are general cultural traits of computerization. They befall every field of activity with which it makes contact, and FD is not an exception. Now that this new world is here, it is to us to make sure the only blood spilled is that of a happy wedding night.

1—Ideas developed around virtual agents by Sengers 2004, starting from Kennedy 1989 and Ritzer 1996.
2—Seltzer 2007: 61.   3—Foucault 1995, Lyon 2003 [9/11], Jensen and Draffan 2004 [biometrics].

Fact sheets

— Are you still on the right side?

— For God's sake, you've left out a whole eagle.

— You want to sabotage? Here in the concentration camp?!

— I guess the fun is about to begin.

— Mark handles the trafficking of money. […]
What else to have your own man in the police!

— Frank, would you be interested in working with the FBI's Financial
Crimes Unit? […] We have the power to take you out of prison.

— [Hoover, recollecting] It was 1919, before anyone respected criminal science... [...]

— Consider your pay doubled. You work for your country now, Mr. Osborn. Congratulations. [...]
— Mr. Osborn, tell us what you need.
— Bright lights, a microscope, measuring instruments, magnifying glasses. A projector.
— You have the full resources of the Bureau — don't be shy.
— Paper samples from every regional manufacturer.
— Mr. Osborn, this is Mr. Tolson [deputy director]. Supply Mr. Osborn whatever he needs to conclude without a doubt that these letters came from the same author. [...]
— [Osborn, some time later] The ink is different, but the handwriting is a match.

— [Hoover] Clyde, the President of the United States is afraid.
— [Tolson] What, he's afraid of you? [...]
— [Hoover] The president signed a secret order granting me increased power of surveillance, secret surveillance of communists and radicals, without warrant.
— [Tolson] Is that legal? [...]
— [Hoover] Even great men can be corrupted, can't they?

— They didn't program you about stealing, shoplifting, robbery?

MORAL ISSUES

Cinema offers glimpses into some of the ethical aspects of FD. For example, its use by dictatorial regimes in *The Lives of Others* (2006) [1]: the plot revolves around a member of the East German secret police, who, by removing an incriminating typewriter, saves the people he was spying on.

The small brother of bank robbery, money counterfeiting is a movie staple that allows the investigation of an astonishingly rich spectrum of moral issues: the survival of Jews in a WWII concentration camp in exchange of fabricating millions of pounds, dollars, and other currencies for the Nazis (*The Counterfeiters* [2007] [3]), the true story of the redeeming of a confidence man helping the FBI hunt down check forgers (*Catch Me If You Can* [2002] [6]), the slow slip into crime of a young man who sees no future working in a photocopy shop (*The Man Who Copied* [2003] [4]), or, the predicament of a Hong Kong detective dueling his own brother, a gangster in a counterfeiting ring (*A Better Tomorrow* [1986] [5]). No qualms however for the imprisoned Allied officers forging German documents in *The Great Escape* (1963) [2].

Incidentally, the Hong Kong counterfeiters use a computerized printing system, in contrast with the FBI agents, who's capacity to judge documents by touch and smell is what qualifies them as experts.

J. Edgar (2011) [7] portrays Albert Osborn being hired by FBI Director Hoover in the Lindbergh case. In the scene seen here he explains before a jury a ransom note, a further popular item in cinema.[1] Unlike in the previous movies staging document experts of both sides of good and bad being dramatically tormented by ethical dilemmas, the focus of this one is the inherent ambiguity of human actions. Hoover is thus a progressist, advocating scientific methods for investigative purposes—but is what the experts do really science? does he not use it to find what he expects? Osborn works for the country, as Hoover puts it, to trace the kidnapped baby of a famous aviator—yet he also works for an individual who exerts unchecked an immense power, blackmailing even presidents of the United States: a democratic country…

And how is the future going to look like when humans will teach robots how to pick locks and become accomplices in crime (*Robot & Franck* [2012] [8])? Is it ethical in respect to these artifacts to impose upon them, by programming, the whole spectrum of human behavior?

1—Lidz 2011.

An ecosystem

Forensic documents (FD) is one area of forensics, of which one subdivision dealing with writing is connected to a number of not necessarily forensic disciplines, referred to as graphonomics: art history, biometrics, cognitive sciences, graphology, history, linguistics, medicine, paleography, paper studies, primary education, security documents, signage, typography, and more. ("Graphonomics" is not to be confounded with "graphonomy," an advanced form of graphology, vocable coined by Edmond Solange Pellat (1875–1931), or its delicious synonym "chirogrammatomancy" [Locard 1935–1937 (5): 14–16, 227–237, Guiral 1927: 17].)

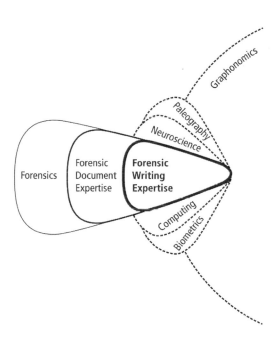

Basic forensic fields

A rough estimation of the relative size of different forensic areas is reflected in two statistics. ▶ The **top** figure reflects the amount of research by area through the number of proceedings pages (numbers in the circles) in each of the sessions of the 2012 conference of the American Association of Forensic Sciences [AAFS 2012b; for similar figures using other bibliometrical data see Sauvageau et al. 2009]. ▶ The **bottom** figure gives the types of requests for forensic services in the publicly funded laboratories in 2005 in the United States [Durose 2008: 10, appendix table 10]. ▶ Note that although forensic documents (FD) is marginal, it maintains independence.

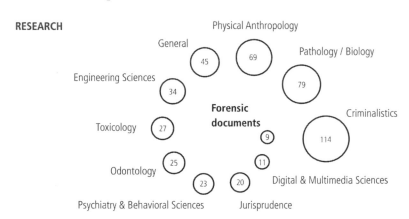

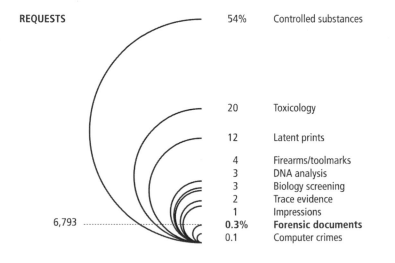

Common topics

This table should help readers gain an idea about the diversity and relative importance of various areas and topics within forensic documents (FD). The typology covers the presentations in the FD sessions of the American Association of Forensic Sciences conferences during the period 2002–2012 [AAFS 2011, 2012b]. The proportions should be considered as approximate, some articles having been allocated to several subjects. For the exact values of the cumulative summary consult the detailed table.

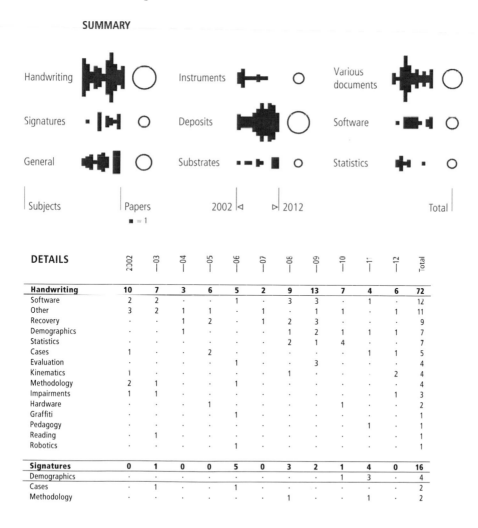

SUMMARY

Handwriting · Instruments · Various documents

Signatures · Deposits · Software

General · Substrates · Statistics

Subjects · Papers · 2002 ◁ ▷ 2012 · Total

■ = 1

DETAILS	2002	–03	–04	–05	–06	–07	–08	–09	–10	–11	–12	Total
Handwriting	**10**	**7**	**3**	**6**	**5**	**2**	**9**	**13**	**7**	**4**	**6**	**72**
Software	2	2	.	.	1	.	3	3	.	1	.	12
Other	3	2	1	1	.	1	.	1	1	.	1	11
Recovery	.	.	1	2	.	1	2	3	.	.	.	9
Demographics	.	.	1	.	.	.	1	2	1	1	1	7
Statistics	.	.	.	.	.	.	2	1	4	.	.	7
Cases	1	.	.	2	.	.	.	.	.	1	1	5
Evaluation	.	.	.	.	1	.	.	3	.	.	.	4
Kinematics	1	.	.	.	.	.	1	.	.	.	2	4
Methodology	2	1	.	.	1	.	.	.	.	.	.	4
Impairments	1	1	.	.	.	.	.	.	.	.	1	3
Hardware	.	.	.	1	.	.	.	.	1	.	.	2
Graffiti	.	.	.	.	1	.	.	.	.	.	.	1
Pedagogy	.	.	.	.	.	.	.	.	.	1	.	1
Reading	.	1	.	.	.	.	.	.	.	.	.	1
Robotics	.	.	.	.	1	.	.	.	.	.	.	1
Signatures	**0**	**1**	**0**	**0**	**5**	**0**	**3**	**2**	**1**	**4**	**0**	**16**
Demographics	.	.	.	.	.	.	.	.	1	3	.	4
Cases	.	1	.	.	1	.	.	.	.	.	.	2
Methodology	.	.	.	.	.	.	1	.	.	1	.	2

DETAILS	2002	–03	–04	–05	–06	–07	–08	–09	–10	–11	–12	Total
Other	·	·	·	·	1	·	·	1	·	·	·	2
Robotics	·	·	·	·	1	·	1	·	·	·	·	2
Evaluation	·	·	·	·	·	·	·	1	·	·	·	1
Hardware	·	·	·	·	1	·	·	·	·	·	·	1
Kinematics	·	·	·	·	·	·	1	·	·	·	·	1
Software	·	·	·	·	1	·	·	·	·	·	·	1
Instruments	**3**	**5**	**1**	**1**	**1**	**2**	**1**	**1**	**0**	**0**	**0**	**15**
Printers, Pens...	2	2	·	1	·	1	·	1	·	·	·	7
Hardware	·	2	·	·	1	·	·	·	·	·	·	3
Imperfections	·	·	1	·	·	1	1	·	·	·	·	3
Cases	1	·	·	·	·	·	·	·	·	·	·	1
Demographics	·	1	·	·	·	·	·	·	·	·	·	1
Deposits	**4**	**3**	**3**	**3**	**5**	**7**	**10**	**7**	**10**	**9**	**5**	**66**
Hardware	1	1	3	2	4	4	8	6	8	7	4	48
Inks, Dyes, Erasers...	1	1	·	·	·	1	1	·	·	·	1	5
Methodology	·	·	·	1	·	·	1	·	2	1	·	5
Aging, Dating	2	·	·	·	·	1	·	1	·	·	·	4
Software	·	·	·	·	1	1	·	·	·	·	·	2
Datasets	·	1	·	·	·	·	·	·	·	·	·	1
State of the Art	·	·	·	·	·	·	·	·	·	1	·	1
Substrates	**1**	**0**	**1**	**1**	**0**	**2**	**1**	**0**	**0**	**3**	**3**	**12**
Hardware	1	·	1	·	·	2	·	·	·	2	2	8
Dating	·	·	·	·	·	·	·	·	·	1	1	2
Fibers	·	·	·	1	·	·	·	·	·	·	·	1
Watermarks	·	·	·	·	·	·	1	·	·	·	·	1
Other Topics	**3**	**1**	**6**	**12**	**7**	**3**	**5**	**2**	**4**	**2**	**5**	**50**
Digital Images & Docs	·	·	2	·	·	1	1	·	·	1	1	6
Computer Forensics	·	·	·	·	2	·	·	·	·	·	·	2
Software Identification	·	·	·	·	·	·	·	·	1	·	·	1
Banknotes	·	1	·	·	1	1	·	1	·	·	·	4
Seals, Stamps	1	·	1	1	1	·	·	·	·	·	·	4
Adhesives	·	·	·	·	·	·	1	·	1	·	·	2
Barcodes	·	·	·	·	·	·	1	·	·	·	1	2
Envelopes	1	·	·	·	1	·	·	·	·	·	·	2
Identity Documents	·	·	·	2	·	·	·	·	·	·	·	2
Checks	·	·	·	·	·	·	·	·	·	·	1	1
Photographs	·	·	·	·	·	·	·	·	1	·	·	1
Typography	·	·	·	·	·	·	·	·	·	·	1	1
Charred Docs	·	·	·	1	·	·	1	1	·	·	·	3
Soaked	·	·	·	2	·	·	·	·	·	·	1	3
Shreds Software	1	·	·	1	·	·	·	·	·	·	·	2
Holes	·	·	·	1	·	·	·	·	·	·	·	1
Shreds Other	·	·	·	1	·	·	·	·	·	·	·	1
Other	·	·	1	2	·	·	·	·	·	·	·	3
Stylistics (Stylometry)	·	·	1	·	1	·	·	·	1	·	·	3
Preservation	·	·	·	1	1	·	·	·	·	·	·	2
Acquisition	·	·	·	·	·	1	·	·	·	·	·	1
Cryptography	·	·	·	·	·	·	1	·	·	·	·	1
Indentations	·	·	·	·	·	·	·	·	·	1	·	1
Other Software	·	·	1	·	·	·	·	·	·	·	·	1
General	**2**	**3**	**4**	**1**	**4**	**5**	**3**	**0**	**6**	**6**	**0**	**34**
Instruction	·	1	1	·	1	1	1	·	2	1	·	8
Methodology	2	·	·	1	·	1	·	·	2	1	·	7
State of the Art	·	1	2	·	·	·	·	·	·	2	·	5
Statistics	·	·	1	·	·	·	·	·	1	2	·	4
Cases	·	·	·	·	2	·	·	·	·	·	·	2
Law	·	1	·	·	·	·	·	·	1	·	·	2
Other	·	·	·	·	1	1	·	·	·	·	·	2
Software	·	·	·	·	·	2	·	·	·	·	·	2
Evaluation	·	·	·	·	·	·	1	·	·	·	·	1
Management	·	·	·	·	·	·	1	·	·	·	·	1

Diverse goals + aspects

A number of **aspects** define what a forensic document (FD) is. To use a simple example, an *author* (the *source* in signal theory terms) writes with a pen (the *instrument* or *transmitter*) on paper (the *substrate* or *carrier*) and leaves an inked *trace* (the *deposit* or *matter*) which is visible to the eye as a *pattern* and contains a *message* (or *information*). The time of writing, the body posture of the writer, and her or his education are some of the *physical*, *biological*, and *sociocultural* aspects defining the document's *context*. How a forensic laboratory handles the document and the *opinion* (or *hypothesis*) expressed about it by an *expert* (the *observer*) is part of the document's *meta-aspects*. The deposit and the substrate form the tangible core of an FD (the *medium/memory*), with the other aspects attached to it cognitively or (for the archival arrangements) materially. Sample FD **datasets** can be constructed by taking any of the aspects as theme, hence this nomenclature can serve also as a datasets design guide. The principal **goals** of FD expertise are to establish a *link* (or *channel*) between a *suspect* and a *trace* (*identification*), test the genuineness of a link (*verification*), recover the written message (*recovery*), and generate *intelligence* (*inference*) — supported by auxiliary tasks (*support*) such as identifying the pen model used for writing.

Information theory / Computing	Forensic documents		
	aspects	example	goals
source	author / suspect	writer	
message / information	message	Hold-up!	
transmitter	instrument	pen	
carrier	substrate	paper	
medium / memory	medium	letter	
matter	deposit	ink	
signal / data	trace	text	recovery
pattern	pattern	handwriting	identification
channel / link	link / evidence	bank robbery	verification
sensor	equipment	eyes / microscope	support
decoder / algorithm	methodology	reading / thinking	
receiver	addressee / victim	bank director	
context / knowledge	context	demographics	
hypothesis	opinion	opinion	
observer / metadata	expert	expert	
inference	intelligence	juvenile criminality	intelligence

SAMPLE TYPOLOGY OF FD ASPECTS AND DERIVABLE DATASETS

PATTERN

age (of the pattern style) • *contemporary* (spanning three living generations) • *historical* (including antiquated scripts and styles practiced by living individuals)

artificiality (technology involvement) • *handwriting*: *direct* (writing with a finger), *mediated* (using an implement such as a pen) • *machine writing*: *mechanical* (typewriters…), *electronic* (printers…)

cursivity & **segmentation** (scalars; curvature is a major shape-defining feature in human vision, reflected in FD classifications of handwriting [Huber and Headrick 1999: 95–96])

quality (of aesthetics and legibility) • *informal* • *formal* • *artistic*

regularity of allographs and layout: scalar varying from • *low* (handwriting) to • *high* (typography). Main variability factors are nonconstant biomechanical performance, quality of writing implements, physical decay of documents. The layout might consist of a • *grid* and • *baselines*

style (the subject of many conflicting typologies whenever touched by FD, paleography, typography, or computer science [Huber and Headrick 1999: 16–29, 42–45, 95–96, 175–186]. A sample of such a misunderstanding: many FD examiners (FDEs) refer to "handprint" or simply "print" for what paleographers call "capitals," the latter pointing to the fact that "handprint" is an oxymoron (the writing is either handwritten or machine printed!); printed characters exist in both capital and lowercase styles; capitals exist independently of printing and preceded it; it would be an anachronism, respectively an instrument misnomer, to use the term "handprint" for such monuments of Roman epigraphy as the Trajan column in Rome and the contemporary lettering on the Vietnam memorial wall in the Arlington Cemetery, VA. The disappearance of cursive script from the daily reading experience and in some countries also from the handwriting styles [Sassoon 2007, Zezima 2011], gives, however, some credit to the use of the term "handprint," in a reversal of the original styling of typography on handwriting; some styles useful in FD computing: • *cursive* (connected characters, difficult to segment) • *capitals* (for printed forms, but also manifest in many natural handwriting styles) • *graffiti*

stylization (the degree to which the linguistic content is present or legible, such as in signatures or graffiti)

volume (text length) • *short* (a few words) • *medium* (one page) • *long* (more than one page)

INSTRUMENT

body part (finger, foot, mouth…) • *pens* (quill, reed, brush, nib pen, fountain pen, ballpoint pen, porous tip pen, ceramic tip… [Franke 2005: 34]) • *pantograph* • *stamps* and *seals* (rubber, metal, stone, wood, bone…) • *typewriters* (mechanical, electrical) • *typography* (xylography, lithography, manual hot metal, mono- and linotype, photocomposer, offset…) • *printers* (laser, ink jet, dot matrix, heat transfer… [Kipphan 2001]) • *photocopiers* • *faxes* • *electronic devices* (keyboards, e-pens, digitizing tablets…) • *writing robots* (plotters, robotic arms…) • *software* for synthetic writing generation

DEPOSIT

material: common: • *solid* (pencil graphite) • *powder* (laser printer toner) • *viscous* (ballpoint pen gel) • *fluid* (fountain pen ink)… ; not uncommon in forensics: • *blood* • *lipsticks*… ; exotic, not likely in forensics: petroglyphs, floral writing, human bodies, pyroglyphs, aerial acrobatics with colored smoke, edible writing: alphabet soup, writing on pastry… A common distinction in forensics is between • *inks* (made for producing patterns such as writing and investigated in FD) and • *paints* (made for covering surfaces, for example, for protection of car bodies; falls outside FD), but these classes do not include graphite, toner, and other deposits. • *Colorants* are one constituent of these substances and are either • *pigments* (insoluble) or • *dyes* (soluble). Furthermore they can be *inorganic* • *organic* • *biological* (from plants or animals) • *synthetic*. • The *vehicle* of the colorants is made of solvents and other components: corrosion inhibitors, insect repellents, drying agents… [Cantu 2009: 1541–1546]

SUBSTRATE

alterations: • *erasing* • *charring* • *soaking* • *freezing* • *tearing* • *shredding*…

indentations • *reproduction*: tangent light, 3D surface scanning…

material • *common*: paper, polycarbonates… • *not uncommon* for FD: human skin (tattoos, involuntary brandings or criminal scarifications)… • *modern technology*: electronic screens (e-ink, liquid crystal, cathode ray tube, plasma)

paper structure • *elements*: watermarks, chain and laid lines, pulp distribution • *reproduction*: transmitted light, rubbing, radiography (beta, X-rays)

MESSAGE

authenticity (of documents and writing [handwriting, signature, print...]; further classification proposals in [Found 2009: 1444–1447, Matuszewski 2011, Pal et al. 2011: 1–2, Locard 1935–1937 (5): 23–30]; symbology by this author; the terminology of authenticity is a source of considerable confusion, see for example the perplexing use of "random forgery" for using one's own signature when impersonating a victim and "simple forgery" when using, well, a random trace [Impedovo and Pirlo 2008: 621a])
1. *genuine* O (class): • 1.1 *natural* O • 1.2 *altered* ◇ (unintentional substantial change of writing (fatigue, alcohol, aided writing [guided by instruments or another person's hand]...) or document appearance [soaked...]) • 1.3 *delegated* →O (a legal or informal authorized reproduction of a genuine identity mark, especially signatures, by a delegate holding "signature authority" [manually, using stamps of the signature, electronically...]; for a medieval example on French royal deeds see Fraenkel 1992: 30; for a modern legislation sample see Ulowa 2012)
2. *forgery* O (class): • 2.1 *usurped* or *fraudulent* →● (unlawfully acquired genuine signature, handwriting or security document [stolen electronic signature, stolen blank ID card...]) • 2.2 *coerced* ◉ (class; writing or document produced involuntary): • 2.2.1 *cooperative* →◉ (the genuine writer or issuer complies to act as demanded) • 2.2.2 *uncooperative* ◉→ (exertion under psychological and/or physical duress; e.g., the genuine writer holds the pen while the forger moves her or his hand [type of guided writing] [Huber and Headrick 1999: 275–279]) • 2.3 *simulated* ●→ (class; impersonating somebody's writing or a genuine document): • 2.3.1 *transfered* O→● (tracing, cut and paste, photographic tampering...) • 2.3.2 *altered* O→◆ (scratching, adjunction...) • 2.3.3 *copied* O●→ (the genuine writing is next to the forged, the forger copies *de visu*) • 2.3.4 *remembered* O◖●→ (the genuine writing is accessible to the forger from memory) • 2.3.5 *fictitious* ◌→● (arbitrary writing; fantasy document) • 2.3.6 *disguise* ●→◌ (altering one's own handwriting to make it look as somebody's else, having or not a particular individual in mind) • 2.3.7 *autoforgery* ●↔◌ (altering one's own handwriting to make it look as an attempt by somebody else at forging it)
constraint (e.g. forms limit the information and its location, thus facilitating machine reading) • *semantic*: free text, forms, envelopes, checks, letters... • *graphical*: free text, forms...

function (of document) • *writing samples* (threat letter, postal envelope, check, signature, form, diary...) • *security documents*: • *currency:* banknotes, checks... • *identity:* travel and access documents, driver license, diplomas...
instance • *original* • *copy*
meaning (possible applications: stylistic analysis [Chaski 1997], allographs determined by the meaning of words [Atanasiu 2003]...)
notation • *language* • *signatures* (hybrid symbols of writing and drawing, function as personal identity and legal validation marks [Fraenkel 1992: 7, 17–25], onomatogram for short) • *digits* (checks) • *symbols:* mathematical, musical...
readership • *human* (natural writing systems) • *machine* (artificial writing systems: barcodes, QR-codes; usually dealt with by digital forensics, not FD)
script: the notation of a linguistic message has four aspects: • *system* (alphabetic [Latin], consonantal or abjad [Arabic], syllabic [Japanese kana], semanto-phonetic, which is a mix between phonetic, ideographic, and pictographic elements [Chinese, Mayan]) • *character set* (English vs. French alphabet) • *style* (bold vs. italic) • *genealogy:* family, source, derivate (the English and French scripts belong to the same Latin family and are derived from the Latin script, itself a Phoenician avatar, created from hieroglyphs; Persian and Arabic belong to the Arabic script family) • Caveat: do not confound "script" and "language": a statement like "written in Chinese" is thrice ambiguous, since it can refer to the language or the script, which could be hanzi characters or Latin pinyin.

CONTEXT

biological: writer • *sex/gender* and • *age* • *ethnicity* • *body posture* during writing • *body part* used in writing: hand, foot, mouth [Pellat 1927] • *pen hold/grip* • *handedness* • *visual feedback* (optimal, nonoptimal [obstructed, deformed, blurred, crowded, disproportionate small/big], absent) • *emotional state* of writer • *medical condition* • *substance intake* • *writing proficiency*: *linguistic* (language, vocabulary), *graphical* (script, style)
physical • *time* of production • *location* • *support* (table...) • *environmental* conditions...
sociocultural • *social* • *educational* • *professional* background of writer...

COMMON ASPECTS

dimensionality (of document or data during analysis) • *static*: *2D* (photography...), *3D* (stereo-microscopy, laser scanner…) • *dynamic* (from live recordings or recovered from static data): stroke *sequence*, trajectory *dynamics* (kinematics), *pressure* of instrument on substrate and fingers on pen (kinetics)

history (what happens to the document); important moments: • *manufacture* (of implements) • *production* of pattern (e.g., time of writing) • *retrieval* at crime scene • *expression* of opinion by the FDE

nature • *physical* • *digital*

processing speed (at which the data was acquired) • *real time*: handwriting recognition of document flux in postal triage machines • *offline*: handwriting recognition of scanned documents

stability (scalar; rate of inscription decay; factors: quality and interaction of materials [exfoliation of metallo-gallic inks, crumbling of acid paper…] and conservation conditions [fading of ink exposed to light, insects, humidity…]) • *permanent* (engravings, controlled conservation conditions, inscriptions on acid-free paper or with a water-resistant marker…) • *stable* (quality materials…) • *unstable* (in time chemically active inks "eat" through the paper [ink corrosion]…) • *ephemeral* or *fugitive* (writing with fire, in the air, on water, on sand…)

META-ASPECTS

accessibility • *public* • *commercial* • *private* • *classified* (governmental)

intelligence (the usage that is made of document and dataset aspects for intelligence purposes and the underlying organizational and technological processes) • *operational and case level*: for specific law enforcement operations • *policy and phenomena level*: for a broader use, to shape law enforcement policy and understand crime phenomena • *raw*: FD information used "as is" • *processed*: FD information substantially processing by analysts • *surveillance*: criminal surveillance carried out by means of FD (e.g., automated mail surveillance)

management • *retrieval* process from crime scene • *handling* conditions in laboratory • *conservation* conditions in archives • *description* (of document and its management process)

quality of dataset • *representativeness* (measure on how well the dataset represents a modeled population) • *nature*: *natural* (samples not produced at the demand of surveyors), *controlled* (surveyors ask subjects to write for them), *synthetic* (computer-generated samples)

Example curricula

List of forensic degree-awarding universities
http://www.aafs.org/colleges-universities/

PROPOSAL

[Huber and Headricks 1999: 40, 369-370]

FORENSIC DOCUMENTS (FD)

Introduction, testing, orientation
History of handwriting
Class characteristics
Individual characteristics
Identification
Standards for comparison
Microscopy
Evidence of genuineness
Evidence of spuriousness
Disguised and miscellaneous writings
Graphology

ADDITIONAL

English
Philosophy
Chemistry
Physics
Mathematics
Psychology
Computer Science
Foreign Languages

ÉCOLE DES SCIENCES CRIMINELLES

University of Lausanne, Switzerland
http://www.unil.ch/esc/

CORE

Forensic crime analysis
Forensic Sciences III
Police Techniques
Forensic Intelligence
The judicial inquiry
Policing
Interpretation II–III (lecture, practice)
Complex expert cases (practice)
Statistical data processing
Dating and Chronology
Crime scene coordination
Forensic Identification of Persons II
   (lecture, practice)
Master Project in Forensic Identification (practice)

Identification through forensic genetics
   (lecture, practice)
Forensic Medicine
Illicit Drugs
Illicit Drugs II & Fire Investigation II
   (analytical practice)

MATERIALS

Fire and Explosions II (lecture, practice)
Firearms II (lecture, practice)
Microtraces II (lecture, analytical practice)
Kinematic Reconstruction of Car Accidents
   (lecture, practice)
Crime scene investigation and identification of ob-
   jects and tools

CHEMISTRY & BIOLOGY

Chemical criminalistics
Analytical chemistry in safety matters
Biological traces

INFORMATION

Questioned documents II
   (lecture, analytical practice)
Cryptology and Identities in the Information Society

OKLAHOMA STATE UNIVERSITY

Tulsa, OK
http://www.healthsciences.okstate.edu/forensic/

GENERAL

Physical Aspects of Forensic Sciences
Biological Aspects of Forensic Sciences
Trace Evidence Analysis
Instrumental Analysis
Crime Scene Investigation I–II
Crime Scene Investigation for Lab Personnel
Homicide Investigation
Selected Topics
Graduate Seminar
Research
Forensic Sciences Practicum
Thesis Research

LAW & ETHICS

Criminal Law I
Criminal Law II: Evidence
Criminal Law III: Moot Court
Ethics and Leadership

MEDICINE

Forensic Psychiatry
Forensic Psychology
Investigation of Child Abuse
Forensic Pathology
Medicolegal Death Investigation

BIOLOGY & CHEMISTRY

Forensic Biology
Forensic Molecular Biology
Principles of Toxicology
Analytical Toxicology
Forensic Toxicology I–II
Medicinal Chemistry I–II
Forensic Chemistry I–II
Forensic Drug Analysis
Forensic DNA Profiling
Population Genetics

MATERIALS

Firearms and Toolmark Identification
Examination of Questioned Documents
Photography in the Forensic Sciences

COMPUTING

Introduction to Computer Systems for Security Professionals
Introduction to Network Systems for Security Professionals
Computer Forensics I: Investigation and Data Gathering
Computer Forensics II: Evidence and Analysis
Computer Forensics III: Advanced Techniques
Incidence Response: Understanding and Identifying Network-Based Attacks
Advanced Incidence Response: Investigating Network-Based Attacks
Linux for Computer Forensics
Video Forensic Analysis
Protection of Information Systems
Steganography and Electronic Watermarking
High-Technology Crime Investigation Capstone Course
The Investigative Process for Computer Forensics
Computer-Related Law

SECURITY

Security Case Law
Security Management
Forensic Accounting
Risk Analysis and Loss Prevention
Industrial Espionage and Corporate Privacy Issues
Issues in Crisis and Disaster Management for Security Professionals
Emergency Planning and Business Continuity
Terrorism

Foremost organizations

List
   http://forensic.to/links/pages/General_information_resources/Associations_and_Societies/

FORENSIC DOCUMENTS (FD)

American Board of Forensic Document Examiners (ABFDE)
   http://www.abfde.org
American Society of Questioned Document Examiners (ASQDE)
   http://www.asqde.org
Association of Forensic Document Examiners (AFDE)
   http://www.afde.org
Australian Academy of Forensic Sciences
   http://forensicacademy.org
European Document Experts Working Group (EDEWG)
   http://www.enfsi.eu/page.php?uid=55
European Network of Forensic Handwriting Experts (ENFHEX)
   http://www.enfsi.eu/page.php?uid=64
Gesellschaft für Forensische Schriftuntersuchung (GFS)
   http://www.gfs2000.de
Institut für Schrift- und Urkundenuntersuchung [Institute for Writing and Document Examination| (ISU,
   1993), Mannheim University, Germany
   http://www.isu-mannheim.de
International Graphonomics Society (IGS, 1985, conferences since 1982, interdisciplinary forum)
   http://www.graphonomics.org
Scientific Working Group for Forensic Document Examination [Burkes 2011]
   http://www.swgdoc.org
Southeastern Association of Forensic Document Examiners (SAFDE)
   http://www.safde.org
Southwestern Association of Forensic Document Examiners (SWAFDE)
   http://www.swafde.org

FORENSICS

Australian Academy of Forensic Sciences (AuAFS)
   http://www.forensicacademy.org
American Academy of Forensic Sciences (AAFS)
   http://www.aafs.org
Canadian Society of Forensic Sciences (CSFS)
   http://www.csfs.ca
European Academy of Forensic Science (EAFS)
   http://www.enfsi.eu/page.php?uid=181
Forensic Science Society (FSS)
   http://www.forensic-science-society.org.uk/home
International Association for Identification (IAI)
   http://www.theiai.org
Technical Committee on Computational Forensics (IAPR-TC6, part of the International Association for Pattern Recognition [IAPR])
   https://sites.google.com/site/compforgroup/

BIOMETRICS

Biometric Consortium (United States, est. 1992, liaison between government, industry, academia)
  http://www.biometrics.org
European Biometrics Forum (European Union, est. 2003, for biometrics coordination and support)
  http://www.eubiometricsforum.com, https://twitter.com/EBF_Manager
IEEE Biometrics Council
  http://ieee-biometrics.org
International Biometric Society
  http://www.biometricsociety.org

SECURITY DOCUMENTS

International confederation for printing and allied industries (Intergraf)
  http://www.intergraf.eu

Gender demographics

The data presented here is intended to present the gender gaps in the two fields that are to collaborate in computational forensic documents (FD) projects: FD and computer science. Note how they relate to the general fields they belong to, forensics and science, and how they vary with such factors as time, career stage, degrees, and cultures.

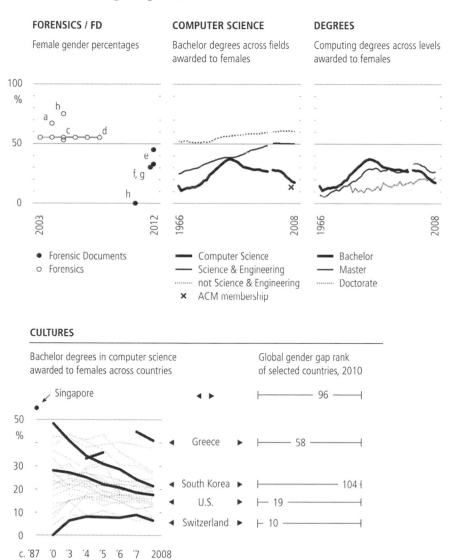

FORENSICS / FD

Female gender percentages

COMPUTER SCIENCE

Bachelor degrees across fields awarded to females

DEGREES

Computing degrees across levels awarded to females

- ● Forensic Documents
- ○ Forensics

- ▬ Computer Science
- — Science & Engineering
- ⋯⋯ not Science & Engineering
- ✗ ACM membership

- ▬ Bachelor
- — Master
- ⋯⋯ Doctorate

CULTURES

Bachelor degrees in computer science awarded to females across countries

Global gender gap rank of selected countries, 2010

◄ ►	├─── 96 ───┤
Greece ►	├─── 58 ────────┤
◄ South Korea ►	├──────── 104 ┤
◄ U.S. ►	├─ 19 ──────┤
◄ Switzerland ►	├ 10 ──────┤

Legend and references

Left — *Percentage of women in forensics and FD.* **a:** 68.5% women, United Kingdom, c. 2004, bachelor students from six universities and 14 out of 16 forensics-oriented courses [SEMTA 2004: 27, 48]. **b:** 75% women, United States, 2005, student membership of the American Association of Forensic Sciences (AAFS), with over 6,200 members from 63 countries the leading generalist forensic society, founded in 1948 [Houck 2009: 67]. **c:** 53%, professional cohort of AAFS (see previous reference). **d:** 53.4% women, United States, 2003–2008, bachelor and masters students in 41, respectively 12 of the 120 higher education curricula accredited by AAFS's Forensic Science Education Programs Accreditation Commission (FEPAC) [Tregar and Proni 2010: 1490, 1491]. **e:** 45% women (out of 11 FD examiners [FDEs]), France, 2012, FDEs at the Institut national de police scientifique (INPS) [Langlois-Peter 2012]. **f:** 33% women, United States, 2012, membership of the American Society of Questioned Document Examiners (ASQDE), founded 1942, 104 members, data tabulated by this author from the online members list [ASQDE 2012]. **g:** 32% women, United States, 2012, American Board of Forensic Document Examiner (ABFDE), founded 1977, 105 members, data from online members list [ABFDE 2012]. **h:** 0% women (out of six to seven FDEs), France, 2011, FDEs with the Gendarmerie nationale [Langlois-Peter 2012].

Middle — *Percentage of bachelor degrees awarded to women in computer science, science and engineering, and nonscience and engineering fields.* A literature review of women in IT is found in McGrath Cohoon and Aspray 2006; for a history of women in computing see Abbate 2012; and for personal accounts, the male geek culture, and a successful program for improving women participation in computing at Carnegie Mellon University see Margolis and Fisher 2001. **Trend lines:** United States, 1966–2008, women bachelors [NSF–NCSES 2011: tables 3, 4, and 33; see also DuBow 2010]. **x:** 13% women, worldwide, 2007, membership in the Association of Computing Machinery (ACM), largest association in the field of computing, with more than 100,000 members [Hall et al. 2008: 9].

Right — *Percentage of computer science degrees awarded to women according to degree level.* **Trend lines:** United States, 1966–2008, women bachelors, masters, and doctors [NSF–NCSES 2011: table 33].

Bottom — **Trend lines:** *Percentage of bachelor degrees awarded to women in computer science in 31 countries, 1987, 2000, 2003–2009.* To improve legibility the extrema for the first and last years and the values for the United States are highlighted by the bold lines. Data for Greece is cut in two segments, since none was available for 2006. [NSF–DSRS 2011: tables C-16 (2000), C-15 (2003–2006), 5-14 (2007–2008); see also OECD 2006: 6–7, 15–16] **Dot ●:** >50% women, Singapore, graduates — this is one of the rare examples of women overrepresentation in computing, typical of Asian countries of the period [Galpin 2002: 97, with a discussion of possible factors in the cultural variability of computing education and gender]. Bulling, another factor in women underrepresentation in computer science, is interestingly also perceived and handled differently according to race [Camacho and Lord 2011]. **Horizontal bars:** Ranking of five highlighted countries by their global gender gap, 2010 [Hausmann et al. 2010: 8–9]. Note the inverse relationship between global and computing education gender gap for the selected countries.

Health trends

To judge the health trends of the forensic documents (FD) market we can look
at the evolution of forensic activity in the publicly funded laboratories in
the United States over the years 2002, 2005, and 2009 [Peterson and Hickman 2005,
Durose 2008, 2012]. The figures for FD (bold line) are compared to the total figures for forensics (fine line) in terms of budget, laboratories performing FD
expertise, employees carrying out forensic services, requests for services,
and median requests per FD examiner (FDE). Depicted in the graph are the
trends for 2002–2005 (first segment of the trend line) and for 2005–2009 (second segment). Some figures were adjusted to the total number of laboratories. We observe that while overall the indicators for forensics are positive,
FD is on a markedly declining slope.

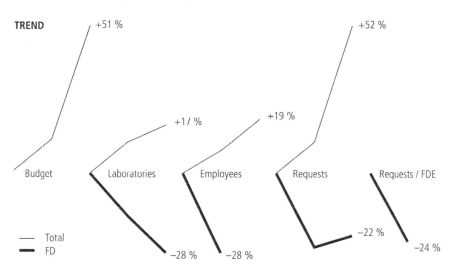

	year	2002	2005	%	2009	%	2002–9
Budget	total (millions)	1,036	1,155	+11	1,562	+35	+51
Laboratories	total	351	389	+11	411	+6	+17
	FD	91	78	−15	66	−15	−28
Employees	total	11,000	11,900	+8	13,100	+10	+19
	FD	137	99	−28	na	na	na
Requests	total	2,706,785	2,997,610	+11	4,120,000	+37	+52
	FD	16,683	12,291	−26	13,000	+6	−22
Requests / FDE	FD (median)	98	74	−24	na	na	na

shown in graph

Information sources

MONOGRAPHS

ESSENTIALS

Forensic Documents (FD) — [Huber and Headrick 1999]: a Bible of handwriting expertise, [Levinson 2001]: lightweight and luminous, [Harrison 1966, Locard 1935–1937]: dated, but contain many basic ideas still waiting to be implemented into software, [Renesse 2005]: optical features in security documents
Forensics — [Jamieson and Moenssens 2009]: encyclopedia; [Houck and Siegel 2010]: textbook
Social background — [Cole 2001]: a social history of fingerprinting, parallels handwriting expertise
Hardware manuals — [UNODC 2010, 2011]
Standards — see Fact sheet "Just standards" [p. 111]
Writing systems — *systems*: [Ager 2012, Daniels and Bright 1996, Everson 2012] • *languages*: [Lewis 2009] • *evolution*: [Christin 2002, Fraenkel 1992] • *context*: [Petrucci 1993, Sassoon 2007] • *typography*: [Bringhurst 2002] • *education*: [Sassoon 1995] • *encoding*: [Everson 2012, Haralambous 2007, LOC 2012, Pedersen 2012, Unicode 2012a, 2012b]

LITERATURE DATABASES

Guide to Information Sources in the Forensic Sciences [Holt 2006]
Mannheimer Bibliographie für Schriftvergleichung und Urkundenprüfung (Mannheim University)
    http://www.isu-mannheim.de/mabi2007.htm
KrimLit (German government criminal research and documentation Institute)
    http://www.krimz.de/dokumentation.html
KrimDok (Heidelberg and Tübingen Universities)
    http://avanti.jura.uni-tuebingen.de/~avanti-x/cgi-bin/acwww25/krimdok.htm
Forensic Bibliographic Database (FORS, Forensic Science Service, United Kingdom)
FBI Library (United States)
    http://fbilibrary.fbiacademy.edu

PERIODICALS

FD

Online list
    http://www.aafs.org/international-Conferences
Annual Meeting of the American Society of Questioned Document Examiners
    http://www.asqde.org/AGM/agm.html
ENFHEX Conference
    http://www.enfsi.eu/page.php?uid=223
International Graphonomics Society Conferences
    http://www.graphonomics.org/
International Journal of Forensic Document Examiners
    http://www.elsevier.com/wps/find/journaldescription.cws_home/505512/description#description
Journal of the American Society of Questioned Document Examiners
    http://www.asqde.org/journal/journal.html
Journal of Forensic Document Examination
    http://afde.org/journal.html
Mannheimer Hefte für Schriftvergleichung (Germany)

FORENSICS

Australian Journal of Forensic Sciences (by the Australian Academy of Forensic Sciences)
http://www.tandf.co.uk/journals/tAJF
American Academy of Forensic Sciences
http://www.aafs.org/aafs-2012-annual-meeting
Canadian Society of Forensic Science Journal (by the Canadian Society of Forensic Sciences)
http://www.csfs.ca/eng/journal
European Academy of Forensic Science Conference (EAFS)
http://www.eafs2012.eu
Forensic Science Communications (by the Federal Bureau of Investigation)
http://www.fbi.gov/about-us/lab/forensic-science-communications
Forensic Science International
http://www.fsijournal.org
Forensic Science Policy & Management
http://www.tandfonline.com/action/aboutThisJournal?journalCode=ufpm20
International Criminal Police Review
Journal of Criminal Law, Criminology and Police Sciences
Journal of Forensic Identification (by the International Association for Identification)
http://www.theiai.org/publications/jfi.php
Journal of Forensic Sciences (by the American Academy of Forensic Sciences)
http://www.aafs.org/journal-forensic-sciences
Journal of Police Science and Administration
Kriminologie
Medicine, Science and the Law
Police Journal
Revue Internationale de Police Criminelle
Science & Justice (formerly Journal of the Forensic Science Society)
http://www.scienceandjusticejournal.com

NEWSLETTERS, MAGAZINES, WEB SITES

Evidence Technology Magazine
http://www.evidencemagazine.com
Forensic-Evidence.com
http://www.forensic-evidence.com
ForensicScience.org (crime infographics)
http://www.forensicscience.org
Forensic Magazine
http://www.forensicmag.com
Global Forensic Science Today
http://www.globalforensicsciencetoday.net
IDentification News
https://www.theiai.org/publications/
Zeno's Forensic Site (digital evidence expert, Netherlands Forensic Institute)
http://4N6site.com

COMPUTING: DOCUMENTS

Conferences of the International Graphonomics Society (IGS)
http://www.graphonomics.org
International Conference on Document Analysis and Recognition (ICDAR)
International Conference on Digital Image Analysis for Libraries (ICDIP)
International Journal on Document Analysis and Recognition (IJDAR)
International Workshop and Tutorial on Automated Forensics Handwriting Analysis (AFHA)
International Workshop on the Frontiers in Handwriting Recognition (IWFHR)
International Workshop on Document Analysis Systems (DAS)

COMPUTING: FORENSICS

International Workshop on Computational Forensics (IWCF)
http://iwcf12.arsforensica.org
International Annual Workshop on Digital Forensics & Incident Analysis (WDFIA)
http://www.wdfia.org

COMPUTING: GENERAL

Annals of Applied Statistics
Biological Cybernetics
Electronic Imaging Conference (IS&T/SPIE)
IEEE Transactions on Pattern Analysis and Machine Learning (PAMI)
IEEE Transactions on Systems, Man and Cybernetics
International Journal of Pattern Recognition and Artificial Intelligence
Pattern Recognition
Pattern Recognition Letters
Progress in Image Analysis and Processing

HUMAN PERCEPTION AND MOTOR SYSTEM

Acta Psychologica
Human Movement Science
Journal of Motor Behavior
Journal of Vision
Perceptual and Motor Skills

WRITING, PALEOGRAPHY

Gazette du livre médiéval
http://www.palaeographia.org/glm/glm.htm
Scripta. International Journal of Codicology and Palaeography
http://www.libraweb.net/riviste.php?chiave=89&h=426&w=300
Visible Language (interdisciplinary)
http://visiblelanguagejournal.com
Writing Systems Research (acquisition, processing, and analysis of writing systems)
http://www.oxfordjournals.org/our_journals/writsy/

PRINTING, INK, SUBSTRATES / CHEMISTRY, METROLOGY

InfoSECURA Newsletter
http://www.intergraf.eu/Content/NavigationMenu/SecurityPrinters/Infosecura/default.htm
International conference on digital printing technologies (NIP) (nonimpact and digital printing technologies)
http://www.imaging.org/IST/conferences/nip/index.cfm
Journal of the American Society for Mass Spectrometry
http://www.sciencedirect.com/science/journal/10440305
Journal of Chromatography
http://www.journals.elsevier.com/journal-of-chromatography-a/
http://www.journals.elsevier.com/journal-of-chromatography-b/
Journal of Pulp and Paper Sciences
http://www.tappi.org/bookstore/technical-papers/journal-articles/archive/jpps.aspx
Measurement Science and Technology
http://iopscience.iop.org/0957-0233
Talanta (International Journal of Pure and Applied Analytical Chemistry)
http://www.journals.elsevier.com/talanta/`

Just standards

FD

Prepared by the Scientific Working Group for Questioned Documents (SWGDOC, est. 1997) and ASTM International, Committee E30.90 Executive (prior to February 2012 by Committee E30.02 on Questioned Documents), http://www.swgdoc.org.

GENERAL

E444   Standard Guide for Scope of Work of Forensic Document Examiners
E2388   Standard Guide for Minimum Training Requirements for Forensic Document Examiners
E2195   Standard Terminology Relating to the Examination of Questioned Documents
WK18965 New Practice for the Case Review of Forensic Document Examinations
WK29498, WK29635   New Guide for Minimum Requirements For Forensic Document Examination Notes
E1658   Standard Terminology for Expressing Conclusions of Forensic Document Examiners

TASKS

WK32033 New Guide for the Dating of Documents
WK29496, WK29633   New Guide for Examination of Sequence of Intersections on Documents
E2331   Standard Guide for Examination of Altered Documents
WK19398 New Guide for Examination of Counterfeit Documents

CURATION

WK25302 New Practice for Collection of Request Writing
E2765   Standard Practice for Use of Image Capture and Storage Technology in Forensic Document Examination
E2710   Standard Guide for Preservation of Charred Documents
E2711   Standard Guide for Preservation of Liquid Soaked Documents

PATTERNS

E2290   Standard Guide for Examination of Handwritten Items
WK29388 New Classification for Typewritten Text
E2289   Standard Guide for Examination of Rubber Stamp Impressions
E2286   Standard Guide for Examination of Dry Seal Impressions
E2285   Standard Guide for Examination of Mechanical Checkwriter Impressions

INSTRUMENTS

WK32034 New Guide for the Classification of Writing Instruments
E2494   Standard Guide for Examination of Typewritten Items
WK29495, WK29632   New Guide for Classification of Conventional Printing Processes

DEPOSITS

E1789   Standard Guide for Writing Ink Identification
E1422   Standard Guide for Test Methods for Forensic Writing Ink Comparison

E2389   Standard Guide for Examination of Documents Produced with Liquid Ink Jet Technology
E2390   Standard Guide for Examination of Documents Produced with Toner Technology
WK29497, WK29634 New Guide for Examination of Documents Produced with Thermal Printing Technology

SUBSTRATE

E2325   Standard Guide for Non-destructive Examination of Paper

DAMAGES

E2291   Standard Guide for Indentation Examinations
E2288   Standard Guide for Physical Match of Paper Cuts, Tears, and Perforations in Forensic Document
         Examinations
E2287   Standard Guide for Examination of Fracture Patterns and Paper Fiber Impressions on Sin-
         gle-Strike Film Ribbons and Typed Text

BIOMETRICS

ISO/IEC JTC1 Subcommittee 37 (JTC1/SC37), Biometrics, http://www.iso.org

Topics: application programming interface; data interchange formats; performance testing and reporting;
calibration, augmentation, and fusion data; sample quality

Pertaining to FD: ISO/IEC 19794-7:2007, Information technology, Biometric data interchange formats,
Part 7: Signature/sign time series data

See also: INCITS/M1, Biometrics Technical Committee, International Committee on Information Technology Standard (INCITS), http://standards.incits.org/a/public/group/m1

Key datasets + databases

This annex is not an extensive review of datasets and databases, but meant to gain an understanding of typical examples useful for computational forensic documents (FD) and provide links to further information. Contents: sources, FD and law enforcement, computing, signatures, security documents, linguistics, paleography.

SOURCES

Digital datasets

Computer science research datasets (mostly collected for writing recognition, but basically any dataset can be used for writer identification and verification too, even if some are more appropriate than others, as is the case for the popular IAM dataset [Marti and Bunke 2002]).

Signature datasets (mostly produced for biometrics by computer scientists and the biometrics industry).

Security documents (extensive data, superb facilities [online access, multispectral reproductions, database management…], commercial products).

Classified digital datasets (e.g.: FISH in Europe, US Secret Service handwriting database in the United States).

Public libraries, archives, museums with online selected items and collections (mostly printed matter and handwritten works of art such as illuminated manuscripts; data is predominantly historical, although contemporary material also exists in archives).

Corporate: Substantial amounts of handwriting data is handled daily by companies as part of document triage, handwriting recognition, and digital archiving of incoming correspondence, but such data is usually not available for research purposes.

Physical datasets

Handwriting samples from **FD research** (many studies exist, but the data is not published).

Archives of **law enforcement agencies** (every national police force has some amount of FD archives).

Books (atlases of handwriting, seals, font catalogs, or copy books, produced by paleographers, typographers, and educators; i.e., outside the FD field).

Art and autographs market (a lucrative field).

Libraries, archives, museums (vast amounts of data).

FD AND LAW ENFORCEMENT

Austrian Federal Criminal Police Office (BKA-AT) — Autographed CVs of inmates, paper archives.

European Network of Forensic Handwriting Experts (ENFHEX) — International Handwriting Information System (IHIS); copybook samples from European and other countries; [ENFHEX 2012a], http://www.enfsi.eu/page.php?uid=76.

Federal Bureau of Investigation (FBI) — Holds reference files (drawn from casework) and standard files (font catalogs for example); datasets containing handwriting and signatures include: ▶ 1. Anonymous Letter File, ▶ 2. Bank Robbery Note File, ▶ 3. National Fraudulent Check File (est. 1936), ▶ 4. National Motor Vehicle Certificate of Title File, ▶ 5. National Stolen Art File, ▶ 6. Government Issued Documents (e.g., drivers licenses, social security cards) [FBI 1994: 27–28, Kelly and Lindblom 2006: 69, Wayman and Orlans 2008], ▶ 7. the modified "London Letter" dataset (created in the late 2000s to calibrate and evaluate the FLASH ID software; five print and five cursive handwriting samples from 500 volunteers at the FBI, training classes, forensic conferences, and personal acquaintances; documents of at least 100 writers were manually segmented into characters by Gannon Technologies) [Buscaglia et al. 2006: 57–58, Saunders et al. 2011: 7–9].

German Federal Criminal Police Office (BKA) — The FISH database [see p. 123] contained 55,000 handwriting samples from 25,000 individuals in 1991 [Phillipp 1992], 77,000 documents in 1997 [Franke 2001: 2b].

Netherlands Forensic Institute (NFI) — About 2,000 handwriting samples, of which at least 1,311 are digitized, collected by the Dutch police from suspects in civil and criminal cases, written under dictation, about two pages in cursive and capitals, in Dutch, exhibiting heterogeneous stylistic quality [Brink et al. 2007: 825, Fagel 2012].

US Secret Service (USSS) — ▶ 1. Collection of threat letters addressed to high-ranking members of the US government (the President, the Vice President, members of the Congress), ambassadors, foreign officials under USSS protection; stored in the US FISH system; [NARA 2007]; ▶ 2. International Ink Library, Digital Ink Library, has >9,500 ink samples dating back to the 1920s; physical and digital access; acquired by purchase and supplied yearly by writing instrument and ink manufacturers; contains: company files (metadata), ink samples (in vials), scribble sheets (ink on paper), thin-layer chromatographs (TLC) (chemical components analysis); managed by the USSS and the Internal Revenue Service; [Bowen and Schneider 2007, Cantu 2009: 1541–1546, Wayman and Orlans 2008].

Other — See Huber and Headrick 1999: 45, 152–164.

COMPUTING

This is a list of handwriting datasets. There exist a number of datasets originating in the computing community that could be used for FD, but with one exception and as already mentioned, these all suffer from the issue of sampling representativeness, which limits their usefulness for FD. A succinct description is provided. Note the mix between datasets specifically designed for writer identification and those for text recognition.

CEDAR/USPS—USPS Office of Advanced Technology Database of Handwritten Cities, States, ZIP Codes, Digits, and Alphabetic Characters; CEDAR (Buffalo, NY), US Postal Service (USPS); offline handwritten samples of about 500 city names, 5,000 state names, 10,000 ZIP codes, 50,000 alphanumeric characters; [CEDAR 2012, Hull 1994].

CEDAR offline—CEDAR; about 1,500 writers representative of the US population; one page of a modified "London Letter" text; specifically designed for writer identification and verification; [Srihari et al. 2002].

CEDAR online—CEDAR; online cursive and capitals samples from 200 writers; [Wayman and Orlans 2008: 5–11].

Chaski—Chaski Writer Sample Database; Institute for Linguistic Evidence (Georgetown, DE); up to a page of spontaneous handwriting from circa 175 known writers; writing implements and content freely chosen to simulate natural writing conditions and "topics which are sociolinguistically determined to evoke different communicative functions and emotive states"; "demographic information includes the age, race, sex, educational level, dialectal information, graphic type (cursive, print, mixed), and legibility"; [Chaski and Walch 2009: 28], http://www.linguisticevidence.org.

Demokritos—National Center for Scientific Research "Demokritos" (Athens, Greece); 26 writers, eight cursive pages per writer; text in English, French, German, and Greek; writer origin mainly Greek; used in the first international writer identification contest (ICDAR 2011), similar dataset used in the subsequent contest (ICFHR 2012); [Louloudis et al. 2011], http://users.iit.demokritos.gr/~louloud/{Writer_Identification_Contest/, WritIdentCont2012/, ICFHR2012WritIdentCont/}.

Firemaker—Nijmegen University (Netherlands), Netherlands Forensic Institute (The Hague, Netherlands), Unipen Foundation (Nijmegen, Netherlands); 431 writers; one page per writer; Dutch; offline; designed for writer expertise; metadata: sex, age, handedness; uses same paper and writing instruments for all writers, special ink to make ruling invisible to the scanner; [Schomaker and Vuurpijl 2000], http://www.unipen.org/products.html.

IAM offline—Institute of Computer Science and Applied Mathematics (IAM) (Bern, Switzerland); 657 writers, 1,539 documents, English; mostly Swiss writers from the canton of Bern, some German, Greek, Chinese, and other writers; [Marti and Bunke 2002].

ICROW-2003—(The ICDAR 2003 Informal Competition for the Recognition of Online Words: The Unipen-ICROW-03 benchmark set, Version 0.0) Unipen Foundation (Nijmegen, Netherlands); 72 writers, 13,119 isolated words, online, Dutch, English, Italian languages, demography: Dutch, Irish, Italian, and mixed; http://www.unipen.org/products.html.

Lehigh Notebook—Lehigh University (Bethlehem, PA); nine writers, 499 pages, 18 notebooks (targets: >50 writers, >3,000 pages, >100 notebooks);

English; students; [Chen et al. 2011], http://dae.cse.lehigh.edu/DAE/?q=browse/ dataitem/554570.

MADCAT/OpenHaRT—University of Pennsylvania (Philadelphia, PA); 46,185 documents and 453 writers; coverage: Arabic speaking countries; [NIST 2012b, Strassel 2009], http://www.ldc.upenn.edu/Catalog/CatalogEntry.jsp?cat alogId={LDC2012T15, LDC2013T09}.

NIST Special Database 19—National Institute of Standards and Technology (NIST, Gaithersburg, MD); based on census forms; offline capitals and cursive handwriting by 3,699 writers; designed for writing recognition, not FD; [Geist et al. 1994, Grother 1995, NIST 2012c], http://www.nist.gov/srd/nistsd19.cfm.

PSI—PSI Laboratory, University of Rouen (Rouen, France); 88 writers, French; Rouen, Thierry Paquette; [Bensefia et al. 2005: 74].

Qatar—Qatar University (Qatar); subset of a larger dataset; >50 writers, 3 paragraphs, Arabic; part of the first and second Arabic writer identification contests (ICDAR 2011, ICFHR 2012); [Hassaïne et al. 2011], http://wic2011.qu.edu. qa, http://awic2012.qu.edu.qa.

RIMES—A2iA (Paris, France), Institut Télécom, Télécom & Management SudParis (Evry, France), Direction générale de l'armement [General Directorate for Military Procurement] (DGA) (Paris, France); RIMES dataset; 1,600 writers, each producing five letters, one page long; French; [Augustin et al. 2006], http://www.rimes-database.fr.

Tobacco800—Tobacco800 Document Image Database; Illinois Institute of Technology (Urbana, IL); 1,290 complex document images; public subset drawn from 42 million pages of a lawsuit involving tobacco companies; [Lewis et al. 2006], http://ir.iit.edu/projects/CDIP.html, http://www.umiacs. umd.edu/~zhugy/tobacco800.html.

TriGraph slant—Institute of Artificial Intelligence and Cognitive Engineering (ALICE), University of Groningen (Netherlands), Donders Institute for Brain, Cognition and Behavior, Radboud University Nijmegen (Nijmegen, Netherlands), Netherlands Forensic Institute (The Hague, Netherlands); 47 writers, c. 200 words in four documents: two natural handwriting, one slanted to the left and one to the right; Dutch; demography: Dutch, average age 27; offline; [Brink et al. 2011], http://unipen.org/trigraphslant.html.

Twins—US Secret Service; handwriting from 206 pairs of twins; used by CEDAR to investigate the variability of twins' handwriting; [Srihari 2010: 7, 2008].

Unipen—Unipen Foundation (Nijmegen, Netherlands); >2,200 writers, >5 million characters (October 1995), online; donated by >40 institutions; [Guyon et al. 1994], http://unipen.nici.kun.nl.

Other datasets—Bensefia et al. 2005: 2083 [links], Bunke 2003: 453–454 [links, synthetic datasets], Chen et al. 2011: 2 [unconstrained Latin, links], Dimauro et al. 2002 [checks], El Abed and Märgner 2007 [Arabic], Farrahi et al. 2010 [Arabic], Frank and Asuncion 2012 [repository], Impedovo et al. 2012 [checks], Jin et al. 2010 [online Chinese], Junaidi et al. 2011 [Lampung], Kavallieratou et al. 2001 [Greek], Khosravi and Kabir 2007 [Perisan digits], Liu et al. 2011 [online and offline Chinese], Slimane et al. 2009 [printed Arabic], Tagougui et al. 2012 [online Arabic links]

SIGNATURES

Signature datasets have been recently extensively reviewed [Impedovo and Pirlo 2008, Liwicki et al. 2012, Martinez-Diaz and Fiérrez 2009]. A summary of the size of these datasets is, however, useful to provide. Compiling the relevant references, up to 64 datasets are found, representative of academic computing research until 2011 — more data is supposed to be held by private companies. The datasets are about equally divided in offline and online, and principally in Latin script from European writers, with some datasets in Chinese, Japanese, and Arabic scripts.

With few exceptions these datasets have been developed in the framework of biometrics and are typically divided into genuine and forged signatures. FD datasets are organized slightly differently: part of the data represents known samples of a single writer (less than 10, usually), and another part questioned samples, a subset that can be a mix of genuine, simulated, and disguised samples from various writers (hundreds of samples or, in the targeted real-life applications, virtually without limit) [Liwicki et al. 2010: 716].

Signature dataset size	min	median	max	total
datasets	—	—	—	64
authors	2	51	667	4,147
signatures / author	3	40	783	—
signatures	40	1,720	33,350	190,156
genuine	18	805	20,010	78,160
forgeries	22	800	13,340	78,908

Sources: Blankers et al. 2009: 1404, Impedovo and Pirlo 2008: 622, 624, Liwicki et al. 2010: 715, 2011: 1481, Martinez-Diaz and Fiérrez 2009: 1179–1182, Munich and Perona 2003: 202, Pu et al. 2009: 132–133, Srihari 2010: 8. • Note: Author figures should be regarded as approximate: some datasets might appear twice in the surveys; author figures are not provided for all datasets; when the same figures are given for both training and test datasets it was assumed that they involve the same authors; when the training and test figures differed the higher one was retained.

SECURITY DOCUMENTS

Note: Most datasets are accessed via proprietary database systems.

Commercial databases

Documentchecker.com — Over 90,000 images of 7,000 identity documents (ID), banknote and forgery samples from >195 countries; online access; multilingual (Dutch, English, French, German, Italian, Spanish); used by more than 1,300 organizations worldwide, by Keesing, Netherlands, est. 1923, https:// keesingreferencesystems.com.

Documentchecker Banknotes — Images and principal security features of >4,500 banknotes (>70,000 images) and sample forgeries from >180 countries, by Attestor, Germany, http://attestor-forensics.com.

Documentchecker Identity Documents—Images and principal security features of >1,800 passports, driving licenses, and other IDs from >180 countries, by Attestor, cf. supra.

Reference Data System "Autodocs"—Over 2,300 images (visible light, ultraviolet, 365 nm and 254 nm wavelengths, infrared, special materials) and security features of >475 driving licenses, vehicle certificates, and related documents from 77 countries; multilingual (English, German, Chinese...), by Regula, Belarus, est. 1992; http://regula.ws.

Reference Data System "Currency"—Over 65,000 images (visible light, infrared, ultraviolet, IR luminescence, magnetic ink pattern, anti–Stokes luminescence) and security features of >2,068 banknotes from 176 countries; multilingual (English, German, Chinese...), by Regula, cf. supra.

Reference Data System "Passport"—Over 24,136 images (visible light, ultraviolet, 365 nm and 254 nm wavelengths, infrared, special materials) and security features of >1,655 passports and other identity documents from 176 countries; multilingual (English, German, Chinese...), by Regula, cf. supra.

Classified, restricted databases

Document Information System for Civil Status (DISCS)—Dutch product; ID verification; free, online; deployed internationally (Australia, Dubai, Hong Kong...); http://www.discs.nl.

Electronic Documentation Information System on Network (EDISON)—Dutch National Police; travel documents (EDISON TD), >2,500 genuine and fake travel document samples from over 190 countries, updated every four months; other docs (EDISON OD); worldwide use: Australia, Canada, China, Dubai, Indonesia, Malaysia, Netherlands, New Zealand, Thailand, United States, Vietnam; [APEC/IEGBM 2003: 6].

European Collection of Automotive Paints (EUCAP)—European crime laboratories from 23 countries, part of European Network of Forensic Institutes (ENFSI); centralized at BKA, Germany; workflow: automotive producers supply paint samples which become part of the collection (BKA, KT13 Dpt.), measurements are performed (BKA KT13, crime lab Berlin, Forensic Institute of the National Gendarmerie [IRCGN], France), stored in the database (BKA KT13), and distributed to members (50 crime labs) and partners (RCMP, Canada, FBI...); [Becker 2007, Masonnet and Monnard 2009: 1946–1947, on paint in general see McCullough 2009].

False and Authentic Documents Online (FADO)—Managed by the Council of the European Union; est. 1998 (legal basis), active since 2003 (?); developed by CRI, Luxembourg, http://www.cri.lu; classified, restricted, online (Intranet FADO, iFADO); goal: combat illegal immigration and organized crime; contains genuine and forged ID images, statistics; available to document experts (authorized persons working for a control authority) in the European Union, Iceland, Norway, Switzerland; uses a closed set glossary in the 22 languages of the European Union, free text translated by professionals; digital development of the European Fraud Bulletin and the Handbook of

Genuine Documents; architecture: Windows 2000 servers, Windows XP clients, Java, Oracle, UML/RUP, HTML-HTTPS, XML-SOAP-Web services, PDF, JPG, PNG, Unicode UTF-8, Teamware used as a secure mail system (CRI Web site); http://europa.eu/legislation_summaries/justice_freedom_security/free_movement_of_persons_asylum_immigration/l33075_en.htm, http://en.wikipedia.org/wiki/FADO.

ID-Check—ORIBI, Netherlands; ID authentication and identification; http://www.oribi.nl.

Informationssystem Urkunden (Document Information System, ISU)—Forensic Science Institute (Kriminaltechnisches Institut, KT), BKA, Germany: all types of documents (travel, vehicles…), forgeries dataset; part of the German Police Information System (est. 1972 [INPOL-alt], 2003 [INPOL-neu] [Dick 2011]); http://www.bva.bund.de > Informationssystem Urkunden.

Informationssystem Stempel (Stamps Information System, ISS)—Forensic Science Institute (Kriminaltechnisches Institut, KT), BKA, Germany: stamps, forgeries dataset; http://www.bva.bund.de > Informationssystem Stempel.

National Automotive Paint File (NAPF)—FBI; maker, model, year; samples sent by car manufacturers; [FBI 2007a].

Paint Data Query (PDQ)—Royal Canadian Mounted Police (RCMP); layer structure (number of layers, color of each layer, and order in which they are applied) and the chemical composition of the individual layers of paint on a factory-applied automotive finish; [FBI 2007a].

Public Register of Travel and Identity Documents Online (PRADO)—Managed by the Council of the European Union; est. 2007; public, online; subset of FADO; http://prado.consilium.europa.eu.

Electronic information systems

These are not specifically dedicated to documents; there are many such systems, and the trend is toward integration [Mathiesen 2000: 186, for a wider perspective see Mathiesen 2006].

European Car and Driving License Information System (EUCARIS)—Electronic text, no document image; has potential for networking; online; est. 1994; contributions from 16 European states; http://www.eucaris.net.

European Dactylographic System (Eurodac), Europol Information System (EIS), Schengen Information System (SIS 1 & SIS II), Supplementary Information Requested at National Entries (SIRENE), Visa Information System (VIS)—Conceived at the European level, these databases are intended to manage visa and asylum applications, track illegal migrants, and, more controversially, used by law enforcement agencies to fight terrorism and crime. Contain electronic text, biometrics (up to 10 fingerprints, facial pictures in SIS II and VIS, possibly DNA, and iris scans), document images (VIS); designed for networking; became progressively operational between the 1990s and 2013; a central IT agency for managing these diverse systems is planned; [primary sources: Europa 2013, Europol 2013; secondary sources: Broeders 2011, Bunyan 1993: 10, 1997: 9–31, Mathiesen 2000: 169–173].

PALEOGRAPHY

In a broad sense paleographic writing datasets are confined to the study of the past, although they can include archived contemporary samples (for which the term "neography" would be more appropriate). The datasets are found in libraries, archives, museums, as well as *extra muros* (public inscriptions). Overwhelmingly in analog format, paleographic datasets cover any form of written messages, down to Babylonian clay tablets, in any language and script—they represent humanity's written memory.

These are tremendous opportunities for understanding writing and creating computing projects, but not without substantial hurdles: physical access to the datasets cannot be taken for granted given cumbersome conservation regulations; digitization necessitates substantial investment, usually the largest part of a project's costs; not rarely, complex preprocessing is needed, for common artifacts like ink bleed-through; usually the writer's identity and the conditions surrounding the document's production are unknown, adding to the difficulty of forming a reference set for writer expertise.

There are also different expertise tasks typical of paleographic datasets, like ascertaining the authorship of calligraphies. Due to models that calligraphers strive to emulate these writing samples can have maddeningly small in-between-writer variability, which is further complicated by purposefully induced artistic variability and writing skills in several styles (for computational paleography see Fischer et al. 2010, Rehbein et al. 2009).

Copybooks used for teaching proper writing in school, are a class of documents useful for FD purposes since they provide normative "vantage points" that can be used to measure distances between styles [see IHIS, p. 114]. A very little-tapped-into resource is the art and autographs market, which has identical goals to FD and can provide substantial document resources (for example, the Musée des lettres et manuscrits [Museum of Letters and Manuscripts], Paris, has a collection of no less than 70,000 documents written by many famous people, from antiquity to this day [Plume 2010]). Good portals to paleographic datasets are major libraries such as the Library of Congress [http://www.loc.gov/rr/mss/], the British Library [http://searcharchives.bl.uk], or the Bibliothèque nationale de France [http://www.bnf.fr/en/collections_and_services/dpts_eng/s.manuscripts_department.html], and various special online libraries such as the Virtual Manuscript Library of Switzerland, which gives access to high-resolution reproductions [http://www.e-codices.unifr.ch/en/], or the Bernstein Project: The Memory of Paper, offering access to hundred of thousands of watermark and paper structure samples from a federation of national and private collections [http://www.memoryofpaper.eu].

Landmark software

This is a survey of software pertaining mostly to forensic writing expertise. The table below is a summary of the following detailed list.

	Used by FDEs			Procurement			Accessibility		
	used	not used	unknown	governmental	commercial	free	has Web site	downloads & installs ok	no Web site
WRITING IMAGE									
AKIM			●	●					●
CEDAR-FOX			●		●		●		
Druide			●		●		●		
FISH	●			●					●
FLASH ID			●	●			●		
FLEX-Tracker			●		●		●		
GIWIS, GRAWIS		●			●		●		
Graphlog	●					●			●
HG4FDE			●		●				●
Script			●	●					●
Wanda		●			●				●
Write-On	●				●		●	●	
WRITING DYNAMICS									
MovAlyzeR			●		●		●		
Oasis			●		●		●		
VISUALIZATION									
MICS	●				●		●		
ScienceGL			●		●		●		
RECONSTRUCTION									
MatchMaker	●			●					●
Unshredder			●		●		●		
PAPER									
AD751		●				●	●	●	
INK									
Color Deconvolution	●					●	●	●	
MARKUP									
Wanda XML		●				●			●

WRITING IMAGE

EARLIER DAYS

The literature mentions a number of handwriting expertise software from the 1970s through the 1990s featuring some particularities when compared to the modern specimens [Huber and Headrick 1999: 154–159, 161]: • the software was developed by the users themselves or under their close supervision; • the users were law enforcement agencies rather than forensic laboratories; and • the programs served the identification of criminals (instead of presenting evidence for conviction). • The methodology was based on script classification and stylistic features frequencies. FISH (q.v.) is among this software breed the one that outlived the others. Some of the developers were: Arkansas State Crime Laboratory, Australian Police [Found et al. 1994], Birmingham Home Office Forensic Science Laboratory, London Metropolitan Police, Zürich Cantonal Police.

AKIM

name—Automatic Classification and Identification of Machinescripts / Automatische Klassifizierung und Identifizierung von Maschinenschriften (AKIM)
developer—German Federal Criminal Police Office / Bundeskriminalamt (BKA), "Technical Research, Development and Testing" team
history—created > 1995 [Heyne 1995: 249]
availability—governmental use
active use—yes
beneficiaries—BKA
purpose—machine writing database and expertise software (similar to FISH, q.v.)
methods—neural networks
screenshots—Web site
references—Heyne 1995
Web site—http://www.bka.de > Search: AKIM

CEDAR-FOX, CEDARAB

name—CEDAR-FOX, CEDARAB
developer—CedarTech, Williamsville (NY), United States; licensing methods developed at the Centre for Excellence in Document Analysis and Recognition (CEDAR), University at Buffalo, The State University of New York (SUNY), Buffalo (NY), United States • Sargur N. Srihari, Venugopal Govindaraju, et al.
history—continuously developed since 1999; awarded funding by the US Department of Justice

availability—commercial, patented
active use—tested among others by the FBI, the US Secret Service, the Canada Border Agency, the Netherlands Forensic Institute; acquired as educational material in the forensic curriculum of the West Virginia University, Morgantown (WV) [Shin 2009: 7]
beneficiaries—primarily the FD community
purpose—handwriting and signature identification and verification
features—*preprocessing*: binarization, deskewing, denoising, skeletonization, stroke thickening, contour extraction, line removal • *interactive measurements*: ruler, protractor • *automatic measurements*: grayscale entropy, total pixels, interior and exterior contour total pixels, 3×3 chain-code distribution, gradient, structural and concavity features, average stroke width, character height and slant, individual interword distance, average interword distance, Palmer metrics (similarity to the Palmer reference characters), character, bigram, word similarity • *recognition*: characters, word spotting • *search*: text to image, image to text, and image to image • *annotation*: ground truthing words • *expertise*: identification and verification
performance—88% top-1 writer identification [Srihari et al. 2002: 12]
evidence—log-likelihood ratio, distance (score), ranking, worded 9 levels opinion scale • the metrics are expressed for most measured features individually and for the document as a whole • based on a model of handwriting styles of the US population and Gamma and Gaussian features distribution models [Srihari 2010: 7, Srihrari et al. 2008: 433–435]
notes—CEDARABIC is a companion software optimized for Arabic script • costs $8,500 (2009) [Shin 2009: 6]
screenshots—Web site, [CedarTech 2008]
references—CedarTech 2008, Srihari 2010, Srihari et al. 2009, 2010, Shin 2009
Web site—http://www.cedartech.com, http://www.cedar.buffalo.edu

DRUIDE

name—Druide. Printer Identification System for forensic applications / Drucker Identifikationssystem für forensische Anwendungen
developer—Druide; Jürgen Holzapfel, Grevenbroich, Germany
history—was available in 2006
availability—commercial
references—Holzapfel and Rottes 2006
Web site—http://www.druidesystem.com

FISH

name—Forensic Information System for Handwriting / Forensisches InformationsSystem Handschriften (FISH)
developer—German Federal Criminal Police Office / Bundeskriminalamt (BKA, Wiesbaden) [Bundestag 2012: 20], "Technical Research, Development and Testing" team • follow-up Windows version by the US Secret Service (USSS)
availability—governmental use
active use—yes
history—project started in 1975 [Phillipp 1996], prototype available in 1986 [Van Erp et al. 2003: 282] or 1989 [Philipp 1994], operational use in 1990 [Levinson 2001: 48], updates scheduled post-2011 [Kerkhoff 2011] • Initially developed in relation to the writing analysis of the German RAF terrorists [Heinrich 2006: 202]. • The USSS uses the system to identify authors of threat letters to high-ranking members of the US government (the President, the Vice President, members of the Congress), ambassadors, foreign officials under the USSS protection [NARA 2007]
beneficiaries—primary: BKA, secondary: USSS; also acquired by: Netherlands Forensic Institute (NFI), Canadian Security Intelligence Service [Huber and Headrick 1999: 157; Kerkhoff 2011, Van Erp et al. 2003: 282]
purpose—FD database; handwriting analysis
features—Preprocessing: ink / background separation. • Analysis: search for documents with similar writing styles based on a number of extracted features. In automatic mode these are binary pixel chain statistics and autocorrelation, and in interactive mode six descriptors: height of character body, ascender, descender and loops, character width, slant. • Database: interactive tracing of character shape, cut of characters from images and save in database, constrained and free-form annotation. • FISH runs on a VAX/VMS machine [Geradts 2002: 23], using the ADABAS database of Software AG, Germany [Bundestag 2012: 21]. • The system is not interconnected with other governmental information systems [Bundestag 2012: 21] or accessible off-site [Kube 1995: 96]. • Contained 55,000 handwriting samples from 25,000 individuals in 1991 [Phillipp 1992], 77,000 documents in 1997 [Franke and Köppen 2001: 2b]
methods—binary pixel chain statistics and autocorrelation, neural networks
screenshots—Web site
references—Bundestag 2012, Hargett 1994, Heyne 1995: 248–249, Kerkhoff 2011, Phillipp 1992, 1994, 1996; US FISH: NARA 2007, FISH vs Script: Schomaker and Vuurpijl 2000
Web site—http://www.bka.de > Search: FISH

FLASH ID, FLEX-TRACKER, FLEX-MINER

name—These are three products: FLEX-Tracker (Forensic Language-Independent Automated System for Handwriting Identification); FLASH ID, its FBI implementation; and FLEX-Miner
developer—1. Gannon Technologies Group, Fairfax (VA), United States; 2. Document Forensics Laboratory, George Mason University, Fairfax (VA) (a joint venture of the Department of Applied Information Technology and the Department of Statistics, funded by Gannon and the FBI); 3. FBI, Quantico (VA) • Mark Walch (GTG), Donald Gantz (GMU), JoAnn Buscaglia (FBI), et al.
history—characters-as-graphs concept patented in 1993, development of FLASH ID initiated during the early 2000s
availability—commercial (FLEX-Tracker), governmental use (FLASH ID); patented
beneficiaries—FBI, public
purpose—FLEX-Tracker, FLASH ID: writer identification and verification in forensics, biometrical applications; FLEX-Miner: word spotting, document triage
features—script- and language-independent, published results on Latin/English, Arabic, and Chinese scripts/languages
methods—Characters from a training dataset are manually segmented and automatically described in terms of graphs, with several measurements taken, such as distances and angles between vertices, Bezier values and curvature [Freeman 2007, Gantz et al. 2005]. The resulting vectors provide a statistical model of the characters that is used to retrieve similar writers from novel documents or compare documents. An automated method for segmentation in arbitrary graphs is also available, with similarities to other allographic approaches (e.g., Bensefia et al. 2005, Bulacu 2007, Bulacu and Schomaker 2007)
performance—100% identification accuracy for >50 Latin characters text length on a 100 writers dataset with manually segmented characters [Saunders et al. 2011]; no published evaluations on public, commonly used datasets were found
evidence—likelihood ratio
notes—tested on the FBI modified "London Letter" dataset [see FBI, p. 114]
references—AAFS 2011: 15, 26, 27, 28, 37, 39, 40, 57–58, Freeman 2007, Gantz et al. 2005, 2006, Walch 1993, 2008, 2010a, 2010b, Walch and Gantz 2004
Web site—http://www.gannontech.com, http://www.gannonintl.com; https://ait.gmu.edu/research

GIWIS, GRAWIS

name—Groningen Intelligent Writer Identification System (GIWIS), Groningen Automatic Writer Identification System (GRAWIS)

developer—Axel Brink (GIWIS), Marius Bulacu (GRAWIS), Institute of Artificial Intelligence and Cognitive Engineering (Alice), University of Groningen

history—GRAWIS was prototyped in the early 2000s in the framework of the Wanda project (q.v.), and the follow-up Trigraph [Niels et al. 2005], and the algorithms incorporated and supplemented with new ones in GIWIS from 2005 onward

availability—free for research purposes; contact the authors

beneficiaries—Netherlands Forensic Institute (NFI), National Archives of the Netherlands; developed for FD examiners (FDEs) and paleographers alike

purpose—writer identification

features—GIWIS: given a written document finds in a collection of written documents those similar to an input image, displays the top-10 results, their metadata, and distance between documents; a clustering of all documents (k-means) is also possible; automatic preprocessing consists in keystoning, scaling, high-pass filtering, binarization; written in Python, C++, XML; GRAWIS: Web browser based

methods—GIWIS: run length, brush, hinge, hinge2, directions, ink width, quill, quill hinge; does not include fraglets (used in GRAWIS)

performance—73% to 98% top-1 writer identification

evidence—ranked document distance scores

notes—GIWIS: tested on Dutch, French, and German documents of the 14th to 17th centuries, and modern Dutch and Swiss handwriting (Firemaker, IAM, Trigraph slant, q.v. in datasets list)

screenshots—GIWIS: Brink 2011: 120, Smit 2011; GRAWIS: Bulacu 2007: 109–113, Bulacu and Schomaker 2007: 713–714

references—GIWIS: Brink 2011: 93–99, 105–114, Brink et al. 2012, Smit 2011; GRAWIS: Bulacu 2007: 107–115, Bulacu and Schomaker 2005

Web site—http://unipen.org/GIWIS/

GRAPHLOG

developer—Institute of Forensic Research (IFR), Krakow, Poland

history—released in 2007

availability—to be freely made available in the near future to scientists and FDEs

active use—research and case work at IFR

beneficiaries—IFR presently

purpose—interactive measurement of simple geometric features

features—measures: distance between two points, proportion of two distance values, slant of an arbitrary line in respect to the image horizontal, angle between two arbitrary lines, surface of an arbitrary polygon; • the measured values are linked to custom or predefined entities (height character body, ascender, descender, interword distance…), stored in files for later processing

methods—interactive

performance—accuracy, repeatability, and reproducibility of measurements obtained with Graphlog are statistically identical to those performed on physical documents

evidence—none

notes—designed by FDEs for FDEs • An Open Source JView plug-in with practically identical measurement capabilities to Graphlog has been developed in the field of paleography: Graphoskop, released in 2009, by Maria Gurrado and Giancarlo Lestingi for the École Nationale des Chartes, Paris, France [Gurrado 2009], http://palaeographia.org

screenshots—Fabianska et al. 2006: 397, Fig. 9

references—Fabianska et al. 2006, Dziedzic 2012

Web site—http://ies.krakow.pl/en/

HG4FDE, ANONYMOUS

name—HG4FDE (provisional name), Anonymous (not yet christened)

developer—Natural Technologies for Handwriting (NITe), Salerno, Italy

history—first release 2012; Anonymous is not described due to its awaiting patenting

availability—commercial

beneficiaries—FDE community

purpose—handwriting expertise

features—HG4FDE: semiautomated segmentation in words, characters, and strokes; automated measurement of spacing, slant, slope, ascender/descender/body character ratio, local curvature; followed by a similarity estimation between known and questioned document, and report generation • Anonymous: more complex

methods—segmentation described in Cordella et al. 2010, De Stefano et al. 2004

evidence—weighted sum of Kullback-Leibler divergences between feature pairs in known and questioned document

references—Marcelli and Chiaviello 2012

SCRIPT

name—Script
developer—TNO, Netherlands
history—initiated by the Netherlands Institute for Forensic Examinations and Research in 1986, field deployed in 1996
beneficiaries—The Hague Police
purpose—quantified approach to handwriting measurement, supported by digitized documents database
features—frequency analysis of certain manually identified features; similar descriptors as in FISH, but more automatization; interactive measurements of height of character body, ascender and descender, character width, slant, word width, interlinear distance [Franke et al. 2005]
references—Jong et al. 1994, Kroon 1996; Script vs FISH: Schomaker and Vuurpijl 2000

WANDA

name—Wanda Workbench
developer—1. Fraunhofer Institute, Division of Security and Testing Technology, Berlin, Germany (FHI); 2. Artificial Intelligence Institute, Groningen University, Netherlands (RUG); 3. Nijmegen Institute for Cognition and Information, University of Nijmegen (NICI); 4. International Unipen Foundation; 5. in addition to over 30 participants and collaborators from more than 10 organizations • led by Katrin Franke (FHI), Lambert R.B. Schomaker (RUG), Louis Vuurpijl (NICI)
history—2002–2005, with funding from the BKA (2002–2003) and collaboration of the Netherlands Forensic Institute and US agencies, as a replacement to FISH (q.v.) [Franke 2012, Franke and Köppen 2001, Franke et al. 2005]
active use—not in active use [Franke 2008]
beneficiaries—BKA, NFI
purpose—complete FD software framework
features—Wanda is a complete FD software framework, with capabilities for image acquisition (scanning, tablet input), preprocessing (including ink/background separation), interactive measurements (height of character body, ascender, descender and loops, character width, slant, interlinear distance), automated feature extraction (prototype), writer identification, report preparation, data annotation, storage, retrieval, and networking (access via Web clients). • Follows a plug-in philosophy of modulable resources. • Technologies: the annotation format WandaXML (q.v.), Java, SQL, PHP, HTTP, TCP/IP
methods—allograph comparison (user draw allograph instances and the machine finds other occurrences; implemented as a proof of concept)

notes—Trivia: The software's name is a wink to BKA's FISH software and the crime comedy movie A Fish Called Wanda (1988)
screenshots—Franke 2004b: 5, 2005
references—Franke 2012, Franke and Köppen 2001, Franke et al. 2003b, 2004b, 2005, Van Erp et al. 2003, 2004

WRITE-ON

name—Write-On. Document Comparison Software
developer—Pikaso Software, Ottawa (ON), Canada; Pierre Goudreault
history—started mid-1990s; last release 2010
availability—commercial
active use—yes
beneficiaries—initially designed for FDEs, enhanced for wider use
purpose—document image annotation and database tool
features—classification of document images in a database, annotation of documents and regions of images, search documents and images by annotations, generate frequency lists of annotated words and characters; Latin script support only
methods—database
evidence—none
screenshots—Web site, [Goudreault 2010]
notes—the company organizes Write-On educational workshops • priced $1,250–$3,250 in 2010
references—Goudreault 2010, Lindblom 2008
Web site—http://www.pikaso.com

WRITING DYNAMICS

BIOMETRIC SMART PEN

name—Biometric Smart Pen (BiSP)
developer—University of Applied Sciences, Regensburg, Germany
history—earlier prototypes produced in 2002
availability—experimental, patented
beneficiaries—biometrics, medicine
purpose—multisensor e-pen
features—x, y, z coordinates, z-pressure, across-pressure, tilt acceleration, writing vibration, finger grip pressure, writing sound • records pen dynamics on the writing surface and in the air • analysis software written in MATLAB™
methods—dynamic time warping (DTW) for signature analysis, neural networks, support vector machines, wavelet transform, statistical features analysis, oscillator models, fuzzy clustering…
performance—above 99% recognition score for signature verification

evidence—score-based
notes—Although an experimental device, BiSP is mentioned because of the unique multisensor handwriting signals it provides FDEs
screenshots—Bashir 2010
references—Bashir 2010, Bashir et al. 2011, Hook 2003
Web site—http://homepages.fh-regensburg.de/~scg39398/biometricsmartpen/

MOVALYZER, MOVALYZERX, SCRIPTALYZER, GRIPALYZER

name—MovAlyzeR ($799, software suite) • MovAlyzeRx ($149, MovAlyzeR without experiments design and databases) • ScriptAlyzeR ($399, MovAlyzeR without visual targets to guide movement, substroke segmentation, and norm database) • GripAlyzeR ($399, bimanual grip-force analysis)
developer—NeuroScript, Tempe (AZ), United States; Hans-Leo Teulings
history—company founded in 1997
availability—commercial
active use—used in 62 countries
beneficiaries—clinical medicine, neurocognitive research, education, forensics, computing
purpose—fine motor control analysis
features—pen position, pressure, orientation, mouse position and finger position at 100–200 Hz; real time, real-size feedback, visual and audible pen pressure feedback; interactive audiovisual stimuli, animated stimuli; substroke segmentation, bitmap image handwriting segmentation, bitmap spirals to movement data; multipage recordings; simulation of handwriting-like trajectories; integration with MATLAB
evidence—none
notes—H.-L. Teulings coorganized in 1982 the first International Graphonomics Conference, precursor of the International Graphonomics Society
screenshots—Web site
references—Gemmert and Teulings 2006
Web site—http://www.neuroscript.net

OASIS

name—Optimized Action Sequence Interpreter System (Oasis)
developer—Kiko Software, Doetinchem, Netherlands; Peter de Jong
history—developed during the 1990s
availability—commercial
active use—research institutions
beneficiaries—medicine, education, forensics, computing
purpose—design experiments for studying human motor control

features—acquire, segment, and analyze pen and mouse movements recorded from a Wacom digitizing tablet; records pen location, velocity, pressure, attitude (24 variables); includes 750 statics for signal analysis; supplemental modules are available for advanced signal processing, such as Power Spectral Density Analysis (PSDA); real-time data acquisition, processing, and feedback; macro programming language; highest fidelity under native DOS (or acquire Oasis Box hardware)
evidence—none
notes—basis price: $2,325
screenshots—Web site
references—De Jong et al. 1996
Web site—http://www.kikosoft.com

VISUALIZATION

MICS

name—Measurement of Internal Consistencies Software (MICS)
developer—LumenIQ (former Limbic Systems), Bellingham (WA), United States
history—prototype 1999, released 2002, patented
availability—commercial
active use—in use by governmental and private forensic laboratories
beneficiaries—forensics (FD, ballistics…), biometrics (fingerprints), medicine…
purpose—surface visualization tool
features—3D representation of a 2D image based on the grayscale intensity
evidence—none
screenshots—Web site
references—Anthony 2002
Web site—http://www.lumeniq.com

SCIENCEGL FORENSIC PRODUCTS

name—ForensicXP (digital forensic spectrograph) • Forensic Hyperspectrum Document Processor • Forensic Image Comparator 3D • Image Comparator 2D Software
developer—ScienceGL, Attleboro (MA), United States
availability—commercial
active use—yes
beneficiaries—forensic experts
purpose—3D visualization
features—side-by-side and superposed comparison; angle, distance, surface, volume measurement; autostitch; real time 3D manipulation, illumination, flyby; annotation; incident, transmitted, oblique, coaxial illumination; absorption,

reflectance, transmission, and fluorescence spectra 400–1000 nm; stand-alone and SDK, API
methods—OpenGL
evidence—none
notes—products can be acquired as stand-alone software or integrated in the ForensicFX spectrograph
screenshots—Web site
references—Ayub 2006
Web site—http://www.sciencegl.com

RECONSTRUCTION

MATCHMAKER

FBI's reconstruction software for shredded documents; [FBI 2007a: 12–13]

UNSHREDDER

Commercial reconstruction software for shredded documents; annual license for $1,250; by Safe Guard, Tel Aviv, Israel. http://www.unshredder.com

PAPER STRUCTURE

AD751

Automatic measurement of laid lines density in digital reproductions of paper structures. Open Source software by Vlad Atanasiu; 2002 v1.0 –2006 v1.14. [Atanasiu 2004a], http://www.waqwaq.info/atanasiu/software/ad751/

INK SEPARATION

COLOR DECONVOLUTION

Interactive separation between inks and between inks and background. Free plug-in for Photoshop compatible hosts written by Charles Berger from the Netherlands Forensic Institute; 2006 v1.10—2008 v1.13. [Berger and Veenman 2009, Berger et al. 2006], http://4N6site.com

MARKUP

WANDAXML

The annotation language WandaXML (2003 v1.0) is an offline and online description format for FD implemented in the documents expertise framework Wanda (q.v.) and developed by some of that project's participants. WandaXML mixes features of other formats, namely InkXML (the XML format idea, dynamic writing data), Unipen (annotation tags, dynamic writing data), and SVG (shapes). [Franke et al. 2003a, 2004a], http://unipen.nici.kun.nl/wandaML/

Main descriptors

This annex presents a hierarchical descriptive system of writing, similar to the Document Object Model (DOM) typical of Web pages: the forensic *document* is seen as having *aspects*, which refer to *entities*, the properties of which are changed by *modifiers*, through the values of *quantifiers*. The entities are classified according to their semantic and physical scale. Not all entities possess all modifiers. See Atanasiu 2011a for the rationale in using the term "descriptor" rather than "feature." Following an object-oriented notation, a forensic document (FD) described according to this schema is defined as FD = documents.aspects.entities.modifiers.quantifiers.

documents

aspects
    instrument
        trajectory in 2D and 3D
        orientation in 3D
        pen-tip torque
        force (instrument on substrate,
            fingers on instrument)
        grip (finger configuration)
    deposit
    substrate
    pattern (script, graphics)
    context
        physical
        biological
        sociocultural
    content
    functions
    global aspects
    meta-aspects

entities (semantic/physical scale)
    strokes
        extremities (landings & terminations)
        connections (between characters)
        diacritics
        punctuation
        embellishments
    characters
        style (cursive, capitals, blackletter...)
        allographs
        numerals
        symbols
    words
        abbreviations
        hyphenation

    lines
        justification
    paragraphs
        margins (alignment...)
        indentation first & last (length...)
        interlines (spacing, parallelism...)
        insertions
        peri-elements (salutations, dates...)
        envelope addresses
    documents

modifiers
    location
    size (absolute, relative, proportions)
    orientation (average, local)
    shape
    color
    texture
    spacing
    sequence
    speed
    perception (grouping, crowding, regularity,
        rhythm, complexity, fluidity, legibility, skill)
    semantics
        information
        connotations
        aesthetics
        stylistics
    context
        physical
        biological
        informational (semantics, sociocultural)

quantifiers
    values distribution (categorical, ordinal, continuous)

Noticeable hardware

TYPOLOGY

[Chen et al. 2002, UNODC 2010, 2011]

Chemical analysis: liquid chromatography, spectroscopy, gas chromatography, mass spectrometry, elemental analysis, or capillary electrophoresis
Optical analysis: 2D visible light scanning, photography and video capture, video spectral analysis, stereo microscopy
Surface analysis: 3D surface laser, electrostatic detection apparatus

SELECTION OF SUPPLIERS

3D surface analysis
   Cyber-SIGN (Italy), http://www.forinst.it/index_eng.html
Optical analysis
   Carl Zeiss (Germany), http://www.zeiss.com
   JVC (Japan), http://www.jvc.com
   Leica (Germany), http://www.leica-microsystems.com
   Zarbeco LLC (United States), http://www.zarbeco.com
Signature [Fiérrez and Garcia-Ortez 2007]
   Cyber-SIGN (Japan), http://www.cybersign.com
   Softpro (Germany), http://www.signplus.com
   CIC (United States), http://www.cic.com
   Sapura (Malaysia), http://www.sapura.com.my
   Signature Net (Switzerland), http://www.signaturenet.ch
Video spectral analysis
   Foster + Freeman (United Kingdom), http://www.fosterfreeman.com
   Fovea (France), http://www.foveafrance.com
   ScienceGL (United States), http://www.sciencegl.com
   Projectina (Switzerland), http://www.projectina.ch
Video spectral & chemical analysis
   Attestor Forensics (Germany), http://attestor-forensics.com
   ChemImage: http://www.chemimage.com
   Regula (Bielarus), http://regula.ws

INFORMATION SOURCES

Security products companies directory
   http://www.security-technologynews.com
Security documents portal
   http://www.securitydocumentworld.com

Open research geography

Where is computational FD research produced? To answer this question to a historian's satisfaction another book besides this one would be required, but some representative data offer a starting point for further reflection.

Data sources and limitations — The following diagrams and maps represent author locations of articles found with keywords *"writer identification"* in IEEE Xplore, ACM Digital Library, and Science Direct [http://ieeexplore.ieee.org, http://dl.acm.org, http://www.sciencedirect.com, accessed 2013.07.20]. Writer identification is a central FD topic, but evidently not the only one: computational signature verification, for example, also has a long history in both academia and the industry. The consulted repositories are major ones, but obviously do not store all publications on writer identification. Research before the 1990s is lacking, just as various locations are absent due to publications outside these repositories' coverage. Quantitative data also begs to be supplemented with qualitative bibliometrics, such as an impact assessment from number of citations, which raise a host of new issues as is well known. Furthermore, there are other aspects equally pertinent: collaborations, intellectual genealogy, or industrial applications of the research. Because of the limitations of the data the following representations are deliberately at a higher granularity level than the data used to produce them and obfuscate place names.

Observations — At spatial level, research on writer identification roughly parallels that of other fields in computing around the world. There are, however, surprises: in North America, the West Coast seems to find no interest in the topic; Russia, otherwise active in the field of security documents, is absent; there is a substantial unbalance between Japan and China; the tiny emirate of Qatar overtakes Egypt, the traditional center of the Arab world. The timeline doesn't credit the early European contribution to the field, as mentioned before, but shows the striking increase in interest around the years 2002–2003 and its spread across continents.

Interpretation — What might the causes of these observations be? Many of the locations shown here would not appear without the long-term dedication of researchers and the vagaries of their mobility. The proximity to centers of political power, where FD is concentrated, also plays a role at times. A country's level of technologization is another factor visible from the striking contrast between areas like China or India, with their monumental daily output of handwriting, and the United States, where keyboards and printers are replacing the pen. The cultural factor is one of the explanations for the European and Chinese dominance: writer identification is developed for dual application in the fields of FD and cultural heritage.

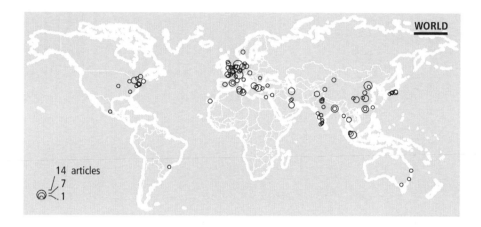

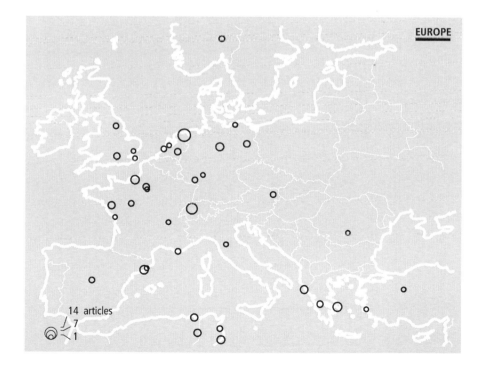

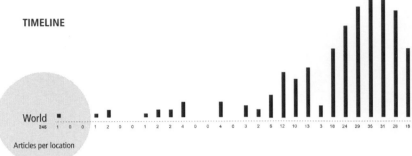

TIMELINE

World
245
Articles per location

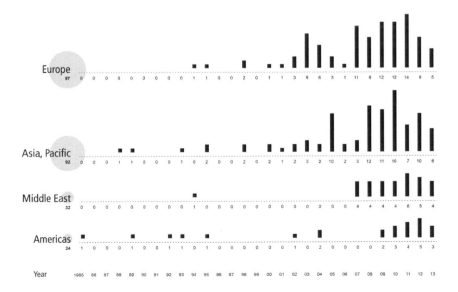

Year   1985 86 87 88 89 90 91 92 93 94 95 96 97 98 99 00 01 02 03 04 05 06 07 08 09 10 11 12 13

Links

ACT EIGHT

— Ballpoints make them press down. When they press
down, they write like monkeys. [...] Penmanship is dying all
across this country.

— He's ambidextrous. He can write with either hand. Didn't you guys know that? In everyday life, Allen uses his left hand. Job applications, letters to friends, et cetera. But he writes the Zodiac letters with his right hand producing a different handwriting that he can't be linked to.

— You see, if I'm married and that's my suitcase, then this letter must be from me. I'm Paul.
— No.
— How do you know?
— Wait a second. Just compare these two handwritings. They are entirely different.
— It is. They are different.

— Um, do you mind?, I am a bit graphologist.
— I thought you were only a hoaxer. […]
— The writer of anonymous letters is driven by far more mysterious reasons, incomprehensible to the average person, all the more to the average policeman.

— Shut up! Do I look like a policeman? [...]
— Tell 'im where he comes from, if you wanna go fortune-telling.
— Cheltenham, Harrow... Cambridge and... India?
— Quite right. [...]
— Do you do this sort of thing for a living at a music hall?
— I have thought of it. Perhaps I will one day. [...]
— How do you do it, may I ask?
— Simple phonetics. The science of speech. That's my profession. Also my hobby. Anyone can spot an Irishman or a Yorkshireman by his brogue... but I can place a man within six miles. I can place 'im within two miles in London. Sometimes within two streets. [...] An Englishman's way of speaking absolutely classifies him.

— What could possibly matter more than to take a human being and change her into a different human being by creating a new speech for her? It's filling up the deepest gap that separates class from class and soul from soul.

— The Queen of Transylvania is here. I'm indispensable to her at these official international parties. I speak 32 languages. I know everyone in Europe. No impostor can escape my detection.

THEMATIC GLIMPSES

Movies are a propagation vector to acquaint the public with various FD themes revolving around handwriting, such as ambidextrous writers (*Zodiac* [2007] [**2**], unsolved case of a serial killing in the 1960s to 1970s California), medical conditions (Charles Bronson playing an amnesiac induced to commit a crime in *Someone Behind the Door* [1971] [**3**]; a detective and murderer discovering his split personality in *So Dark the Night* [1946] by analyzing his footprints and handwriting), or the technologically and socially induced evolution of handwriting styles that makes datasets obsolete (the lamentations of a nun in a 1964 Bronx school in *Doubt* [2008] [**1**]). One cannot resist to take a step aside FD and also mention the charming *My Fair Lady* (1964) [**5**], starring Audrey Hepburn. In this musical, which in a sense is all about disguised biometrics or social impersonation for that matter (passing a flower girl for duchess at an embassy ball), a professor of phonetics is mistaken for a policeman while doing his eavesdropping fieldwork in the streets of London. His proficiency at identifying "within six miles" or less the people's birthplace and their various residence locations during life, just from their speech, is marvelous — it leaves every watching FDE wishing to posses a similar sociogeographical atlas for handwriting.

A "graphical epidemic"[1] is the FD curiosity of *Le Corbeau* [The Raven] (1943) [**4**], fictionalizing the Tulle affair, a wave of anonymous letters in provincial France, were more and more individuals become culprits as they imitate the writing style of the initial perpetrator. This complex masterpiece epitomizes the role of cinema as an effective medium to think about reality by fictionalizing it. Based on actual events — in which Edmond Locard organized a collective dictation to gather writing samples and observe the suspect's behavior — the movie takes the liberty to make even the expert a delinquent for the purpose of illuminating the unpredictability of human nature.[2] The mix of technological and psychological approach in solving the case reflects, however, Locard's own personality.[3] As a medical doctor he was obsessed with both what technology can discover in symptoms (transmuted in forensics as the famous Locard principle of every action leaving a trace) and fascinated with language as an investigative tool in the "criminal mind" (a prolific scientific writer, his *Radio Memoirs* reveal him as an equally good storyteller). Sensitive to the public image of forensics, Locard took pains (and obvious pleasure) to produce books about the police investigator in real life and in literature — and wrote himself a novel on the Tulle affair.[4]

1—Locard 1935–1937 (6): 504–505, 514; Huber and Headrick 1999: 179.   **2**—Maybe inspired by 17th century FDE and forger Raveneau. His work was admired by Locard, whose studies shaped the movie [Locard 1935–1937 (5): 12–13].   **3**—Larriaga 1988.   **4**—Locard 1935–1937 (6): 509–515, Wikipedia 2013a, b.

References

AAFS (American Academy of Forensic Sciences) (2011) — *Proc. of the Annual Meeting of the American Academy of Forensic Sciences 2002–2011: Questioned Documents*, Colorado Springs, CO: AAFS.

——(2012a) — "Colleges and Universities [offering forensic science programs]," *AAFS*, online, accessed 2012.05.22, http://www.aafs.org/colleges-universities/.

——(2012b) — *Proc. of the Annual Meeting of the American Academy of Forensic Sciences 2012*, Colorado Springs, CO: AAFS.

ABBATE Janet (2012) — *Recoding Gender: Women's Changing Participation in Computing*, Cambridge, MA: The MIT Press.

ABFDE (2012) — *American Board of Forensic Document Examiners*, online, accessed 2012.09.06, http://www.abfde.org.

ABOUT Ilsen (2011) — "Classer le corps : l'anthropométrie judiciaire et ses alternatives, 1880–1930" [Body Classification. Judicial Anthropometry and its Alternatives], in Ceyhan and Piazza 2011: 39–61.

ABRAHAMS Paul W. (2013) — "Computer Science Is Not a Science," *Communications of the ACM*, 56 (1): 8.

AGER Simon (2012) — *Omniglot: The Online Encyclopedia of Writing Systems and Languages*, online, accessed 2012.06.05, http://www.omniglot.com.

AITKEN Colin G.G. (2009a) — "Interpreting Expert Opinions: History of," in Allan Jamieson, André Moenssens, eds., *Wiley Encyclopedia of Forensic Science*, Chichester: John Wiley & Sons, 3: 1579–1586.

——(2009b) — "Sampling and Estimation of Quantities," in Allan Jamieson, André Moenssens, eds., *Wiley Encyclopedia of Forensic Science*, Chichester: John Wiley & Sons, 5: 2281–2291.

AMELOTTI Mario, Giorgio Costamagna (1975) — *Alle origini del notariato italiano* [Origins of the Italian Notary], Rome: Consiglio Nazionale del Notariato, 1975.

ANAND Jassy (2011) — "Determination of Variations in the Writing of Rural and Urban People from Their Letter Characteristics in Roman Script," in AAFS (2011), *Annual Meeting 2011, Chicago, IL*, presented paper, 4.

ANDERSON Michael, Susan Leigh Anderson, eds. (2011) — *Machine Ethics*, Cambridge: Cambridge University Press.

ANONYMOUS (1929) — "Bad Handwriting," *The Canadian Medical Association J.*, 20 (4): 442.

——(1967) — "Medical Paleography," *The Canadian Medical Association J.*, 96 (18): 1284.

ANONYMOUS (2002) — "European Fingerprint Standards," *Fingerprint Whorld*, 28 (107): 19.

ANTHONY Arthur T. (2002) — "Validation Study of 'Measurement of Internal Consistencies Software (MICS)' as It Relates to Line Sequence and Line Quality Determinations in Forensic Document Examination," in AAFS (2011), *Annual Meeting 2002, Atlanta, GA*, presented paper, 90.

APEC/IEGBM (Asia–Pacific Economic Cooperation, Informal Experts' Group on Business Mobility) (2003) — *Security Standards for Travel Documents*, draft, Senior Officials' Meeting III, August 2003, Phuket, Thailand, Singapore: APEC.

ARCHIVES DÉPARTEMENTALES DU TARN (2012) — *Inventaire des archives notariales du Tarn* [Inventory of Notary Archives of the Tarn Department], online, accessed 2012.09.20, http://archivesnotaires.tarn.fr/index.php?id=1241.

ARCHIVES MUNICIPALES DE LYON (2010) — *Empreintes d'Edmond Locard* [Edmond Locard's Imprints], exhibition, 2010.04.09–13.07, Lyon, online, accessed 2013.05.07, http://www.archives-lyon.fr/static/archives/edmond_locard/.

ARTIÈRES Philippe, Claire Bustarret, Muriel Salle (2010) — *"Percevoir l'invisible." Le travail de l'expert en écriture selon Edmond Locard (1877–1966)* ["Seeing the Invisible." The Work of the Forensic Handwriting Examiner According to Edmond Locard (1877–1966)], research report, Paris: École des Hautes Études en Sciences Sociales (EHSS) / Centre national de la recherche scientifique (CNRS), accessed 2013.05.15, http://www.gip-recherche-justice.fr/catalogue/PDF/rapports/203-RF -Artieres_Locard.pdf.

ASHBAUGH David (1999) — *Quantitative-Qualitative Friction Ridge Analysis: An Introduction to Basic and Advanced Ridgeology*, Boca Raton, FL: CRC Press.

ASQDE (2012) — *American Society of Questioned Document Examiners*, online, accessed 2012.09.06, http://www.asqde.org.

ASTM (ASTM International) (2012) — *ASTM International*, online, accessed 2012. 05.12, http://www.astm.org.

AŞICIOĞLU Faruk, Nurten Turan (2003) — "Handwriting Changes under the Effect of Alcohol," *Forensic Science International*, 132: 201–210.

ATANASIU Vlad (2000) — "Le Retroencrage. Analyse du ductus des écritures d'après le dégradé du coloris de l'encre" [Retroinking: Finding the Direction of Writing from the Intensity of Ink], *Gazette du Livre médiéval*, 37: 34–42, videos at http:// www.waqwaq.info/atanasiu/studies/retroencrage/.

——(2003) — "Allographic Biometrics and Behavior Synthesis," *TUG-boat*, 24 (3): 998–1002.

——(2004a) — "Assessing Paper Origin and Quality through Large-Scale Laid Lines Density Measurements," *Paper as a Medium of Cultural Heritage. Archeology and Conservation. Proc. of the 26th Congress of the International Paper Historians Association (IPHA), 30 August – 6 September 2002, Rome/Verona, Italy*, 172–184.

ATANASIU Vlad (2004b) — "Les réalités subjectives d'un paléographe arabe du Xe siècle" [Subjective Realities of a 10th Century Paleographer], *Gazette du Livre médiéval*, 43: 14–22.

——(2011a) — "Forensic vs. Computing Writing Features as Seen by Rex, the Intuitive Document Retriever," *Proc. of the 1st International Workshop on Automated Forensic Handwriting Analysis (AFHA)*, Beijing, China, 17–18 September 2011, 16–20.

——(2011b) — *Rex. Retrieve Written Documents by Describing Them*, software, online, online, accessed 2012.05.02, http://glyph.telecom-paristech.fr/rex/.

——(2011c) — "Paleographers and Computer Scientists," *Gazette du livre médiéval*, 56–57: 122–123.

——, Laurence Likforman-Sulem, Nicole Vincent (2011) — "Writer Retrieval—Exploration of a Novel Biometric Scenario Using Perceptual Features Derived from Script Orientation," *Proceeding of the 11th International Conference on Document Analysis and Recognition, 18–21 September 2011, Beijing, China*, 628–632.

AUGUSTIN Emmanuel, Jean-Marie Brodin, Matthieu Carré, Edouard Geoffrois, Emmanuèle Grosicki, Françoise Prêteux (2006) — "RIMES Evaluation Campaign for Handwritten Mail Processing," *Proc. of the 10th Workshop on Frontiers in Handwriting Recognition, 23–26 October 2006, La Baule, France*, 231–235.

AYUB Hina, Diane Williams (2006) — "The Role of Hyperspectral Imaging in the Visualization of Obliterated Writings," *Proc. of the American Physical Society (APS) March Meeting, March 13–17, 2006, Baltimore, MD*.

BAAYEN Harald R. (2001) — *Word Frequency Distributions*, Dordrecht: Kluwer Academic Publishers.

BACKES Michael, Markus Dürmuth, Dominique Unruh (2008) — "Compromising Reflections-or-How to Read LCD Monitors around the Corner," *Proc. of the 29th IEEE Symposium on Security and Privacy, Oakland, CA, 18–21 May 2008*, 158–169.

BANGERTER Adrian, Cornelius J. König, Sandrine Blatti, Alexander Salvisberg (2009) — "How Widespread Is Graphology in Personnel Selection Practice? A Case Study of a Job Market Myth," *International J. of Selection and Assessment*, 17 (2): 219–230.

BANKER [Boston banker in Exeter, NH] (1883) — "Identification by Handwriting," *New York Times*, 1883.01.26.

BARNES Jeffrey G. (2011) — "History," in Alan McRoberts, ed., *The Fingerprint Sourcebook*, Washington, DC: National Institute of Justice, 1-5-1-22.

BARON Cynthia (2008) — *Adobe Photoshop Forensics: Sleuths, Truths, and Fauxtography*, Boston, MA: Thomson Course Technology.

BARTLOW Nick (2009) — "Keystroke Recognition," in Stan Z. Li, Anil K. Jain, eds., *Encyclopedia of Biometrics*, Berlin: Springer, 877–882.

BARTOS Leah (2012) — "No Forensic Background? No Problem," *ProPublica*, online, accessed 2012.06.23, http://www.propublica.org/article/no-forensic-background-no-problem/.

BASHIR Muzaffar (2010) — *A Novel Multisensoric System Recording and Analyzing Human Biometric Features for Biometric and Biomedical Applications*, PhD thesis, University Regensburg, Germany.

——, Georg Scharfenberg, Juergen Kempf (2011) — "Person Authentication by Handwriting in Air Using a Biometric Smart Pen Device," *Proc. of the International Conference of the Biometrics Special Interest Group (BIOSIG), 8–9 September 2011, Darmstadt, Germany*, 219–226.

BASSO Keith H. (1996) — *Wisdom Sits in Places: Landscape and Language among the Western Apache*, Albuquerque, NM: University of New Mexico Press.

BAXENDALE D., I.D. Renshaw (1979) — "The Large-Scale Searching of Handwriting Samples," *J. of the Forensic Science Society*, 19: 245–251.

BBC (British Broadcasting Company) (2010) — "Huntingdon Forensic Science Lab Is to Close," *BBC*, online, accessed 2012.05.15, http://www.bbc.co.uk/news/uk-england-suffolk-11993101.

BECKER Stefan (2007) — "Trace Evidence: A European Perspective," *Trace Evidence Symposium 2007, 13–17 August 2007, Clearwater Beach, FL*, presented paper, accessed 2012.06.14, http://projects.nfstc.org/trace/index2007.htm.

BEDOS-REZAK Brigitte Miriam (2008) — "In Search of a Semiotic Paradigm: The Matter of Sealing in Medieval Thought and Praxis (1050–1400)," in Noël Adams, John Cherry, James Robinson, eds., *Good Impressions: Image and Authority in Medieval Seals*, London: British Museum, 1–24.

BENDER Klaus W. (2006) — *Moneymakers*, Weinheim: Wiley-VCH.

BENSEFIA Ameur, Thierry Paquet, Laurent Heutte (2005) — "A Writer Identification and Verification System," *Pattern Recognition Letters*, 26: 2080–2092.

BERGER Charles E.H., Jan A. de Koeijer, W. Glas, H.T. Madhuizen (2006) — "Color Separation in Forensic Image Processing," *J. of Forensic Sciences*, 51: 100–102.

——, Cor J. Veenman (2009) — "Color Deconvolution and Support Vector Machines," *Proc. of the 3rd International Workshop on Computational Forensics (IWCF), 13–14 August 2009, The Hague, Netherlands*, 174–180.

BERNSTEIN (The Bernstein Consortium) (2012) — *Bernstein. The Memory of Paper: Image-Based Paper Expertise and History*, online, accessed 2012.06.17, http://www.memoryofpaper.eu.

BERNSTEIN David E., Jeffrey D. Jackson (2004) — "The Daubert Trilogy in the States," *Jurimetrics J.*, 44: 351–366.

BERTHO Catherine (1981) — *Télégraphes & Téléphones : De Valmy au microprocesseur* [Telegraphs & Telephones: From Valmy to the Microprocessor], Paris: Le Livre de Poche.

BERTSCH MCGRAYNE Sharon (2011) — *The Theory That Would Not Die: How Bayes' Rule Cracked the Enigma Code, Hunted Down Russian Submarines, & Emerged*

Triumphant from Two Centuries of Controversy, New Haven, CT: Yale University Press.

BERWICK Donald M., David E. Winickoff (2006) — "The Truth about Doctors' Handwriting: A Prospective Study," *British Medical J.*, 313 (7072): 1657–1658.

BICKNELL Danna E., Gerald M. Laporte (2009) — "Forged and Counterfeit Documents," in Allan Jamieson, André Moenssens, eds., *Wiley Encyclopedia of Forensic Science*, Chichester: John Wiley & Sons, 3: 1255–1276.

BIRD Carolyne, Bryan Found, Douglas Rogers (2007) — "Forensic Document Examiners' Opinions on the Process of Production of Disguised and Simulated Signatures," *Proc. of the 13th Conference of the International Graphonomics Society (IGS), 11–14 November 2007, Melbourne, Australia*, 171–175.

——, Bryan Found, Kaye Ballantyne, Doug Rogers (2010) — "Forensic Handwriting Examiners' Opinions on the Process of Production of Disguised and Simulated Signatures," *Forensic Science International*, 195 (1–3): 103–107.

BISOTTI Anne (2011) — personal communication, Institut National de Police Scientifique, Section documents, Paris, 2011.05.03.

BKA (Bundeskriminalamt [Criminal Police Agency]) (1995) — *Aktuelle Methoden der Kriminaltechnik und Kriminalistik. BKA-Arbeitstagung 1994* [Contemporary Forensic Methods. BKA Workshop 1994], Wiesbaden: BKA, 77–100.

——(2013) — "Ausstellung in BKA zu '100 Jahre Daktyloskopie' (2003), Bild b085" [BKA Exhibition '100 Years of Fringerprinting' (2003), Picture b085], *BKA Fotogalerie Kriminaltechnische Untersuchungen und Personenidentifizierung* [BKA Photogallery Forensic Investigations and Person Identification], 2009.12.21, online, accessed 2013.04.25, http://www.bka.de/nn_232524/DE/Presse/Fotogalerie/Ktu/fotogalerieKtu,templateId=renderZoom,param=30.html.

BLACK Bert, Francisco J. Ayala, Carol Saffran-Brinks (1994) — "Science and the Law in the Wake of Daubert: A New Search for Scientific Knowledge," *Texas Law Review*, 72: 715–802.

BLANCHETTE Jean-François (2012) — *Burdens of Proof: Cryptographic Culture and Evidentiary Law in the Age of Electronic Documents*, Cambridge, MA: The MIT Press.

BLANKERS Vivian L., Ralph M.J. Niels, Louis G. Vuurpijl (2007) — "Writer Identification by Means of Explainable Features: Shapes of Loop and Lead-In Strokes," *Proc. of the 19th Belgian–Dutch Conference on Artificial Intelligence (BNAIC), 5–6 November 2007, Utrecht, Netherlands*, 17–24.

——, Elisa C. van den Heuvel, Katrin Y. Franke, Louis G. Vuurpijl (2009) — "The ICDAR 2009 Signature Verification Competition," *Proc. of the 10th International Conference on Document Analysis and Recognition (ICDAR), 26–29 July 2009, Barcelona, Spain*, 1403–1407.

BLUME Fred H., Timothy Kearley, eds. (2012) — *Annotated Justinian Code*, 2nd ed., online, accessed 2012.08.12, http://uwacadweb.uwyo.edu/blume&justinian/.

BLUMENSTEIN Michael, Miguel A. Ferrer, Jesus Francisco Vargas Bonilla (2010) — "The 4NSigComp2010 Offline Signature Verification Competition: Scenario 2," *Proc.*

of the 12th International Conference on Frontiers of Handwriting Recognition (ICFHR), 16–18 November 2010, Kolkata, India, 721–726.

BOHAN Thomas L. (2010) — "Review of: Strengthening Forensic Science in the United States: A Path Forward," *J. of Forensic Sciences*, 55 (2): 560–564.

BORGES Jorge Luis, etchings by Erik Desmazières (2000) — *The Library of Babel*, Jaffrey, NH: David R. Godine.

BOTTOMORE Stephen (1984) — "Dreyfus and Documentary," *Sight & Sound*, 53 (4): 290-293.

BOWEN Robin, Jessica Schneider (2007) — "Forensic Databases: Paint, Shoe Prints, and Beyond," *NIJ J.*, 258, accessed 2012.06.12, http://www.ojp.usdoj.gov/nij/journals/258/forensic-databases.html.

BRADBERRY Trent J., Rodolphe J. Gentili, José L. Contreras-Vidal (2010) — "Reconstructing Three-Dimensional Hand Movements from Non-Invasive Electroencephalographic Signals," *The J. of Neuroscience*, 30 (9): 3432–3437.

BRANSTON Barry (1989) — *Graphology Explained. A Workbook*, London: Piatkus.

BRASSIL Jack (2002) — *Tracing the Source of a Shredded Document*, Palo Alto, CA: Hewlett-Packard, technical report HPL-2002-215.

BRECKENRIDGE Keith (2011) — "Capitaliser sur les pauvres : les enjeux de l'adoption de services financiers biométriques au Nigeria" [Capitalizing on the Poor: The Stakes in Biometric Financial Services in Nigeria], in Ceyhan and Piazza 2011: 176–193.

BRIDGEMON Rondal (2007) — "Letter to the Editor: No Time for Research?," *Forensic Science Communications*, 9 (3).

BRINGHURST Robert (2002) — *The Elements of Typographic Style*, Vancouver, BC: Hartley & Marks Publishers.

BRINK Axel A. (2011) — *Robust and applicable handwriting biometrics*, PhD thesis, Groningen: Institute of Artificial Intelligence and Cognitive Engineering (Alice), University of Groningen.

——, Lambert R.B. Schomaker, Marius Bulacu (2007) — "Towards Explainable Writer Verification and Identification Using Vantage Writers," *Proc. of the International Conference on Document Analysis and Recognition (ICDAR), 23-26 September 2007, Curitiba, Paraná, Brazil*, 824–828.

——, Ralph M.J. Niels, R.A. van Batenburg, Elisa C. van den Heuvel, Lambert R.B. Schomaker (2011) — "Towards Robust Writer Verification by Correcting Unnatural Slant," *Pattern Recognition Letters*, 32 (3): 449–457.

——, Jinna Smit, Marius L. Bulacu, Lambert R.B. Schomaker (2012) — "Writer Identification Using Directional Ink-Trace Width Measurements," *Pattern Recognition*, 45: 162–171.

BRITT S. Henderson, Ivan N. Mensh (1943) — "The Identification of One's Own Handwriting," *J. of Criminal Law and Criminology*, 34 (1): 50–60.

BROEDERS Dennis (2011) — "Le virage biométrique dans la 'lutte contre l'immigration clandestine' de l'UE : l'établissement d'un contrôle migratoire intérieur '2.0'" [The Biometric Turn within the European Union in the 'Fight against Illegal

Immigration': The Establishment of an Internal Migratory Control 2.0], in Ceyhan and Piazza 2011: 235–256.

BROWN Sharon, Laser Sin-David (2005) — "Diary of an Astronaut: Examination of the Remains of the Late Israeli Astronaut Ilan Ramon's Crew Notebook Recovered after the Loss of NASA's Space Shuttle Columbia," in AAFS (2011), *Annual Meeting 2005, New Orleans, LA*, presented paper, 71–73.

BStU (Der Bundesbeauftragte für die Unterlagen des Staatssicherheitsdienstes der ehemaligen Deutschen Demokratischen Republik [The Federal Representative for the Documents of State Security Service of the Former German Democratic Republic]) (2012) — *BStU*, online, accessed 2012.04.27, http://www.bstu.bund.de > Rekonstruktion von Unterlagen.

BULACU Marius L. (2007) — *Statistical pattern recognition for automatic writer identification and verification*, PhD thesis, Groningen: Artificial Intelligence Institute, University of Groningen.

——, Lambert R.B. Schomaker (2005) — "GRAWIS: Groningen Automatic Writer Identification System," *Proc. of the 17th Belgium–Netherlands Conference on Artificial Intelligence (BNAIC), 17–18 October, Brussels, Belgium*, 413–414.

——, Lambert R.B. Schomaker (2007) — "Text-Independent Writer Identification and Verification Using Textural and Allographic Features," *IEEE Transactions on Pattern Analysis and Machine Intelligence*, 29 (4): 701–717.

BUNDESDRUCKEREI (2013) — *Bundesdruckerei*, online, accessed 2013.04.05, http://www.bundesdruckerei.de.

BUNDESTAG (Deutscher Bundestag [German Parliament]) (2012) — *Antwort der Bundesregierung auf die Kleine Anfrage der Abgeordneten Andrej Hunko, Jan Korte, Herbert Behrens, weiterer Abgeordneter und der Fraktion DIE LINKE. Drucksache 17/8257. Computergestützte Kriminaltechnik bei Polizeibehörden* [Answer of the Federal Government to a Minor Question of Representatives Andrej Hunko, Jan Korte, Herbert Behrens and Others, of the Faction THE RIGHT. Publication 17/8257. Computer Aided Forensics of Police Organizations], Berlin: Deutscher Bundestag, Drucksache 17/8544 (neu), 17. Wahlperiode, 2012.02.06.

BUNGE Mario Augusto (1999) — *The Sociology-Philosophy Connection*, New Brunswick, NJ: Transaction.

BUNKE Horst (2003) — "Recognition of Cursive Roman Handwriting: Past, Present and Future," *Proc. of the 7th International Conference on Document Analysis and Recognition (ICDAR), 3–6 August 2003, Edinburgh, Scotland*, 1: 448–61.

BUNYAN Tony (1993) — "Trevi, Europol and the European State," *Statewatch News online*, online, accessed 2012.06.14, http://www.statewatch.org/news/handbook-trevi.pdf.

——(1997) — *Key Texts on Justice and Home Affairs in the European Union. Volume 1 (1976-1993): From Trevi to Maastricht*, London: Statewatch, online, accessed 2012.06.1, http://www.statewatch.org/semdoc/index.php?id=903.

BURKES Ted M. (2011) — "SWGDOC: Where We've Been, Where We Are, and Where We're Going," in AAFS (2011), *Annual Meeting 2011, Chicago, IL*, presented paper, 8.

BUSCAGLIA JoAnn, Mark Walch, Donald T. Gantz, John J. Miller (2006) — "Development and Validation of an Automated Biometric Handwriting Comparison System," in AAFS (2011), *Annual Meeting 2006, Denver, CO*, presented paper, 57–58.

BUSEY Thomas A., Itiel E. Dror (2011) — "Special Abilities and Vulnerabilities in Forensic Expertise," in Alan McRoberts, ed., *The Fingerprint Sourcebook*, Washington, DC: National Institute of Justice, 15-3–15-23.

BYRNE Joseph P. (2004) — "Notaries," in Christopher Kleinhen, ed., *Medieval Italy: An Encyclopedia*, London: Routledge, 2: 780–784.

CAHALAN Anthony (2008) — *Type, Trends and Fashion: A Study of the Late Twentieth Century Proliferation of Typefaces*, New York: Mark Batty.

CALANDRINO Joseph A., William Clarkson, Edward W. Felten — "Bubble Trouble: Off-Line De-Anonymization of Bubble Forms," *Proc. of the 20th USENIX Security Symposium, 8–12 August 2011, San Francisco, CA*, 267–280.

CALIGIURI Michael P., Hans-Leo Teulings, Charles E. Dean, Alexander B. Niculescu, James B. Lohr (2007) — "Handwriting Movement Analyses for Monitoring Drug-Induced Motor Side Effects in Schizophrenia," *Proc. of the 13th Conference of the International Graphonomics Society (IGS), 11–14 November 2007, Melbourne, Australia*, 75–78.

——, Linton A. Mohammed (2012) — *The Neuroscience of Handwriting: Applications for Forensic Document Examination*, Boca Raton, FL: CRC Press.

CAMACHO Michelle Madsen and Susan M. Lord (2011) — "'Microaggressions' in Engineering Education: Climate for Asian, Latina and White Women," *Proc. of the 41st ASEE/IEEE Frontiers in Education Conference, October 12–15, 2011, Rapid City, SD*, Session 3H: 1-6.

CAMPBELL William B., Thomas P. Wood, Zachariah Gibson, Chadwick Cox (2004) — "Integrity of Digital Documents: A Technique for Authentication of Digitally Recorded Information," in AAFS (2011), *Annual Meeting 2004, Dallas, TX*, presented paper, 78.

CANTU Antonio A. (2009) — "Ink Analysis," in Allan Jamieson, André Moenssens, eds., *Wiley Encyclopedia of Forensic Science*, Chichester: John Wiley & Sons, 3: 1541–1546.

CARAVALE Mario (1982) — "La legislazione de Regno di Sicilia sul notariato durante il Medio Evo" [The Legislation of the Kingdom of Sicily on the Notary during the Middle Age], in *Per une storia del notariato meridionale* [For a History of the Southern Notary], Roma: Consiglio Nazionale del Notariato, 95–176.

CARTER James (2013) — *Starring the Computer: Computers in Movies and Television*, online, accessed 2013.05.17, http://www.starringthecomputer.com.

CAUDILL David S. (2008) — "Idealized Images of Science in Law: The Expert Witness in Trial Movies," *St. John's Law Review*, 82: 921–949.

CEDAR (2012) — *USPS Office of Advanced Technology Database of Handwritten Cities, States, ZIP Codes, Digits, and Alphabetic Characters*, online, accessed 2012.06.13, http://www.cedar.buffalo.edu/Databases/CDROM1/.

CEDARTECH (2008) — *CEDAR-FOX User Manual v1.3*, Williamsville, NY: Cedartech.

CERF Vinton G. (2013) — "Where Is the Science in Computer Science?," *Communications of the ACM*, 55 (10): 5.

CEYHAN Ayse (2011) — "'Acceptabilité' de la biométrie : linéaments d'un cadre analytique" ["Acceptability" of Biometrics: Outline of an Analysis Framework], in Ceyhan and Piazza 2011: 395–415.

——, Pierre Piazza, eds. (2011) — *L'identification biométrique: Champs, acteurs, enjeux et controverses* [Biometric Identification: Topics, Players, Issues and Controversies], Paris: Éditions de la Maison des Sciences de l'Homme.

CHA Sung-Hyuk (2007) — "Comprehensive Survey on Distance/Similarity Measures between Probability Density Functions," *International J. of Mathematical Models and Methods in Applied Sciences*, 4 (1): 300–307.

CHAMPOD Christophe (2009) — "Identification and Individualization," in Allan Jamieson, André Moenssens, eds., *Wiley Encyclopedia of Forensic Science*, Chichester: John Wiley & Sons, 5: 1508–1511.

——, Chris Lennard, Pierre Margot, Milutin Stoilovic (2004) — *Fingerprints and Other Ridge Skin Impressions*, Boca Raton, FL: CRC Press.

——, Ian W. Evett (2009) — "Evidence Interpretation: A Logical Approach," in Allan Jamieson, André Moenssens, eds., *Wiley Encyclopedia of Forensic Science*, Chichester: John Wiley & Sons, 2: 968–976.

——, Joëlle Vuille (2011) — "Scientific Evidence in Europe: Admissibility, Evaluation and Equality of Arms," *International Commentary on Evidence*, 9 (1), 1–68.

CHASKI Carole E. (1997) — "Who Wrote It? Steps toward a Science of Identification," *National Institute of Justice J.*, September 1997: 15–22.

——, Mark A. Walch (2009) — "Validation Testing for FLASH ID on the Chaski Writer Sample Database," in AAFS (2011), *Annual Meeting 2009, Denver, CO*, presented paper, 28.

CHEN Hu-Sheng, Hsien-Hui Meng, Kun-Chi Cheng (2002) — "A Survey of Methods used for the Identification and Characterization of Inks," *Forensic Science J.*, 1: 1–14.

CHEN Jin, Daniel Lopresti, Bart Lamiroy (2011) — "A Real-World Noisy Unstructured Handwritten Notebook Corpus for Document Image Analysis Research," *Proc. of the 2011 Joint Workshop on Multilingual OCR and Analytics for Noisy Unstructured Text Data (MOCR_AND), 17 September 2011, Beijing, China*, 2: 1–8.

CHENG Nellie, Gek Kwee Lee, Bei Sing Yap, Lee Tiang Lee, Sock Kim Tan, Koon Puay Tan (2005) — "Investigation of Class Characteristics in English Handwriting of the Three Main Racial Groups: Chinese, Malay and Indian in Singapore," *J. of Forensic Sciences*, 50 (1): 177–84.

CHESEN Jeff (2008) — "The '*CSI* Effect'—There's No Such Thing as Questions, Just Hidden Answers," *It's Evident... NCSTL's [National Clearinghouse for Science, Technology and the Law] Quarterly e-Newsletter*, July 2008, accessed 2012.05.23, http://www.ncstl.org/evident/July,%202008.

CHM (Computer History Museum) (2013) — "Catalog Search," *CHM*, online, accessed 2013.04.29, http://www.computerhistory.org/collections/search/ > Search: "sage."

CHRISTIN Anne-Marie, ed. (2002) — *History of Writing*, Paris: Flammarion.

CLANCHY M.T. (1993) — *From Memory to Written Record: England 1066–1307*, Oxford: Blackwell.

COLE Simon A. (2001) — *Suspect Identities: A History of Fingerprinting and Criminal Identification*, Cambridge, MA: Harvard University Press.

——(2005) — "More Than Zero: Accounting for Error in Latent Fingerprint Identification," *J. of Criminal Law & Criminology*, 95 (3): 985–1078.

——(2009) — "A Cautionary Tale about Cautionary Tales about Intervention," *Organization*, 16 (1): 121–141.

——(2010) — "Acculturating Forensic Science: What Is 'Scientific Culture', and How Can Forensic Science Adopt It?," *Fordham Urban Law J.*, 38 (2): 435–471.

——(2011) — "La saisie de l'ADN aux États-Unis et au Royaume-Uni à des fins d'identification des individus : origines et enjeux" [Sizing DNA in the United States and United Kingdom for Identifying Individuals: Origins and Stakes], in Ceyhan and Piazza 2011: 63–78.

COLLINS H.M. (1990) — *Artificial Experts: Social Knowledge and Intelligent Machines*, Cambridge, MA: The MIT Press.

COMMONS (House of Commons Science and Technology Committee) (2005) — *Forensic Science on Trial*, London: The Stationery Office.

——(2011) — *The Forensic Science Service*, London: The Stationery Office.

CONDUIT Russell (2008) — "The Effect of Sleep Deprivation on the Spatial Characteristics of Handwriting," *J. of Forensic Document Examination*, (19): 29–40.

CORDELLA Luigi P., Claudio De Stefano, Angelo Marcelli, Adolfo Santoro (2010) — "A New Graph Search Algorithm for Writing Order Recovery," *Proc. of the International Conference on Pattern Recognition (ICPR), 23–26 August 2010, Istanbul, Turkey*, 1896–1900.

COUNCIL of the European Union (2009) — *The Council of the EU Glossary of Security Documents, Security Features and other Related Technical Terms*, Brussels: European Communities, General Secretariat of the Council of the European Union, General Directorate for Justice and Home Affairs, online, last updated 2009, online, accessed 2012.04.19, http://prado.consilium.europa.eu/en/glossaryPopup.html.

CRAUSER Jean-Pierre (2010) — *Edmond Locard, le Sherlock Holmes français* [Edmond Locard, the French Sherlock Holmes], Lausanne: Société d'études holmésiennes de la Suisse romande.

CRICHTON Michael (1999) — "Ritual Abuse, Hot Air, and Missed Opportunities," *Science*, 283 (5407): 1461–1463.

CURRAN James M. (2009) — "Use of Knowledge-Based Systems in Forensic Science," in Allan Jamieson, André Moenssens, eds., *Wiley Encyclopedia of Forensic Science*, Chichester: John Wiley & Sons, 5: 2590–2593.

DANIELS Peter T., William Bright, eds. (1996) — *The World's Writing Systems*, Oxford: Oxford University Press.

DARMÉ E. (1909) — *Signature des actes notariés* [Signature of Notary Documents], PhD thesis, Toulouse: Law Faculty, University of Toulouse.

DARPA (Defense Advanced Research Projects Agency) (2011) — *DARPA's Schredder Challenge Solved*, Arlington, VA: DARPA, online, accessed 2012.04.30. http://www.darpa.mil/NewsEvents/Releases/2011/12/02_.aspx.

DAVIS Jesse, Mark Goadrich (2006) — "The Relationship between Precision-Recall and ROC Curves," *Proc. of the 23rd International Conference on Machine Learning (ICML), 25–29 June 2006, Pittsburgh, PA*, 233–240.

DAVIS Linda J., Christopher P. Saunders, Amanda Hepler, JoAnn Buscaglia (2012) — "Using Subsampling to Estimate the Strength of Handwriting Evidence via Score-Based Likelihood Ratios," *Forensic Science International*, 216 (1–3): 146–157.

DAY Stephen P. (2009) — "Handwriting and Signatures, Interpretation of Comparison Results," in Allan Jamieson, André Moenssens, eds., *Wiley Encyclopedia of Forensic Science*, Chichester: John Wiley & Sons, 3: 1451–1458.

DE STEFANO Claudio, Gianluca Guadagno, Angelo Marcelli (2004) — "A Saliency-Based Segmentation Method for On-Line Cursive Handwriting," *International J. of Pattern Recognition and Artificial Intelligence*, 18 (7): 1139–1156.

DEHARO Gaëlle (2011) — "L'identification biométrique dans l'entreprise" [Biometric Identification in Companies], in Ceyhan and Piazza 2011: 143–160.

DEHAENE Stanislas (2009) — *Reading in the Brain: The New Science of How We Read*, New York: Viking.

DEMARCO Tom (1997) — *The Deadline: A Novel about Project Management*, New York: Dorset House.

DENIS Vincent (2011) — "Identifier par le corps avant la biométrie aux XIVe–XIXe siècles" [Identification through the Body before Biometrics, during the 18th and 19th Centuries], in Ceyhan and Piazza 2011: 25 37.

DENNING Peter J. (2013) — "The Science in Computer Science," *Communications of the ACM*, 56 (5): 35–38.

DEROCHE Jean-Claude, Michel Prieur (2003) — *1€: Argus des €monnaies & des €billets*, Paris: Les Chevau-légers.

DESSIMOZ Damien, Jonas Richiardi, Christophe Champod, Andrzej Drygajlo (2007) — "Multimodal Biometrics for Identity Documents," *Forensic Science International*, 167: 154–159.

——, Christophe Champod (2008) — "Linkages between Biometrics and Forensic Science," in Anil K. Jain, Patrick Flynn, Arun Ross, eds., *Handbook of Biometrics*, Berlin: Springer, 425–459.

DEZA Michel M., Elena Deza (2009) — *Encyclopedia of Distances*, Berlin: Springer.

DICK René [alias Stefan Winkler?] (2011) — *Die Polizeilichen Online-Informationssysteme in der Bundesrepublik Deutschland* [Online Police Information Systems in the Federal German Republic], Norderstedt: Books on Demand, accessed 2012.05.08, http://www.nadir.org/nadir/initiativ/linksrhein/dokus/innen/inpol/.

DIDIER Bernard, Carole Pellegrino (2011) — "Technologies identitaires biométriques : que fait l'Europe face aux États-Unis?" [Identity Biometric Technologies: What Does Europe Do in response to the United States?], in Ceyhan and Piazza 2011: 101–110.

DIMAURO Giovanni, Sebastiano Impedovo, Raffaele Modugno, Giuseppe Pirlo (2002) — "A New Database for Research on Bank-Check Processing," *Proc. of the 8th International Workshop on Frontiers in Handwriting Recognition (IWFHR), 6–8 August 2002, Niagara-on-the-Lake, Ontario, Canada*, 524–528.

DIRKS Tim (2013) — "Robots in Film: A Complete Illustrated History of Robots in the Movies," *Filmsite*, online, accessed 2013.05.17, http://www.filmsite.org/robotsin film1.html.

DoD (Department of Defense) (2007) — *Department of Defense Fiscal Year (FY) 2008/ 2009 Budget Estimates, Volume 1. Defense Advanced Research Projects Agency*, Washington, DC: DoD, February 2007, 54.

DoJ (Department of Justice) (2006) — *A Review of FBI's Handling of the Brandon Mayfield Case*, Washington, DC: DoJ, Office of the Inspector General.

——(2010) — *Amerithrax Investigative Summary*, Washington, DC: DoJ.

DOERMANN David S., Venugopal Varma, Azriel Rosenfeld (1994) — "Instrument Grasp: A Model and Its Effects on Handwritten Strokes," *Pattern Recognition*, 27 (2): 233–245.

——, Azriel Rosenfeld (1995) — "Recovery of Temporal Information from Static Images of Handwriting," *International J. of Computer Vision*, 15: 143–164.

DOUD Donald B. (2010) — *Witness to Forgery: Memoir of a Forensic Document Examiner*, Elm Grove, WI: Orchard Knoll.

DOURISH Paul, Genevieve Bell (2013) — "'Resistance Is Futile': Reading Science Fiction alongside Ubiquitous Computing," *Personal and Ubiquitous Computing*, online, accessed 2013.05.26, http://link.springer.com/content/pdf/10.1007%2Fs00779-013-0678-7.pdf.

DRESBOLD Michelle, James Kwalwasser (2006) — *Sex, Lies, and Handwriting*, New York: Free Press.

DROR E. Itiel, Ailsa E. Péron, Sara-Lynn Hind, David Charlton (2005) — "When Emotions Get the Better of Us: The Effect of Contextual Top-Down Processing on Matching Fingerprints," *Applied Cognitive Psychology*, 19: 799–809.

——, Robert Rosenthal (2008) — "Meta-Analytically Quantifying the Reliability and Biasability of Forensic Experts," *J. of Forensic Sciences*, 53 (4): 900–903.

DuBow Wendy M. (2010) — *NCWIT Scorecard. A Report on the Status of Women in Information Technology*, Boulder, CO: National Center for Women & Information Technology (NCWIT), accessed 2012.09.05, http://www.ncwit.org/resources/ncwit-scorecard-report-status-women-information-technology.

DUNSTONE Ted, Neil Yager (2008) — *Biometric System and Data Analysis Design, Evaluation, and Data Mining*, Berlin: Springer.

DUROSE Matthew R. (2008) — *Census of Publicly Funded Forensic Crime Laboratories, 2005*, Washington, DC: US Department of Justice, Bureau of Justice Statistics.

——, Kelly A. Walsh, Andrea M. Burch (2012) — *Census of Publicly Funded Forensic Crime Laboratories, 2009*, Washington, DC: US Department of Justice, Bureau of Justice Statistics.

DZIEDZIC Tomasz (2012) — personal communication, Institute of Forensic Research, Krakow, Poland, 2012.05.16.

EDMOND Gary, Andrew Roberts (2011) — "Procedural Fairness, the Criminal Trial and Forensic Science and Medicine," *Sydney Law Review*, 33: 359–394.

EDWARDS Harry T. (2009) — *Strengthening Forensic Science in the United States: A Path Forward*, statement before the US Senate Committee on the Judiciary, 2009. 04.18.

EFROS Alexei A., Thomas K. Leung (1999) — "Texture Synthesis by Non-Parametric Sampling," *Proceeding of the 7th IEEE International Conference on Computer Vision, 20–25 September 1999, Kerkyra, Corfu, Greece*, 2: 1033–1037.

EL ABED Haikal, Volker Märgner (2007) — "The IFN/ENIT-database: A Tool to Develop Arabic Handwriting Recognition Systems," *Proc. of the 9th International Symposium on Signal Processing and Its Applications (ISSPA), 12–15 February 2007, Sharjah, United Arab Emirates*, 1–4.

ELDA (2012) — *Evaluations and Language resources Distribution Agency*, online, accessed 2012.06.17, http://www.elda.org.

ENFHEX (European Network of Forensic Handwriting Experts) (2002) — *European Network of Forensic Handwriting Experts (ENFHEX). Final Report*, The Hague: ENFHEX.

——(2012a) — "Copybook Models and Handwriting Samples Database," *European Network of Forensic Institutes*, online, accessed 2012.05.12, http://www.enfsi. eu/page.php?uid=76.

——(2012b) — *European Network of Forensic Institutes*, online, accessed 2012.06.05. http://www.enfsi.eu/page.php?uid=64.

ENSMENGER Nathan (2010) — *The Computer Boys Take Over: Computers, Programmers, and the Politics of Technical Expertise*, Cambridge, MA: The MIT Press.

EPSTEIN Richard G. (1997) — *The Case of the Killer Robot*, Chichester: John Wiley & Sons.

ERP Merijn van, Luis G. Vuurpijl, Katrin Franke, Lambert R.B. Schomaker (2003) — "The WANDA Measurement Tool for Forensic Document Examination," *Proc. of the 11th Conference of the International Graphonomics Society (IGS), 2–5 November 2003, Scottsdale, AZ*, 282–285.

——, Luis G. Vuurpijl, Katrin Franke, Lambert R.B. Schomaker (2004) — "The WANDA Measurement Tool for Forensic Document Examination," *J. of Forensic Document Examination*, 16: 103–118.

EU (Council of the European Union) (2012) — "The Council of the EU Glossary of Security Documents, Security Features and Other Related Technical Terms," *Public Register of Authentic Identity and Travel Documents Online (PRADO)*, online, accessed 2012.06.06, http://prado.consilium.europa.eu/en/glossarypopup.html.

EUROPA (Official Web site of the European Union) (2013) — *Free Movement of Persons, Asylum and Immigration*, online, accessed 2013.04.24, http://europa.eu/legislation_summaries/justice_freedom_security/free_movement_of_persons_asylum_immigration/.

EUROPOL (European Police Office) (2013) — *Europol Information System (EIS)*, online, accessed 2013.04.24, https://www.europol.europa.eu/content/page/europol-information-system-eis-1850.

EVETT W. Ian (1998) — "Towards a Uniform Framework for Reporting Opinions in Forensic Science Casework," *Science & Justice*, 38 (3): 198-202.

FABIAŃSKA Ewa, Marcin Kunicki, Grzegorz Zadora, Tomasz Dziedzic, Dariusz Bułka (2006) — "Graphlog: Computer System Supporting Handwriting Analysis," *Problems of Forensic Sciences*, 68: 394–408.

FAGEL Wil (2011) — "The Netherlands Register of Court Experts," *ENFHEX Conference, 26–29 October 2011, Delft, Netherlands*, presented paper.

——(2012) — personal communication, Netherlands Forensic Institute, The Hague, Netherlands, 2012.07.10.

FAIGMAN David L. (1999) — *Legal Alchemy: The Use and Misuse of Science in the Law*, New York: W.H. Freeman and Co.

FARRAHI Reza, Mohamed Cheriet, Mathias M. Adankon, Kostyantyn Filonenko (2010) — "IBN SINA: A Database for Research on Processing and Understanding of Arabic Manuscripts Images," *Proc. of the 9th IAPR International Workshop on Document Analysis Systems (DAS), 9–11 June 2010, Boston, MA*, 11–18.

FAWCETT Tom (2006) — "An Introduction to ROC Analysis," *Pattern Recognition Letters*, 27: 861–874.

FBI (Federal Bureau of Investigation) (1994) — *Handbook of Forensic Science*, Washington, DC: FBI.

——(2005) — "Press Release: FBI Laboratory Announces Discontinuation of Bullet Lead Examinations," *FBI*, online, accessed 2012.07.03, http://web.archive.org/web/20060614104823/http://www.fbi.gov/pressrel/pressrel05/bullet_lead_analysis.htm.

——(2007a) — *FBI Laboratory 2007 Report*, Quantico, VA: FBI.

——(2007b) — *Questioned Documents Unit Protocols*, Quantico, VA: FBI.

——(2008) — *The FBI: A Centennial History, 1908–2008*, Washington, DC: FBI.

——(2010a) — *The Lindbergh Kidnapping*, FBI, online, accessed 2012.04.10, http://www.fbi.gov/about-us/history/famous-cases/the-lindbergh-kidnapping.

——(2010b) — *The Weinberger Kidnapping*, FBI, online, accessed 2012.04.10, http://www.fbi.gov/about-us/history/famous-cases/the-weinberger-kidnapping.

FBI (Federal Bureau of Investigation) (2012a) — *CODIS Brochure*, online, accessed 2012.06.18, http://www.fbi.gov/about-us/lab/codis/codis_brochure.

——(2012b) — *Integrated Automated Fingerprint Identification System (IAFIS): Fact Sheet*, online, accessed 2012.06.18, http://www.fbi.gov/about-us/cjis/finger prints_biometrics/iafis/iafis_facts.

FIENBERG Stephen E. (2003) — "When Did Bayesian Inference Become 'Bayesian'?," *Bayesian Analysis*, 1(1): 1–41.

——, ed. (1989) — *The Evolving Role of Statistical Assessments as Evidence in the Courts*, Berlin: Springer.

FIÉRREZ Julian, Javier Ortega-Garcia (2007) — "On-Line Signature Verification," in Anil K. Jain, Patrick Flynn, Arun Ross, eds., *Handbook of Biometrics*, Berlin: Springer, 189–209.

——, Javier Galbally, Javier Ortega-Garcia et al. (2010) — "BiosecurID: A Multimodal Biometric Database," *Pattern Analysis and Applications*, 13: 235–246.

FINEGOLD Len (1999) — "Pens Are Certainly More Portable Than Computers," *British Medical J.*, 319 (7216): 1073.

FISCHER Franz, Christiane Fritze, Georg Vogeler (2010) — *Codicology and Palaeography in the Digital Age 2*, Norderstedt: Books on Demand.

FISHER Jim (2008) — *Forensics under Fire: Are Bad Science and Dueling Experts Corrupting Criminal Justice?*, Piscataway, NJ: Rutgers University Press.

FLASH Tamar, Neville Hogan (1985) — "The Coordination of Arm Movements: An Experimentally Confirmed Mathematical Model," *J. of Neuroscience*, 5: 1688–1703.

——, Amir A. Handzel (2007) — "Affine Differential Geometry Analysis of Human Arm Movements," *Biological Cybernetics*, 96: 577–601.

FLEMING Jenny (2010) — "Learning to Work Together: Police and Academics," *Policing*, 4 (2): 139–145.

FLICKER Eva (2008) — "Women Scientists in Mainstream Film: Social Role Models—A Contribution to the Public Understanding of Science from the Perspective of Film Sociology," in Bernd Hüppauf, Peter Weingart, eds., *Science Images and Popular Images of the Sciences*, New York: Routledge, 241–256.

FLORENCE (2003) — *Florence v. Commonwealth*, 120 S.W.3d 699, 701, Kentucky.

FLORES David M., James T. Richardson, Mara L. Merlino (2010) — "Examining the Effects of the Daubert Trilogy on Expert Evidence Practices in Federal Civil Court: An Empirical Analysis," *Southern Illinois University Law J.*, 3: 533–564.

FONTFONT (2012) — "Search for FontFonts," *FontFont*, online, accessed 2012.05.02, https://www.fontfont.com/find/.

FOUCAULT Michel (1995) — *Discipline & Punish: The Birth of the Prison*, New York: Vintage.

FOUND Bryan (2009) — "Handwriting and Signatures, Comparison of," in Allan Jamieson, André Moenssens, eds., *Wiley Encyclopedia of Forensic Science*, Chichester: John Wiley & Sons, 3: 1436–1451.

FOUND Bryan, Douglas Rogers, R. Schmittat (1994) — "A Computer Program Designed to Compare the Spatial Elements of Handwriting," *Forensic Science International*, 68: 195–203.

——, Douglas Rogers, eds. (1999) — "Documentation of Forensic Handwriting Comparison and Identification Method: A Modular Approach," *J. of Forensic Document Examination*, 12: 1–68.

——, Jodi Sita, Douglas Rogers (1999) — "The Development of a Program for Characterising Forensic Handwriting Examiners' Expertise: Signature Examination Pilot Study," *J. of Forensic Document Examination*, 12: 69–80.

——, Douglas Rogers (2007) — "The Probative Character of Forensic Document Examiners' Identification and Elimination Opinions on Questioned Signatures," *Proc. of the 13th Conference of the International Graphonomics Society (IGS), 11–14 November 2007, Melbourne, Australia*, 175–178.

FRAENKEL Béatrice (1992) — *La signature* [The Signature], Paris: Gallimard.

FRANGIN Bernard (1964) — "Tournage du film 'Docteur Locard : l'heure du crime'" [Film Shooting of "Doctor Locard: The Crime Hour"], *Rhône Alpes actualités*, Lyon: Office national de radiodiffusion télévision française, accessed 2013.05.06, http://www.ina.fr/video/LXF99004238/tournage-du-film-docteur-locard-l-heure-du-crime-video.html.

FRANK Andrew, Arthur Asuncion (2010) — *UCI Machine Learning Repository*, online, accessed 2012.06.16, http://archive.ics.uci.edu/ml/.

FRANKE Y. Katrin (2005) — *The Influence of Physical and Biomechanical Processes on the Ink Trace. Methodological Foundations for the Forensic Analysis of Signatures*, PhD thesis, Groningen: University of Groningen.

——(2008) — personal communication, Norwegian Information Security Laboratory, Gjøvik University College, Gjøvik, Norway, 2008.01.26.

——(2012) — *Katrin Y. Franke Home Page*, online, accessed 2012.04.20. http://www.kyfranke.com.

——, Mario Köppen (2001) — "A Computer-Based System to Support Forensic Studies on Handwritten Documents," *International J. on Document Analysis and Recognition*, 3 (4): 218–231.

——, Isabelle Guyon, Lambert R.B. Schomaker, Luis G. Vuurpijl (2003a) — *WandaXML: A Data Standard for the Annotation and Storage of Handwriting Samples in the Context of (Computer-Based) Forensic Handwriting Analysis and Writer Identification*, Nijmegen: International Unipen Foundation, technical report.

——, Lambert R.B. Schomaker, Christian Veenhuis, Christian Taubenheim, Isabelle Guyon, Louis G. Vuurpijl, Merijn van Erp, Geertje Zwarts (2003b) — "WANDA: A Generic Framework Applied in Forensic Handwriting Analysis and Writer Identification," in Ajith Abraham, Mario Köppen, Katrin Franke, eds., *Design and Application of Hybrid Intelligent Systems*, Amsterdam: IOS Press, 927–938.

FRANKE Y. Katrin, Isabelle Guyon, Lambert R.B. Schomaker, Luis G. Vuurpijl (2004a) — "WandaML: A Markup Language for Digital Document Annotation," *Proc. of the 9th International Workshop on Frontiers in Handwriting Recognition (IWFHR), 26–29 October 2004, Tokyo, Japan*, 563–568.

——, Lambert R.B. Schomaker, Christian Veenhuis, Luis G. Vuurpijl, Merijn van Erp, Isabelle Guyon (2004b) — "WANDA: A Common Ground for Forensic Handwriting Examination and Writer Identification," *ENFHEX news: Bulletin of the European Network of Forensic Handwriting Experts*, 1 (4): 23–47.

——, Lambert R.B. Schomaker, Luis G. Vuurpijl, Stefan Giesler (2005) — "FISH-new = Wanda: A Common Ground for Writer Identification," *NICI/NFI meeting*, August 2005, presentation paper.

——, Sargur N. Srihari (2008) — "Computational Forensics: An Overview," *Proc. of the 2nd International Workshop on Computational Forensics, (IWCF), 7–8 August 2008, Washington, DC*, 1–10.

FRAYLING Christopher (2006) — *Mad, Bad and Dangerous? The Scientist and the Cinema*, London: Reaktion Books.

FREEMAN Jennifer (2007) — "Bringing Scientific Certainty to Handwriting Analysis," *Mason Research*, 28–30.

FRIEDMAN Batya, ed. (1997) — *Human Values and the Design of Computer Technology*, Stanford: CSLI Publications.

FSS (Forensic Science Service) (2012) — *Forensic Science Service Home Page*, online, accessed 2012.05.15. http://www.forensic.gov.uk.

FUJI (2000) — *Fuji v. U.S.*, 152 F.Supp.2d 939 (N.D.Ill. 2000).

GABEL Jessica D., Margaret D. Wilkinson (2008) — "'Good' Science Gone Bad: How the Criminal Justice System Can Redress the Impact of Flawed Forensics," *Hastings Law J.*, 59: 1001–1030.

GACEK Adam (2000) — "Tazwir," in P.J. Bearman et al., *The Encyclopaedia of Islam*, Leiden: Brill, 10: 408–409.

GALBALLY Javier, Réjan Plamondon, Julian Fierrez, Javier Ortega-Garcia (2012) — "Synthetic On-Line Signature Generation. Part I: Methodology and Algorithms," *Pattern Recognition*, 45: 2610–2621.

GALBRAITH Oliver III, Craig S. Galbraith, Nannette Galbraith (1995) — "The Principle of the 'Drunkard's Search' as a Proxy for Scientific Analysis: The Misuse of Handwriting Test Data in a Law Journal Article," *International J. of the Forensic Society Examiners*, 7.

GALPIN Vashti (2002) — "Women in Computing around the World," *SIGCSE [Special Group on Computer Science Education] Bulletin*, 34 (2): 94–100.

GANAGADHAR Garipelli, Denny Joseph, V. Srinivasa Chakravarthy (2007) — "A Computational Neuromotor Model of Parkinson," *Proc. of the 13th Conference of the International Graphonomics Society (IGS), 11–14 November 2007, Melbourne, Australia*, 75–78.

GANTZ Donald T., John J. Miller, Mark A. Walch (2005) — "Multi-Language Handwriting Derived Biometric Identification," *Proc. of the Symposium on Document Image Understanding Technology (SDIUT), 2–4 November 2005, College Park, MD*, 197–209.

GANTZ Donald T., John J. Miller, Mark A. Walch (2006) — "Application of Pictographic Recognition Technology for Spotting Handwritten Chinese Words," *Proc. of the Summit on Arabic and Chinese Handwriting (SACH), 27–28 September 2006, College Park, MD*, 75–86.

GARRETT Brandon L. (2008) — "Judging Innocence," *Columbia Law Review*, 108: 55–142.

GARRIS Michael D. (1992) — "Design and Collection of a Handwriting Sample Image Database," *Social Science Computer Review*, 10 (2): 196–214.

——(1994) — "Design, Collection, and Analysis of Handwriting Sample Image Database," in Allen Kent, James G. Williams, eds., *Encyclopedia of Computer Science and Technology*, New York: Marcel Dekker, 189–213.

GAUTHIER Jean-Paul (2000) — *Expertise en écritures : quel poids dans la balance ? Les affaires Dreyfus, Villemin, Omar Raddad* [Handwriting Expertise: How Worthy Is It? The Dreyfus, Villemin, and Omar Raddad Cases], Villeurbanne: Golias.

GEIST Jon, R. Allen Wilkinson, Stanley A. Janet, Patrick J. Grother, Bob Hammond, Norman W. Larsen, Randy M. Klear, Mark J. Matsko, Christopher J.C. Burges, Robert Creecy, Jonathan J. Hull, Tomas P. Vogl, Charles L. Wilson (1994) — *The Second Census Optical Character Recognition Systems Conference*, technical report, Gaithersburg, MD: National Institute of Standards and Technology.

GEMMERT Arend W.A. van, Hans-Leo Teulings, eds. (2006) — "Advances in Graphonomics: Studies on Fine Motor Control, Its Development and Disorders," *Human Movement Science*, 25 (4–5): 447–694.

GERKE Paul Konstantin (2010) — *Kinetic Online Trajectory Recovery from Static Images*, BA thesis, Nijmegen: Radboud University.

GIANNELLI Paul C. (2003) — "The Supreme Court's 'Criminal' Daubert Cases," *Seton Hall Law Review*, 33: 1071–1112.

GIESECKE Ⅎ DEVRIENT (2013) — *Giesecke & Devrient*, online, accessed 2013.04.05, http://www.gi-de.com.

GLADWELL Malcom (2007) — "Dangerous Minds: Criminal Profiling Made Easy," *The New Yorker*, 2007.11.12: 36–45.

GLISSON James K., Mary E. Morton, Allyn H. Bond, Michael Griswold (2011) — "Does an Education Intervention Improve Physician Signature Legibility? Pilot Study of a Prospective Chart Review," *Perspectives in Health Information Management*, 8 (Summer): 1–14.

GOMMEL Matthias, Martina Haitz, Jan Zappe (2010) — "The Bible Scribe," *Robotlab*, online, accessed 2012.12.26, http://www.robotlab.de/bios/bible_engl.htm.

GOODSTEIN David (2000) — "How Science Works," in Federal Judicial Center, *Reference Manual on Scientific Evidence*, Washington, DC: Federal Judicial Center, 2nd ed., 67–82.

GOUDREAULT Pierre (2010) — *Write-On 2.0 User Manual*, Ottawa, ON: Pikasso Software.

GRISSINGER Matthew (2010) — "Remote Computerized Prescriber Entry Errors—More Than 'Remotely' Possible," *Pharmacy and Therapeutics*, 35 (11): 594–595.

GROFF Elizabeth, Tom McEwen (2006) — *Exploring the Spatial Configuration of Places Related to Homicide*, technical report, Alexandria, VA: Institute for Law and Justice, 4–5.

GROTHER Patrick J. (1995) — *NIST Special Database 19. Handprinted Forms and Characters Database*, technical report, Gaithersburg, MD: National Institute of Standards and Technology.

GUCHET Xavier (2011) — "La biométrie à l'école : une approche anthropologique" [Biometrics in Schools: Anthropological Approach], in Ceyhan and Piazza 2011: 161–176.

GUIRAL Maggie (1927) — *La valeur de la preuve dans l'expertise des écritures* [The Probatory Value of Handwriting Expertise], PhD thesis, Lyon: Faculty of Law, University of Lyon.

GURRADO Maria (2009) — "Graphoskop, uno strumento informatico per l'analisi paleografica quantitative" [Graphoskop, an Computer Tool for the Quantitative Paleographical Analysis], in Malte Rehbein, Patrick Sahle, Torsten Schaßan, eds., *Codicology and Palaeography in the Digital Age*, Norderstedt: Books on Demand, 251–259.

GUYON Isabelle, Lambert R.B. Schomaker, Réjan Plamondon, M. Liberman, S. Janet (1994) — "UNIPEN Project of On-Line Data Exchange and Recognizer Benchmarks," *Proc. of the 12th International Conference on Pattern Recognition (ICPR), 9–13 October 1994, Jerusalem, Israel*, 2: 29–33.

HAIGHTON Angela (2010) — "Roman Methods of Authentication in the First Two Centuries AD," *J. of the Society of Archivists*, 31 (1): 29–49.

HALL Wendy, Lillian Israel, Tracy Camp, Paula Gabbert, Lucy Sanders, Telle Whitney (2008) — "ACM Membership Gender Study," *The Grace Hopper Celebration of Women in Computing, 1–4 October 2008, Keystone Resort, CO*.

HANUSIAK R.K., L.S. Oliveira, E. Justino, R. Sabourin (2012) — "Writer Verification using Texture-Based Features," *International J. on Document Analysis and Recognition*, 15: 213–226.

HARALAMBOUS Yannis (2007) — *Fonts & Encodings*, Sebastopol, CA: O'Reilly.

HARGETT John W. III (1994) — "The Utilization of Automated Handwriting Technology for Assisting Law Enforcement," *4th European Handwriting Conference for Police and Government Handwriting Experts, 12–14 October 1994, London*, presented paper.

HARRALSON Heidi H. (2013) — *Developments in Handwriting and Signature Identification in the Digital Age*, Waltham, MA: Anderson Publishing.

HARRIS John J. (2005) — "How Much Do People Write Alike: A Study of Signatures," *J. of Criminal Law, Criminology, and Police Science*, 48 (6): 647–651.

HARRISON Diana, Danielle P. Seiger (2003) — "Meeting the Daubert Challenge: A Bibliography of Handwriting Articles for the Forensic Document Examiner," *Forensic Science Communications*, 5 (1).

HARRISON Diana, Ted M. Burkes, Danielle P. Seiger (2009) — "Handwriting Examination: Meeting the Challenges of Science and the Law," *Forensic Science Communications*, 11 (4).

HARRISON Wilson R. (1966) — *Suspect Documents: Their Scientific Examination*, London: Sweet & Maxwell.

HASSAÏNE Abdelâali, Somaya Al-Ma'adeed, Jihad Mohamad Alja'am, Ali Jaoua, Ahmed Bouridane (2011) — "The ICDAR2011 Arabic Writer Identification Contest," *Proc. of the 11th International Conference on Document Analysis and Recognition (ICDAR), 18–21 September 2011, Beijing, China*, 1470–1474.

HAUSMANN Ricardo, Laura D. Tyson, Saadia Zahidi (2010) — *The Global Gender Gap Report 2010*, Geneva: World Economic Forum.

HAYNES Roslynn D. (1994) — *From Faust to Strangelove: Representation of the Scientist in Western Literature*, Baltimore, MD: The John Hopkins University Press.

HEINGARTNER Douglas (2003) — "Back Together Again," *New York Times*, online, accessed 2013.05.29, http://www.nytimes.com/2003/07/17/technology/back-together-again.html.

HEINRICH Stephan (2006) — *Innere Sicherheit und neue Informations- und Kommunikationstechnologien. Veränderungen des Politikfeldes zwischen institutionellen Faktoren, Akteursorientierungen und technologischen Entwicklungen* [National Security and the New Information and Communication Technologies. Transformations in Politics: Institutional Factors, Actors' Interests and Technological Developments], PhD thesis, Duisburg/Essen: University of Duisburg–Essen.

HEPLER Amanda B., Christopher P. Saunders, Linda J. Davis, JoAnn Buscaglia (2012) — "Score-Based Likelihood Ratios for Handwriting Evidence," *Forensic Science International*, 219 (1–3): 129–140.

HERBERTSON Gary (2002) — *Document Examination on the Computer: A Guide for Forensic Document Examiners*, Berkeley, CA: WideLine.

HEUVEL Elisa C. van den (2008) — personal communication, Netherlands Forensic Institute, The Hague, Netherlands, 2008.04.28.

HEYNE Wolfgang (1995) — "Mustererkennung und künstliche Intelligenz" [Pattern Recognition and Artificial Intelligence], in BKA (1995): 245–255.

HIRSHHORN Caryn (2000) — "Poor Penmanship Costs MD $225000," *The Canadian Medical Association J.*, 162 (1): 91.

HOFSTADTER Douglas R. (1996) — *Fluid Concepts & Creative Analogies: Computer Models of the Fundamental Mechanisms of Thought*, New York: Basic Books.

HOLT Cynthia (2006) — *Guide to Information Sources in the Forensic Sciences*, Englewood, CO: Libraries Unlimited.

HOLZAPFEL Jürgen, T. Rottes (2006) — "Toner Analysis. Methods for Classification and Identification of Toner-based Printed Material," *Digital Technology: The Document Examiner's Friend and Foe, 4th Conference of the European Document Experts Working Group (EDEWG), 27–30 September 2006, The Hague, Netherlands*, presented paper.

HOOK Christian, Juergen Kempf, Georg Scharfenberg (2003) — "New Pen Device for Biometrical 3D Pressure Analysis of Handwritten Characters, Words and Signatures," *Proc. of the 2003 ACM SIGMM Workshop on Biometrics Methods and Applications (WBMA), 8 November 2003, Berkley, CA*, 38–44.

HORTON Richard A. (1996) — "A Study of the Occurrence of Certain Handwriting Characteristics in a Random Population," *International J. of Forensic Document Examiners*, 2: 95–102.

HOUCK Max M. (2009) — "Is Forensic Science a Gateway for Women in Science?," *Forensic Science Policy and Management*, 1: 65–69.

——, Jay A. Siegel (2010) — *Fundamentals of Forensic Science*, Burlington, MA: Academic Press.

HUBER Peter (1993) — *Galileo's Revenge: Junk Science in the Courtroom*, New York: Basic Books.

HUDER Roy A. (1990) — "The Uniqueness of Writing," *48th Conference of the American Society of Questioned Document Examiners (ASQDE), 26 August 1990, San Jose, CA*, presented paper.

——(2000) — "The Heterogeneity of Handwriting," *J. of the American Society of Questioned Document Examiners*, 3 (1): 2–10.

——, Alfred M. Headrick (1999) — *Handwriting Identification: Facts and Fundamentals*, Boca Raton, FL: CRC Press.

HUGHES Thomas P. (2004) — *Human-Build World: How to Think about Technology and Culture*, Cambridge, MA: The MIT Press.

HULL Jonathan J. (1994) — "A Database for Handwritten Text Recognition Research," *IEEE Transactions on Pattern Analysis and Machine Intelligence*, 16 (5): 550–554.

IBG (International Biometric Group) (2005) — *Biometrics Market and Industry Report 2006–2010*, New York: IBG.

——(2008) — *Biometrics Market and Industry Report 2009–2014*, New York: IBG.

ICAO (International Civil Aviation Organization) (2006) — *Machine Readable Travel Documents (Doc 9303), Part 1: Machine Readable Passports, Volume 1: Passports with Machine Readable Data Stored in Optical Character Recognition Format*, Montréal, QC: ICAO.

ICAO (International Civil Aviation Organization) (2007) — *Machine Readable Travel Documents (MRTDs): History, Interoperability, and Implementation*, Montréal, QC: ICAO.

IDENTIFONT (2012) — *Identifont*, online, accessed 2012.05.02, http://www.identifont.com.

IFSA (Institute for Forensic Science Administration) (2012) — *IFSA*, online, accessed 2012.05.23, http://view.fdu.edu/default.aspx?id=3935.

IMPEDOVO Donato, Guiseppe Pirlo (2008) — "Automatic Signature Verification: The State of the Art," *IEEE Transaction on Systems, Man, and Cybernetics, Part C: Applications and Reviews*, 38 (5): 609–635.

IMPEDOVO Sebastiano, Giuseppe Facchini, Francesco Maurizio Mangini (2012) — "A New Cursive Basic Word Database for Bank-Check Processing Systems," *Document Analysis Systems*, 450–454.

INQUIRY (The Fingerprint Inquiry, Scottish Parliament) (2011) — *The Fingerprint Inquiry*, Edinburgh: APS Group Scotland.

INTERPOL (2012) — "The INTERPOL Global Complex for Innovation," *Interpol*, online, accessed 2012.05.24, http://www.interpol.int/About-INTERPOL/The-INTERPOL -Global-Complex-for-Innovation.

JACKSON Glen Paul (2009) — "The Status of Forensic Science Degree Programs in the United States," *Forensic Science Policy and Management*, 1: 2–9.

JAMIESON Allan (2008) — "The Philosophy of Forensic Scientific Identification," *Hastings Law J.*, 59: 1031–1046.

——, André Moenssens, eds. (2009) — *Wiley Encyclopedia of Forensic Science*, Chichester: John Wiley & Sons.

JENSEN Derrick, George Draffan (2004) — *Welcome to the Machine: Science, Surveillance, and the Culture of Control*, White River Junction, VT: Chelsea Green.

JIN Lianwen, Yan Gao, Gang Liu, Yunyang Li, Kai Ding (2010) — "SCUT-COUCH 2009: A Comprehensive Online Unconstrained Chinese Handwriting Database and Benchmark Evaluation," *International J. on Document Analysis and Recognition*, 14 (1): 53–64.

JOHNSON B. David (2010a) — "Science Fiction for Scientists!! An Introduction to SF Prototypes and Brain Machines," *Workshops Proc. of the 6th International Conference on Intelligent Environments, 18–19 July 2010, Kuala Lumpur, Malaysia*, 195–203.

——(2010b) — "Brain Machines," *Workshops Proc. of the 6th International Conference on Intelligent Environments, 18–19 July 2010, Kuala Lumpur, Malaysia*, 204–220.

JOHNSON Deborah G., John W. Snapper, eds. (1985) — *Ethical Issues in the Use of Computers*, Belmont, CA: Wadsworth.

JOHNSON Janet H. (1987) — "Ptolemaic Bureaucracy from an Egyptian Point of View," in M. Gibson, R. Biggs, eds., *The Organization of Power: Aspects of Administration in the Ancient, Medieval and Ottoman Middle East*, 141–49.

JOHNSON John (2011) — "Bank Robber Foiled by... Lousy Handwriting," *Newser*, online, accessed 2013.01.17. http://www.newser.com/story/133587/memo-to-bank-robbers-penmanship-counts.html.

JONG W.C. de, L.N. Kroon–van der Kooij, D.Ph. Schmidt (1994) — "Computer Aided Analysis of Handwriting, the NIFO–TNO Approach," *4th European Handwriting Conference for Police and Government Handwriting Experts, 12–14 October 1994, London*, presented paper.

JONG W.C. de, W. Hulstijn, B.J.M. Kosterman, B.C.M. Smits-Engelsman (1996) — "OASIS Software and Its Application in Experimental Handwriting Research," in M.L. Simner, C.G. Leedham, A.J.W.M. Thomassen, eds., *Handwriting and Drawing*

Research: Basic and Applied Issues, Amsterdam: IOS, 429–440.

JULIAN R.D., S.F. Kelty, C. Roux, P. Woodman, J. Robertson, A. Davey, R. Hayes, P. Margot, A. Ross, H. Sibly, R. White (2011) — "What Is the Value of Forensic Science? An Overview of the Effectiveness of Forensic Science in the Australian Criminal Justice System Project," *Australian J. of Forensic Sciences*, 43 (4): 217–229.

JUNAIDI Akmal, Szilárd Vajda, Gernot A. Fink (2011) — "Lampung: A New Handwritten Character Benchmark: Database, Labeling and Recognition," *Proc. of the 2011 Joint Workshop on Multilingual OCR and Analytics for Noisy Unstructured Text Data (MOCR AND), 17 September 2011, Beijing, China*, 105–112.

KAESTLE Frederika A., Ricky A. Kittles, Andrea L. Roth, Edward J. Ungvarsky (2006) — "Database Limitations on the Evidentiary Value of Forensic Mitochondrial DNA Evidence," *American Criminal Law Review*, 43: 53–88.

KADMON Naftali (2000) — *Toponymy: The Lore, Laws, and Language of Geographical Names*, New York: Vantage Press.

KAFKA Ben (2012) — *The Demon of Writing: Power and Failures of Paperwork*, New York: Zone Books.

KAM Moshe, Joseph Wetstein, Robert Conn (1994) — "Proficiency of Professional Document Examiners in Writer Identification," *J. of Forensic Sciences*, 39 (1): 5–14.

KAVALLIERATOU Ergina, N. Liolios, E. Koutsogeorgos, N. Fakotakis, G. Kokkinakis (2001) — "The GRUHD Database of Modern Greek Unconstrained Handwriting," *Proc. of the 6th International Conference on Document Analysis and Recognition (ICDAR), 10–13 September 2001, Seattle, WA*, 561–565.

KAYE David H. (2010) — "Probability, Individualization, and Uniqueness in Forensic Science Evidence: Listening to the Academies," *Brooklyn Law Review*, 75: 1163–1185.

KELLY Jan Seaman, Brian S. Lindblom, eds. (2006) — *Scientific Examination of Questioned Documents*, Boca Raton, FL: CRC Press.

KELTY Sally F., Roberta D. Julian, (2011) — "Success in Forensic Science Research and Other Collaborative Projects: Meeting Your Partners' Expectations," *Forensic Science Policy and Management*, 2 (3): 141–147.

KENNEDY Donald (2003) — "Forensic Science: Oxymoron?," *Science*, 2003.12.5 (302): 1625.

KENNEDY Noah (1989) — *The Industrialization of Intelligence: Mind and Machine in the Modern Age*, Boston, MA: Unwin Hyman.

KERKHOFF Axel (2011) — "Giving FISH a KISS: Current Developments in the German Handwriting Identification Service," *ENFHEX Conference, 26–29 October 2011, Delft, Netherlands*, presented paper.

KERMORVANT Christopher (2012) — personal communication, A2iA, Paris, France, 2012.04.24.

KERZNER Harold (2009) — *Project Management: A Systems Approach to Planning, Scheduling, and Controlling*, Chichester: John Wiley & Sons, 10th ed.

KHANNA Nitin, Aravind K. Mikkilineni, Edward J. Delp (2009) — "Forensic Camera Classification: Verification of Sensor Pattern Noise Approach," *Forensic Science Communications*, 11 (1).

KHOSRAVI Hossein, Ehsanollah Kabir (2007) — "Introducing a Very Large Dataset of Handwritten Farsi Digits and a Study on Their Varieties," *Pattern Recognition Letters*, 28: 1133–1141.

KIPPHAN Helmut, ed. (2001) — *Handbook of Print Media: Technologies and Production Methods*, Berlin: Springer.

KIRBY David A. (2011) — *Lab Coats in Hollywood: Science, Scientists, and Cinema*, Cambridge, MA: The MIT Press.

KIZZA Joseph Migga (2007) — *Ethical and Social Issues in the Information Age*, Berlin: Springer.

KLEBER Florian, Robert Sablatnig (2009) — "A Survey of Techniques for Document and Archaeology Artefact Reconstruction," *Proc. of the 10th International Conference on Document Analysis and Recognition (ICDAR), 26–29 July 2009, Barcelona, Spain*, 1061–1065.

KOEHLER Jonathan J., Michael J. Saks (2010) — "Individualization Claims in Forensic Science: Still Unwarranted," *Brooklyn Law Review*, 75: 1187–1208.

KOPPL Roger, Lawrence Kobilinsky (2005) — "Forensic Science Administration: Toward a New Discipline," *Proc. of the 31st Annual Northeastern Association of Forensic Scientists (NEAFS) Meeting, 8–12 November 2005, Newport, RI*, online, accessed 2012.05.23, http://alpha.fdu.edu/~koppl/fsa.doc.

KRANE Dan E., Simon Ford, Jason R. Gilder, Keith Inman, Allan Jamieson, Roger Koppl, Irving L. Kornfield, D. Michael Risinger, Norah Rudin, Marc Scott Taylor, William C. Thompson (2008) — "Sequential Unmasking: A Means of Minimizing Observer Effects in Forensic DNA Interpretation," *J. of Forensic Sciences*, 53 (4): 1006–7.

KRIMSKY Sheldon, Tania Simoncelli (2011) — *Genetic Justice: DNA Data Banks, Criminal Investigations, and Civil Liberties*, New York: Columbia University Press.

KROON–van der Kooij L.N. (1996) — "The NIFO–TNO System SCRIPT," *14th Meeting of the International Association of Forensic Sciences (IAFS), 26–30 August 1996, Tokyo, Japan*, presented paper.

KRUGER Diane (2008) — "The LongPen: The World's First Original Remote Signing Device," in AAFS (2011), *Annual Meeting 2008, Washington, DC*, presented paper, 45.

KUBE Edwin (1995) — "Kriminaltechnik zwischen aktuellen Problemen und Zukunftsorientierung" [Forensics between Present Problems and Future Development], in BKA (1994): 77–100.

KUHN Markus G. (2003) — *Compromising Emanations: Eavesdropping Risks of Computer Displays*, technical report UCAM-CL-TR-577, Cambridge: University of Cambridge.

LADD John (1985) — "The Quest for a Code of Professional Ethics: An Intellectual and Moral Confusion," in Deborah G. Johnson, John W. Snapper, eds., *Ethical Issues in the Use of Computers*, Belmont, CA: Wadsworth, 8–13.

LaFollette Marcel Chotkowski (1990) — *Making Science Our Own: Public Images of Science, 1910–1955*, Chicago, IL: University of Chicago Press.

——(2008) — *Science on the Air: Popularizers and Personalities on Radio and Early Television*, Chicago, IL: University of Chicago Press.

——(2013) — *Science on American Television: A History*, Chicago, IL: University of Chicago Press.

Lalam Nacer and Franck Nadaud (2011) — "La biométrie : un secteur rentable soutenu par la commande publique" [Biometrics: A Profitable Sector Supported by Public Procurements], in Ceyhan and Piazza 2011: 81–97.

Lance F. (2012) — "Scientific Theories: The Criteria for Science," *About.com*, online, accessed 2012.04.07, http://atheism.about.com/od/philosophyofscience/tp/Criteria ScientificTheory.htm.

Landauer Thomas K. (1997) — *The Trouble with Computers: Usefulness, Usability, and Productivity*, Cambridge, MA: The MIT Press.

Langlois-Peter Marie-Blanche (2012) — personal communication, National Institute of Scientific Police, Marseille, France, 2012.10.19.

Larriaga Marielle (1988) — *Moi, Edmond Locard, flic de province. Portrait d'un criminalogiste* [Me, Edmond Locard, Provincial Cop], Lyon: France Régions 3, Institut Lumière, accessed 2013.05.06, http://www.ina.fr/video/LXC01039267/ moi-edmond-locard-flic-de-province-video.html.

Lawless Christopher J. (2010) — *A Curious Reconstruction? The Shaping of 'Marketized' Forensic Science*, London: Centre for Analysis of Risk and Regulation, London School of Economics and Political Science.

——(2011) — "Policing Markets: The Contested Shaping of Neoliberal Forensic Science," *British J. of Criminology*, 51 (4): 671–689.

——, Robin Williams (2010) — "Helping with Inquiries or Helping with Profits? The Trials and Tribulations of a Technology of Forensic Reasoning," *Social Studies of Science*, 40 (5): 731–755.

LDC (2012) — *Linguistic Data Consortium*, online, accessed 2012.06.17, http://www. ldc.upenn.edu.

Lentini John J. (2009) — "Forensic Science Standards: Where They Come from and How They Are Used," *Forensic Science and Policy Management: An International J.*, 1 (1): 10–16.

Levinson J. (2001) — *Questioned Documents: A Lawyer's Handbook*, San Diego, CA: Academic Press.

Lewis David D., G. Agam, S. Argamon, O. Frieder, D. Grossman, J. Heard (2006) — "Building a Test Collection for Complex Document Information Processing," *Proc. of the 29th Annual International ACM Special Interest Group on Information Retrieval Conference on Research and Development in Information Retrieval (SIGIR), 6–9 August 2006, Seattle, WA*, 665–666.

Lewis Paul M. (2009) — *Ethnologue: Languages of the World*, Dallas, TX: SIL International, online, accessed 2012.06.05, http://www.ethnologue.com/web.asp.

LI Chi-keung, Nai-leung Poon, Wing-kam Fung, Chi-ting Yang (2005) — "Individuality of Handwritten Arabic Numerals in Local Population," *J. of Forensic Sciences*, 50 (1): 185–191.

LI Stan Z., Anil K. Jain, eds. (2009) — *Encyclopedia of Biometrics*, Berlin: Springer.

Lidz Franz (2011) — "We're Holding Your Plot Device. If You Want It Back, Send Us…," *The New York Times*, online, accessed 2013.05.29, http://www.nytimes.com/2011/07/03/movies/ransom-note-age-old-device-with-dramatic-payoff.html.

LIN Patrick, Keith Abney, George A. Bekey (2012) — *Robot Ethics: The Ethical and Social Implications of Robotics*, Cambridge, MA: The MIT Press.

LIN Zhouchen, Liang Wan (2007) — "Style-Preserving English Handwriting Synthesis," *Pattern Recognition*, 40: 2097–2109.

LINDBLOM Brian S. (2008) — "The Application of Write-On Document Comparison Software to Complex Handwriting Comparisons," in AAFS (2011), *Annual Meeting 2008, Washington, DC*, presented paper, 45.

LIU Cheng-Lin, Fei Yin, Da-Han Wang, Qiu-Feng Wang (2011) — "CASIA Online and Offline Chinese Handwriting Databases," *Proceeding of the 11th International Conference on Document Analysis and Recognition, 18–21 September 2011, Beijing, China*, 37–41.

LIWICKI Marcus, Horst Bunke (2008) — *Recognition of Whiteboard Notes: Online, Offline and Combination*, Singapore: World Scientific Publishing Co.

——, Elisa C. van den Heuvel, Brian Found, Muhammad Imran Malik (2010) — "Forensic Signature Verification Competition 4NSigComp2010: Detection of Simulated and Disguised Signatures," *Proc. of the 12th International Conference on Frontiers of Handwriting Recognition (ICFHR), 16–18 November 2010, Kolkata, India*, 715–720.

——, Muhammad Imran Malik, Elisa C. van den Heuvel, Xiaohong Chen, Charles Berger, Reinoud Stoel, Michael Blumenstein, Bryan Found (2011) — "Signature Verification Competition for Online and Offline Skilled Forgeries (SigComp2011)," *Proceeding of the 11th International Conference on Document Analysis and Recognition, 18–21 September 2011, Beijing, China*, 1480–1484.

——, Muhammad Imran Malik, Charles Berger, Elisa C. van den Heuvel, Reinoud Stoel, Bryan Found, Michael Blumenstein, Donato Impedovo, Giuseppe Pirlo, Miguel A. Ferrer (2012) — "Automatic Signature Verification: Where Are We Now and Where Should We Go?," submitted.

LOC (Library of Congress) (2012) — *Codes for the Representation of Names of Languages*, online, accessed 2012.06.05, http://www.loc.gov/standards/iso639-2/php/code_list.php.

LOCARD Edmond (1924) — *Policiers de roman et policiers de laboratoire* [Fiction Cops and Laboratory Cops], Paris: Payot.

——(1935–1937) — *Traité de criminalistique : L'expertise des documents écrits ; Les correspondances secrètes ; Les falsifications* [Treatise of Criminalistics: The Expertise of Written Documents; Secret Correspondence; Forgeries], Lyon: Joannès Desvigne, 5–6.

LOCARD Edmond (1937) — *L'affaire Dreyfus et l'expertise des documents écrits* [The Dreyfus affair and the Expertise of Written Documents], Lyon: Joannès Desvigne.

——(1955) — *Entretiens avec Edmond Locard* [Conversations with Edmond Locard], radio interview by Zitrone Léon and Madeleine Finidori, Radiodiffusion française, archives of the Institut national de l'audiovisuel, (2) 1955.09.08. http://www.ina.fr/video/PHD88007686/edmond-locard-2-video.html.

——(1957) — *Mémoires d'un criminologiste* [Recollections of a Criminologist], Paris: Fayard.

LOHR Sharon L. (2010) — *Sampling: Design and Analysis*, Boston, MA: Brooks/Cole.

LONGCAMP Marieke (2003) — *Étude comportementale et neurofonctionnelle des interactions perceptivo-motrices dans la perception visuelle de lettres. Notre manière d'écrire influence-t-elle notre manière de lire?* [Behavioral and Neuro-Functional Study of Somato-Sensory Interactions in Visual Perception of Letters. Does the Way in which We Write Influence the Way in which We Read?], PhD thesis, Aix-en-Provence/Marseille: University of Provence.

LOULOUDIS Georgios, Nikolaos Stamatopoulos, Basilis Gatos (2011) — "ICDAR 2011 Writer Identification Contest," *Proc. of the 11th International Conference on Document Analysis and Recognition (ICDAR), 18–21 September 2011, Beijing, China*, 1475–1479.

LOVE Nathaniel, Michael Genesereth (2005) — "Computational Law," *Proc. of the International Conference for Artificial Intelligence and Law (ICAIL), 6–11 June 2005, Bologna, Italy*, 205–209.

LUCENA-MOLINA Jose-Juan, Virginia Pardo-Iranzo, Joaquin Gonzalez-Rodriguez (2012) — "Weakening Forensic Science in Spain: From Expert Evidence to Documentary Evidence," *J. of Forensic Sciences*, 57 (4): 952–963.

LYNCH Michael, Simon Cole (2005) — "Science and Technology Studies on Trial," *Social Studies of Science*, 35 (2): 269–311.

LYON David (2003) — *Surveillance after September 11*, Cambridge & Oxford: Polity Press & Blackwell.

——(2011) — "Les insignes corporels : la biométrie comme perte de l'histoire personnelle" [Body Signs: Biometrics as Loss of Personal History], in Ceyhan and Piazza 2011: 347–373.

LYONS Ronan, Christopher Payne, Michael McCabe, Colin Fielder (1998) — "Legibility of Doctors' Handwriting: Quantitative Comparative Study," *British Medical J.*, 317 (7162): 863.

MAATEN Laurens van der (2009) — *A New Benchmark Dataset for Handwritten Character Recognition*, technical report 2009–002, Tilburg: Tilburg Centre for Creative Computing, Tilburg University.

MACKENZIE Donald, Judy Wajcman, eds. (1999) — *The Social Shaping of Technology*, Maidenhead: Open University Press, 2nd ed.

MACNEIL Heather (2000) — *Trusting Records: Legal, Historical, and Diplomatic Perspectives*, Dordrecht: Kluwer Academic Publishers.

MAES Pattie (1999) — "*Very* Personal Computers," in Peter J. Denning, ed., *Talking Back to the Machine: Computers and Human Aspirations*, New York: Copernicus, 37–44

MAINGUET Jean-François (2013) — *Movies & Biometrics*, online, accessed 2013.05.13, http://fingerchip.pagesperso-orange.fr/biometrics/movies.htm.

MALTONI Davide, Dario Maio, Anil K. Jain, Salil Prabhakar (2003) — *Handbook of Fingerprint Recognition*, Berlin: Springer.

MANO Junji, Lifeng He, Tsuyoshii Nakamura, Hiroshi Enowaki, Atsuko Mutoh, Hidenori Itoh (1999) — "A Method to Generate Writing-Brush-Style Japanese Hiragana Character Calligraphy," *Proc. of the 6th IEEE International Conference on Multimedia Computing and Systems (ICMCS), 7–11 June 1999, Florence, Italy*, 1: 787–791.

MANSUY Roger, Laurent Mazliak (2013) — "L'analyse controversée d'Alphonse Bertillon dans l'affaire Dreyfus. Polémiques et réflexions autour de la figure de l'expert" [The Controversial Expertise of Alphonse Bertillon in the Dreyfus Affair: Controversies and Reflections around the Character of the Expert], Pierre Piazza, ed., *Aux origines de la police scientifique. Alphonse Bertillon, précurseur de la science du crime* [At the Origins of the Scientific Police: Alphonse Bertillon, forerunner of the science of the crime], Paris: Karthala, 354–370.

MARCELLI Angelo, Carmela Chiaviello (2012) — personal communication, teleconference, Natural Computation Laboratory, University of Salerno, Salerno, Italy, 2012.06.19.

MARCUS Richard L. (2008) — "The Impact of Computers on the Legal Profession: Evolution or Revolution?," *Northwestern University Law Review*, 102: 1827–1867.

MARGOLIS Jane, Allan Fisher (2001) — *Unlocking the Clubhouse. Women in Computing*, Cambridge, MA: The MIT Press.

MARGOT Pierre (2011) — "Commentary on the Need for a Research Culture in the Forensic Sciences," *UCLA Law Review*, 58: 795–801.

MARTI Urs, Horst Bunke (2002) — "The IAM-Database: An English Sentence Database for Off-Line Handwriting Recognition," *International J. on Document Analysis and Recognition*, 5: 39–46. http://www.iam.unibe.ch/fki/databases/iam-handwriting-database.

MARTINEZ-DIAZ Marcos, Julian Fiérrez (2009) — "Signature Databases and Evaluation," in Stan Z. Li, Anil K. Jain, eds., *Encyclopedia of Biometrics*, Berlin: Springer, 1178–1185.

——, Seiichiro Hangai (2009) — "Signature Features," in Stan Z. Li, Anil K. Jain, eds., *Encyclopedia of Biometrics*, Berlin: Springer, 1185–1192.

MASSON Janet F. (2011) — "Scanned Images: How Well Do They Depict the Subtle Features in Handwriting?," in AAFS (2011), *Annual Meeting 2011, Chicago, IL*, presented paper, 5.

MASSONNET Geneviève, Florence Monnard (2009) — "Paint: Interpretation," in Allan Jamieson, André Moenssens, eds., *Wiley Encyclopedia of Forensic Science*, Chichester: John Wiley & Sons, 4: 1943–1953.

MATHIESEN Thomas (2000) — "On the Globalisation of Control: Towards an Integrated Surveillance System in Europe," in Penny Green, Andrew Rutherford, eds., *Criminal Policy in Transition*, Oxford: Hart Publishing, 167–192.

——(2006) — *Prison on Trial*, Winchester: Waterside Press.

MATLEY Marcel B. (2008) — *A Critical Evaluation of: "On the Discriminability of the Handwriting of Twins." 53(2) J. of Forensic Sciences, 430–446 (March 2008), by Sargur Srihari, Chen Huang and Harish Srinivasan*, posting to the members of the National Association of Document Examiners (NADE), online, accessed 2012. 05.15, http://archive.org/details/ACriticalEvaluationOfonTheDiscriminabilityOf TheHandwritingOfTwins.

MATUSZEWSKI Szymon (2011) — "Types of Handwriting Samples," *Problems of Forensic Sciences*, 87: 181–192.

MAXWELL Stephen, Jonathan Morris (2011) — "Validation and Accreditation of Handwriting Examination," *ENFHEX Conference, 26–29 October 2011, Delft, Netherlands,* presented paper.

MAZÉVET Michel (2006) — *Edmond Locard, le Sherlock Holmes français* [Edmond Locard, the French Sherlock Holmes], Lyon: Éditions des Traboules.

McCULLOUGH John (2009) — "Paint," in Allan Jamieson, André Moenssens, eds., *Wiley Encyclopedia of Forensic Science*, Chichester: John Wiley & Sons, 4: 1931–1943.

McGRATH COHOON Joanne, William Aspray (2006) — *Women and Information Technology: Research on Underrepresentation*, Cambridge, MA: The MIT Press.

McNAMARA Tim (2005) — "21st Century Shibboleth: Language Tests, Identity and Intergroup Conflict," *Language Policy*, 4: 351–370.

McQUISTON-SURRETT Dawn, Michael J. Saks (2008) — "Communicating Opinion Evidence in the Forensic Identification Sciences: Accuracy and Impact," *Hastings Law J.*, 59 (5): 1159–1189.

MEINTJES-VAN DER WALT Lirieka (2003) — "The Proof by the Pudding: The Presentation and Proof of Expert Evidence in South Africa," *J. of African Law*, 47 (1): 88–106.

MELSON Kenneth E., Ralph Keaton, John K. Neuner (2009) — "Accreditation: Laboratory," in Allan Jamieson, André Moenssens, eds., *Wiley Encyclopedia of Forensic Science*, Chichester: John Wiley & Sons, 1: 1–10.

MENDES Emilia (2008) — *Cost Estimation Techniques for Web Projects*, Hershey, PA: IGI Publishing.

MENSH Ivan N. (1942) — *The Identification of One's Own Handwriting: A Study in Legal Psychology*, Washington, DC: George Washington University.

MET (Metropolitan Police) (2012) — *Metropolitan Police Crime Mapping*, online, accessed 2012.05.10, http://maps.met.police.uk.

MEYER Bertand (2013) — "When Reviews Do More Than Sting," *Communications of the ACM*, 56 (2): 8–9.

MIYATA Hitomi, Makoto Shinozaki, Tomohito Nakayama, Toshiharu Enomae (2002) — "A Discrimination Method for Paper by Fourier Transform and Cross Correlation," *J. of Forensic Sciences*, 47 (5): 1125–1132.

MNOOKIN Jennifer L. (2001) — "Scripting Expertise: The History of Handwriting Identification Evidence and the Judicial Construction of Reliability," *Virginia Law Review*, 87 (8), 1723–1846.

——(2008) — "Of Black Boxes, Instruments, and Experts: Testing the Validity of Forensic Science," *Episteme: A J. of Social Epistemology*, 5 (3): 343–358.

——(2010) — "The Courts, the NAS, and the Future of Forensic Science," *Brooklyn Law Review*, 75: 1209–1275.

——, Simon A. Cole, Itiel E. Dror, Barry A.J. Fisher, Max M. Houck, Keith Inman, David H. Kaye, Jonathan J. Koehler, Glenn Langenburg, D. Michael Risinger, Norah Rudin, Jay A. Siegel, David A. Stoney (2011) — "The Need for a Research Culture in the Forensic Sciences," *UCLA Law Review*, 58: 725–779.

MOALLA Ikram, Frank Le Bourgeois, Hubert Emptoz, Adel M. Alimi (2006) — "Contribution to the Discrimination of the Medieval Manuscript Texts: Application in the Palaeography," *Proc. of the 7th International Conference on Document Analysis Systems (DAS), 13–15 February 2006*, Nelson, New Zealand, 25–37.

MOENSSENS André (2009) — "Cross-Examination of Experts," in Allan Jamieson, André Moenssens, eds., *Wiley Encyclopedia of Forensic Science*, Chichester: John Wiley & Sons, 2: 662–665.

MOHAMMED Linton A. (2009a) — "Alterations: Erasures and Obliterations of Documents," in Allan Jamieson, André Moenssens, eds., *Wiley Encyclopedia of Forensic Science*, Chichester: John Wiley & Sons, 1: 128–134.

MOSES Kenneth R. (2011) — "Automated Fingerprint Identification System (AFIS)," in Alan McRoberts, ed., *The Fingerprint Sourcebook*, Washington, DC: National Institute of Justice, 6-3–6-33.

MORPHOTRUST (2012) — *MorphoTrust*, online, accessed 2012.06.06, http://www.mor photrust.com.

MULLAN Kenneth (1989) — "Importance of Legible Prescriptions," *J. of the Royal College of General Practitioners*, 39 (325): 347–348.

MUNICH Mario E., Pietro Perona (2003) — "Visual Identification by Signature Tracking," *IEEE Transaction on Pattern Analysis and Machine Intelligence*, 25 (2): 200–217.

MYFONTS (2012) — "WhatTheFont!," *MyFonts*, online, accessed 2012.05.02, http:// www.myfonts.com/WhatTheFont/.

MYHRVOLD Nathan (1999) — "I, Software," in Peter J. Denning, *Talking Back to the Machine: Computers and Human Aspirations*, New York: Copernicus, 45–52.

NACJD (National Archive of Criminal Justice Data) (2012) — *NACJD*, online, accessed 2012.05.22, http://www.icpsr.umich.edu/icpsrweb/NACJD/index.jsp.

NARA (National Archives and Records Administration) (2007) — *Forensic Information System for Handwriting (FISH). Electronic Records Disposition Schedule*, request for records disposition authority, nr. MI-087-06-2, College Park, MD: NARA, online, accessed 2013.07.21, http://www.archives.gov/records-mgmt/rcs/

schedules/departments/department-of-homeland-security/rg-0087/n1-087-06-002_sf115.pdf.

NAS (National Academy of Sciences, Committee on Identifying the Needs of the Forensic Science Community) (2009) — *Strengthening Forensic Science in the United States: A Path Forward*, Washington, DC: The National Academies Press.

NEEF Sonja, José van Dijck, Eric Ketelaar (2006) — *Sign Here! Handwriting in the Age of New Media*, Amsterdam: Amsterdam University Press.

NELSON Lisa S. (2011) — *America Identified. Biometric Technology and Society*, Cambridge, MA: The MIT Press.

NEUMANN Cedric, Ian W. Evett, James E. Skerrett, Ismael Mateos-Garcia (2011) — "Quantitative Assessment of Evidential Weight for a Fingerprint Comparison. I. Generalisation to the Comparison of a Mark with Set of Ten Prints from a Suspect," *Forensic Science International*, 207 (1–3): 101–5.

——, Ian W. Evett, James E. Skerrett, Ismael Mateos-Garcia (2012) — "Quantitative Assessment of Evidential Weight for a Fingerprint Comparison. Part II: A Generalisation to take Account of the General Pattern," *Forensic Science International*, 214 (1–3): 195–9.

NFI (The Netherlands Forensic Institute) (2013) — "State-of-the-Art premises," *NFI Web site*, online, accessed 2013.05.06, http://www.forensicinstitute.nl/about_nfi/organisation_profile/state_of_the_art_premises/.

NGUYEN Daniel M.T., Derek L. Hammond, Michael J. Salyards (2011) — "Signature Frequency and Classification in the Military," in AAFS (2011), *Annual Meeting 2011, Chicago, IL*, presented paper, 4.

NICKOLAY Bertram (2010) — *Automatisierte virtuelle Rekonstruktion* [Automatic Virtual Reconstruction], Berlin: Fraunhofer-Institut für Produktionsanlagen und Konstruktionstechnik IPK.

NIELS Ralph M.J. (2010) — *Allograph based Writer Identification, Handwriting Analysis and Character Recognition*, PhD thesis, Nijmegen: Donders Center for Brain, Behavior and Cognition, Radboud University Nijmegen.

——, Louis Vuurpijl, Lambert R.B. Schomaker (2005) — "Introducing TRIGRAPH: Trimodal Writer Identification," *ENFSI Conference of the European Network of Forensic Handwriting Experts (ENFHEX), 10–12 November 2005, Budapest, Hungary*.

NIELSEN Jakob (1993) — *Usability Engineering*, San Diego: Morgan Kaufmann.

NIJ (National Institute of Justice) (2006) — *Status and Needs of Forensic Science Service Providers: A Report to Congress*, Washington, DC: NIJ.

—— (2011) — *FY 2009-10: Forensic Science Discretionary Awards Made by the National Institute of Justice's (NIJ) Forensic Science Research and Development Program*, Washington, DC: NIJ, Office of Investigative and Forensic Sciences.

—— (2012) — "Questioned Documents: Research and Development Projects," *NIJ*, accessed 2012.06.17, http://nij.gov/topics/forensics/evidence/questioned-documents/projects.htm.

NIST (National Institute of Standards and Technology) (2012a) — "The History of Automatic Speech Recognition Evaluations at NIST," *NIST*, online, accessed 2012. 05.11, http://www.itl.nist.gov/iad/mig/publications/ASRhistory/.

——(2012b) — *NIST 2012 Open Handwriting Recognition and Translation Evaluation Plan*, Gaithersburg, MD: NIST.

——(2012c) — *NIST Special Database 19: NIST Handprinted Forms and Characters Database*, online, accessed 2012.06.13, http://www.nist.gov/srd/nistsd19.cfm.

NOCTIS Jeff (2010) — "Forensics vs Forensic Science," *Qondio*, online, accessed 2012. 05.22, http://textphonic.qondio.com/forensics-vs-forensic-science.

NORDBERG Peter (2012) — *Daubert on the Web*, online, accessed 2012.05.12, http://www.daubertontheweb.com.

NORMAN Donald A. (2002) — *The Design of Everyday Things*, New York: Basic Books.

NPIA (National Policing Improvement Agency) (2012) — "National DNA Database: Statistics," *NPIA*, online, accessed 2012.06.19, http://www.npia.police.uk/en/13338.htm.

NRC (National Research Council: Committee on Technologies to Deter Currency Counterfeiting, Board on Manufacturing and Engineering Design, Division on Engineering and Physical Sciences) (2007) — *A Path to the Next Generation of U.S. Banknotes: Keeping Them Real*, Washington, DC: National Academies Press.

NSF–DSRS (National Science Foundation, Division of Science Resources Statistics) (2011) — *Women, Minorities, and Persons with Disabilities in Science and Engineering: 2011. Special Report NSF 11-309*, Arlington, VA: NSF, accessed 2012.10.24, http://www.nsf.gov/statistics/wmpd/.

NSF–NCSES (National Science Foundation, National Center for Science and Engineering Statistics) (2011) — *Science and Engineering Degrees: 1966–2008. Detailed Statistical Tables NSF 11-316*, Arlington, VA: NSF, online, accessed 2012.10.24, http://www.nsf.gov/statistics/nsf11316/.

NUSSDORFER Laurie (2009) — *Brokers of Public Trust: Notaries in Early Modern Rome*, Baltimore, MD: The John Hopkins University Press.

NVVB (2012) — "ID Protocol: Bijlage 2 overzicht ID instrumenten" [Annex 2 Overview of ID Instruments], *Nederlandse Vereniging voor Burgerzaken* [Dutch Society of Civil Affairs], online, accessed 2012.06.06, http://www.nvvb.nl/pro ducten-en-projecten/id-protocol.

NYT (*The New York Times*) (1899) — "Bertillon Accuses Dreyfus," 1899.08.26.

OBERTHUR (2013) — *Oberthur Technologies*, online, accessed 2013.04.05, http://www.oberthur.com.

OCQUETEAU Frédéric, Philippe Pichon (2011) — "Les impacts discutables de l'identification biométrique et de la traçabilité des personnes dans les pratiques policières" [The Dubious Impact of the Biometrical Identification and Tracking in Law Enforcement], in Ceyhan and Piazza 2011: 217–234.

OECD (Organization for Economic Cooperation and Development) (2006) — *Evolution of Student Interest in Science and Technology Studies: Policy Report*, Paris: OECD.

OED (Oxford English Dictionary) (2012) — "forensic, adj. and n.," *Oxford English Dictionary*, Oxford: Oxford University Press, online, accessed 2012.10.10, http://www.oed.com/view/Entry/73107?result=4&rskey=ENUzMW&.

OLIVE Joseph P. (2007) — *Multilingual Automatic Document Classification Analysis and Translation (MADCAT), BAA 07-38 Proposer Information Pamphlet*, Arlington, VA: Defense Advanced Research Projects Agency (DARPA), Information Processing Techniques Office (IPTO).

OMBELLI Diana, Fons Knopjes (2008) — *Documents: The Developer's Kit*, Geneva, Lisbon: International Organization for Migration, Via Occidentalis.

OSBORN Albert Sherman (1929) — *Questioned Documents*, Albany, NY: Boyd, 2nd ed.

PAGE Mark, Jane Taylor, Matt Blenkin (2011) — "Uniqueness in the Forensic Identification Sciences. Fact or Fiction?," *Forensic Science International*, 206: 12–18.

PAL Srikanta, Michael Blumenstein, Umapada Pal (2011) — "Non-English and Non-Latin Signature Verification Systems: A Survey," *Proc. of the 1st International Workshop on Automated Forensic Handwriting Analysis (AFHA), Beijing, China, 17–18 September 2011*, 1–5.

PALENIK Christopher S., Samuel J. Palenik (2004) — "Forensic Science and Academic Science," *Science*, 303: 1136.

PANCHASI Roxanne (1996) — "Graphology and the Science of Individual Identity in Modern France," *Configurations*, 4.1: 1–31.

PANSEGRAU Petra (2008) — "Stereotypes and Images of Scientists in Fiction Films," in Bernd Hüppauf, Peter Weingart, eds., *Science Images and Popular Images of the Sciences*, New York: Routledge, 257–256.

PARADISE Jordan, Susan M. Wolf, Jennifer Kuzma, Aliya Kuzhabekova, Alison W. Tisdale, Efrosini Kokkoli, Gurumurthy Ramachandran (2009) — "Developing U.S. Oversight Strategies for Nanobiotechnology: Learning from Past Oversight Experiences," *J. of Law, Medicine & Ethics*, 37 (4): 688–705.

PARK Roger C. (2008) — "Signature Identification in the Light of Science and Experience," *Hastings Law J.*, 59: 1101–1157.

PEARSON Greg, A. Thomas Young, eds. (2002) — *Technically Speaking: Why All Americans Need to Know More about Technology*, Washington, DC: National Academy Press.

PEDERSEN Thomas T. (2012) — *Transliteration of Non-Roman Scripts: A Collection of Transliteration and Transcription Tables for Various Writing Systems*, online, accessed 2012.06.05, http://transliteration.eki.ee.

PELLAT Solange (1927) — *Les lois de l'écriture*, Paris: Vuibert.

PETERSON Joseph L., Matthew J. Hickman (2005) — *Census of Publicly Funded Forensic Crime Laboratories, 2002*, Washington, DC: US Department of Justice, Bureau of Justice Statistics.

PETERSON Joseph L., Ira Sommers, Deborah Baskin, Donald Johnson (2010) — *The Role and Impact of Forensic Evidence in the Criminal Justice Process*, Washington, DC: US Department of Justice, National Institute of Justice.

PETRUCCI Armando (1993) — *Public Lettering: Script, Power, and Culture*, Chicago, IL: University Of Chicago Press.

PETTUS (2012) — *Pettus vs. United States*, 08–CF–1361, DCCA.

PHILLIPP M. (1992) — "Efficiency Control Studies of the FISH System under Real World Conditions," *Proc. of the 3rd European Conference of Police Handwriting Experts, 5–7 October 1992, Rome, Italy*, presented paper.

——(1994) — "Expected Future Developments in the Forensic Information System Handwriting (FISH)," *4th European Handwriting Conference for Police and Government Handwriting Experts, 12–14 October 1994, London*, presented paper.

——(1996) — *Fakten zu FISH, Das Forensische Informations-System Handschriften des Bundeskriminalamtes. Eine Analyse nach über 5 Jahren Wirkbetrieb* [Facts about FISH, the Forensic Information System Handwriting of the Federal Criminal Police Agency. An Analysis after More Than Five Years of Operation], technical report, Wiesbaden: Kriminaltechnisches Institut 53, Bundeskriminalamt.

PHILLIPS James G., Friedmann Müller, Rowen P. Ogeil (2007a) — "Alcohol Intoxication and Handwriting: A Kinematic Analysis," *Proc. of the 13th Conference of the International Graphonomics Society (IGS), 11–14 November 2007, Melbourne, Australia*, 83–87.

——, Doug Rogers, Rowen P. Ogeil (2007b) — "Alcohol Intoxication and Handwriting: Spatial Characteristics," *Proc. of the 13th Conference of the International Graphonomics Society (IGS), 11–14 November 2007, Melbourne, Australia*, 162–166.

PIAZZA Pierre (2011) — "Les résistances à la biométrie en France" [The Resistance to Biometrics in France], in Ceyhan and Piazza 2011: 377–394.

PLAMONDON Réjan (1995) — "A Kinematic Theory of Rapid Human Movements, Part I: Movement Representation and Generation," *Biological Cybernetics*, 72: 295–307.

PLOEG Irma Van der (2011) — "Le corps biométrique : différences corporelles, normes intégrées et classifications automatisées" [The Biometric Body: Corporal Differences, Integrated Norms, and Automatic Classifications], in Ceyhan and Piazza 2011: 217–234.

PLUME (2010) — "Musée des Lettres et Manuscrits : Rendez-vous au 222 Boulevard Saint-Germain" [Museum of Letters and Manuscripts: Meeting at 222 Saint-Germain Boulevard], *Plume : Le magasin du patrimoine écrit* [Quill: The Magazine of the Written Heritage], May–June 2010. Also: http://www.museedeslettres.fr.

PNNL (Pacific Northwest National Laboratory) (2013) — *Starlight Information Visualization System*, online, accessed 2013.05.22, http://starlight.pnnl.gov.

PODLAS Kimberlianne (2006) — "'The CSI Effect:' Exposing the Media Myth," *Fordham Intellectual Property, Media and Entertainment Law J.*, 16: 429–465.

PRAKKEN Henry, Giovanni Sartor (2006) — *Logical Models of Legal Argumentation*, Dordrecht: Kluwer Academic Publishers.

PREUSS-LAUSSINOTTE Sylvia (2011) — "L'encadrement juridique des bases de données biométriques européennes" [Juridical Framework of European Biometric Databases], in Ceyhan and Piazza 2011: 303–326.

PRIME (2005) — *United States vs. Prime*, 431 F.3d 1147, 9th Circuit.

PSAPF (Purdue Sensor and Printer Forensics) (2012) — *Purdue Sensor and Printer Forensics*, online, accessed 2012.05.11, https://engineering.purdue.edu/~prints/.

PU Danjun, Gregory R. Ball, Sargur N. Srihari (2009) — "A Machine Learning Approach to Off-Line Signature Verification Using Bayesian Inference," *Proc. of the 3rd International Workshop on Computational Forensics (IWCF), 13–14 August 2009, The Hague, Netherlands*, 125–136.

QUINCHE Nicolas (2011) — *Sur les traces du crime. De la naissance du regard indicial à l'institutionnalisation de la police scientifique et technique en Suisse et en France. L'essor de l'Institut de police scientifique de l'Université de Lausanne* [In the Footsteps of Crime: From the Birth of Identification to the Institutionalization of the Scientific and Technical Police in Switzerland and in France; The Growth of the Forensic Institute at the University of Lausanne], Genève: Slatkine.

——— (2012) — "Taire, transmettre ou prostituer sa science, les experts divergent : utilité et dangers de la vulgarisation du savoir criminalistique en Suisse romande et en France (1900–1960)" [Conceal, Communicate, or Prostitute One's Science — The experts Diverge: The Utility and Dangers of Popularizing the Forensic Knowledge in French-Speaking Switzerland and in France (1900–1960)], in Michaël Meyer, ed., *Médiatiser la police, policer les médias* [Popularizing the Police, Policing the Media], Lausanne: Antipodes, 21–37.

RAVENEAU Jacques (1666) — *Traité des inscriptions en faux et reconnoissances d'escritures et signatures par comparaison et autrement* [Treatise on Forged Writings and the Expertise of Handwriting and Signatures by Comparison and Otherwise], Paris: T. Joly.

REICHMAN Amnon (2007) — "The Production of Law (and Cinema)," *bepress Legal Series*, paper 1997, accessed 2013.05.06, http://law.bepress.com/expresso/eps/1997.

REHBEIN Malte, Patrick Sahle, Torsten Schaßan (2009) — *Codicology and Palaeography in the Digital Age*, Norderstedt: Books on Demand.

RENARD WARD Jean (2006) — *Annotated Bibliography in On-Line Character Recognition, Pen Computing, Gesture User Interfaces and Tablet and Touch Computers*, online, accessed 2012.0528, http://rwservices.no-ip.info:81/biblio.html.

RENESSE Rudolf L. van, ed. (1998) — *Optical Document Security*, Delft: TNO Institute of Applied Physics, 2nd ed.

RENESSE Rudolf L. van (2005) — *Optical Document Security*, Boston: Artech House, 3rd ed.

RIBAUX Olivier, Amélie Baylon, Claude Roux, Olivier Delémont, Éric Lock, Christian Zingg, Pierre Margot (2010a) — "Intelligence-Led Crime Scene Processing. Part I: Forensic Intelligence," *Forensic Science International*, 195: 10–16.

RIBAUX Olivier, Amélie Baylon, Claude Roux, Olivier Delémont, Éric Lock, Christian Zingg, Pierre Margot (2010b) — "Intelligence-Led Crime Scene Processing. Part II: Intelligence and Crime Scene Examination," *Forensic Science International*, 199: 63–71.

RISINGER D. Michael (2007) — "Cases Involving the Reliability of Handwriting Identification Expertise Since the Decision in *Daubert*. Appendix to Goodbye to All That, or a Fool's Errand, by One of the Fools: How I Stopped Worrying about Court Responses to Handwriting Identification (and Forensic Science in General) and Learned to Love Misinterpretations of *Kumho Tire v. Carmichael*," *Tulsa Law Review*, 42 (2): 477–596.

——(2010) — "Whose Fault?—Daubert, The NAS Report, And The Notion Of Error In Forensic Science," *Fordham Urban Law J.*, 38 (2): 519–545.

——, Mark Denbeaux, Michael J. Saks (1989) — "Exorcism of Ignorance as a Proxy for Rational Knowledge: The Lessons of Handwriting Identification Expertise," *University of Pennsylvania Law Review*, 137: 731–792.

——, Michael J. Saks (1996) — "Science and Non-Science in the Courts: *Daubert* Meets Handwriting Identification Expertise," *Iowa Law Review*, 82: 21–74.

——, Mark P. Denbeaux, Michael J. Saks (1998) — "Brave New 'Post-*Daubert* World'—A Reply to Professor Moensses, *Seton Hall Law Review*, 29: 405-490.

——, Michael J. Saks, William C. Thompson, Robert Rosenthal (2002) — "The *Daubert/ Kumho* Implications of Observer Effects in Forensic Science: Hidden Problems of Expectation and Suggestion," *California Law Review*, 90: 1–56.

RITZER George (1996) — *The McDonaldization of Society*, Thousand Oaks, CA: Pine Forge Press.

ROANE Kit R., Dan Morrison (2005) — "The *CSI* Effect: On TV, It's All Slam-Dunk Evidence and Quick Convictions. Now Juries Expect the Same Thing—And That's a Big Problem," *U.S. News & World Report*, 2005.04.25, online, accessed 2013.05.20, http://www.usnews.com/usnews/culture/articles/050425/25csi.htm.

ROBINSON Alex (1994) — "An Ounce of Prevention Could Eliminate Most Prescription-Writing Errors, MDs Advised," *The Canadian Medical Association J.*, 151 (5): 659–661.

RODRIGUEZ-VERA F. Javier, Y. Marin, A. Sanchez, C. Borrachero, E. Pujol (2002) — "Illegible Handwriting in Medical Records," *J. of the Royal Society of Medicine*, 95 (11): 545–546.

ROOT-BERNSTEIN Robert (1984) — "On Defining a Scientific Theory: Creationism Considered," in M.F. Ashley Montagu, ed., *Science and Creationism*, Oxford: Oxford University Press, 64–94.

ROSCHACH Ernest (1866-7) — "Signets authentiques des notaires de Toulouse du XIIIᵉ au XVIᵉ siècle" [Authentical Notary Signs of Toulouse from the 13th to the 16th Century], *Revue archéologique du Midi de la France*, 1: 142–152.

ROSS Arun A., Karthik Nandakumar, Anil K. Jain (2006) — *Handbook of Multibiometrics*, Berlin: Springer.

ROSSMO D. Kim (2000) — *Geographic Profiling*, Boca Raton, FL: CRC Press.

ROWLES Genevieve L., Bryan Found, Ian R. Dadour (2006) — "Graffiti Tagging Behavior and Its Forensic Identification," in AAFS (2011), *Annual Meeting 2006, Denver, CO*, presented paper, 61.

ROYALL Richard M. (1997) — *Statistical Evidence. A Likelihood Paradigm*, New York: Chapman & Hall.

RUSU Amalia, Achint Oommen Thomas, Venu Govindaraju (2009) — "Generation and Use of Handwritten CAPTCHAs," *International J. of Document Analysis and Recognition*, 13 (1): 49–64.

RÜCKERT Peter, Sandra Hodecek, Emanuel Wenger (2009) — *Bull's Head and Mermaid. The History of Paper and Watermarks from the Middle Ages to the Modern Period*, Vienna: Bernstein Consortium.

SAKS Michael J. (2003a) — "Commentary on: Srihari SN, Cha S-H, Arora H, Lee S. Individuality of Handwriting. *J Forensic Sci* 2002; 47(4):856–72," *J. of Forensic Sciences*, (48) 4: 916–918.

—— (2003b) — *Videotaped Deposition of Michael D. Saks, Ph.D.*, in U.S. v. William Emmett Lecroy, Jr., No. 2:02-CR-38, Tempe, Arizona, 2003.12.05.

—— (2010) — "Forensic identification: From a faith-based 'Science' to a scientific science," *Forensic Science International*, 201: 14–17.

——, Jonathan J. Koehler (2008) — "The Individualization Fallacy in Forensic Science Evidence," *Vanderbilt Law Review*, 61 (1): 199-219.

——, Holly VanderHaar (2005) — "On the 'General Acceptance' of Handwriting Identification Principles," *J. of Forensic Science*, 50 (1): 119–126.

——, David L. Faigman (2008) — "Failed Forensics: How Forensic Science Lost Its Way and How It Might Yet Find It," *Annual Review of Law and Social Sciences*, 4: 149–171.

SASSOON Rosemary (1995) — *The Acquisition of a Second Writing System*, Oxford: Intellect.

—— (2007) — *Handwriting of the Twentieth Century*, Bristol: Intellect.

SAUNDERS Christopher P., Linda J. Davis, Andrea C. Lamas, John J. Miller, Donald T. Gantz (2011) — "Construction and Evaluation of Classifiers for Forensic Document Analysis," *The Annals of Applied Statistics*, 5 (1): 381–399.

SAUVAGEAU Anny, Sébastien Desnoyers, Anny Godin (2009) — "Mapping the Literature in Forensic Sciences: A Bibliometric Study of North-American Journals from 1980 to 2005," *The Open Forensic Science J.*, 2: 41–46.

SCHIFFER Beatrice, Eric Stauffer (2009) — "Accreditation: Organizational," in Allan Jamieson, André Moenssens, eds., *Wiley Encyclopedia of Forensic Science*, Chichester: John Wiley & Sons, 1: 10–16.

SCHNEIDER K.A., C.W. Murray, R.D. Shadduck, D.G. Meyers (2006) — "Legibility of Doctors' Handwriting Is as Good (or Bad) as Everyone Else's," *Quality and Safety in Health Care*, 15: 445.

SCHOMAKER Lambert R.B. (2007) — "Writer Identification and Verification," in Nalini K. Ratha, Venu Govindaraju, eds., *Advances in Biometrics: Sensors, Systems and Algorithms*, Berlin: Springer, 247–264.

——, Louis G. Vuurpijl (2000) — *Forensic Writer Identification: A Benchmark Dataset and a Comparison of Two Systems*, technical report, Nijmegen: Nijmegen Institute for Cognition and Information, University of Nijmegen.

SCHÖLL Rudolf, Wilhelm Kroll (2009) — *Corpus Iuris Civilis*, Hildesheim: Weidmann, online, accessed 2012.08.12, http://web.upmf-grenoble.fr/Haiti/Cours/Ak/.

SCHREIBER Marion (1981) — "'Wir fühlten uns einfach stärker': SPIEGEL-Redakteurin Marion Schreiber über Frauen in der Terrorszene" ["We simply felt stronger": SPIEGEL-Editor Marion Schreiber on Women among the Terrorists], *Der Speigel*, 20: 46–51.

SCHWID Bonnie L., Lynn Wilson Marks (1994) — "Forensic Analysis of Handwriting in Multiple Personality Disorder," in Claudie Faure, P. Keuss, Guy Lorette, Annie Vinter, *Advances in Handwriting Drawings: A Multidisciplinary Approach*, Paris: Europia, 501–513.

SCIACCA Emmanuelle, Jean-Luc Velay, Marie-Blanche Langlois, Jean-Claude Gilhodes, Pierre Margot (2007) — "Study of Within-Subject Handwriting Variability under Usual and Unusual Writing Conditions," *Proc. of the 13th Conference of the International Graphonomics Society (IGS), 11–14 November 2007, Melbourne, Australia*, 110–113.

SCOTT Samuel Parsons (1932) — *The Civil Law*, Cincinnati, OH: The Central Trust Co., accessed 2012.08.12, http://www.constitution.org/sps/sps.htm.

SEDEYN Marie-Jeanne (1998) — *Standard Handwriting Objective Examination "SHOE,"* Mereuil: Fovea.

SELIN Ann-Sofie (2003) — *Pencil Grip. A Descriptive Model and Four Empirical Studies*, Åbo: Åbo University Press.

SELTZER Mark (2007) — *True Crime: Observations on Violence and Modernity*, New York: Routledge.

SEMTA (Sector Skills Council for Science, Engineering and Manufacturing Technologies) (2004) — *Forensic Science: Implications for Higher Education 2004*, Hertfordshire: SEMTA.

SENGERS Phoebe (2004) — "The Agents of McDonaldization," in Sabine Payr and Robert Trappl, *Agent Culture: Human–Agent Interaction in a Multicultural World*, Mahwah, NY: Lawrence Erlbaum, 3–19.

SÉROPIAN Audrey, M. Grimaldi, Nicole Vincent (2003) — "Writer Identification Based on the Fractal Construction of a Reference Base," *Proc. of the 7th International Conference on Document Analysis and Recognition (ICDAR), 3–6 August 2003, Edinburgh, Scotland, United Kingdom*, 1163–1167.

SHEDROFF Nathan, Christopher Noessel (2012) — *Make It So: Interaction Design Lessons from Science Fiction*, New York: Rosenfeld Media.

SHF (Signature & Handwriting Forensics) (2012) — *SHF*, online, accessed 2012.05.13, http://www.signatureforensic.com.au.

SHIN Yong (2009) — *Technology Transfer of Forensic Document Analysis System: Final Report*, Williamsville, NY: CedarTech.

SHIVER Farrell C. (1996) — "Case Report: The Individuality of Handwriting Demonstrated through the Field Screening of 1000 Writers," *54th Conference of the American Society of Questioned Document Examiners (ASQDE), 24–28 August 1996, Washington, DC*, presented paper.

SIEGEL Jay A. (2009) — "Education and Accreditation in Forensic Science," in Allan Jamieson, André Moenssens, eds., *Wiley Encyclopedia of Forensic Science*, Chichester: John Wiley & Sons, 2: 897–902.

SIGCOMPO9 (2009) — *Signature Verification Competition: On- and Offline Skilled Forgeries*, online, accessed 2012.06.21, http://sigcomp09.arsforensica.org/index.php/Competition/Competition.

SIRAT Colette, Jean Irigoin, Emmanuel Poulle (1990) — *L'Écriture : le cerveau, l'œil et la main* [Writing: Brain, Eye, and Hand], Turnhout: Brepols.

SITA Jodi, Bryan Found, Douglas K. Rogers (2002) — "Forensic Handwriting Examiners' Expertise for Signature Comparison," *J. of Forensic Sciences*, 47 (5): 1117–1124.

SLIMANE Fouad, Rolf Ingold, Slim Kanoun, Adel M. Alimi, Jean Hennebert (2009) — "A New Arabic Printed Text Image Database and Evaluation Protocols," *Proc. of the 10th International Conference on Document Analysis and Recognition (ICDAR), 26–29 July 2009, Barcelona, Spain*, 946–950.

SMALLWOOD Scott (2002) — "As Seen on TV: 'CSI' and 'The X-Files' Help Build Forensic Programs," *The Chronicle of Higher Education*, 48 (45): A8–A10.

SMIT Jinna (2011) — "The Death of the Palaeographer? Experiences with the Groningen Intelligent Writer Identification System (GIWIS)," *Archiv für Diplomatik: Schriftgeschichte, Siegel- und Wappenkunde*, (57): 413–426.

SOLIS Jorge, Carlo A. Avizzano, Massimo Bergamasco (2002) — "Teaching to Write Japanese Characters Using a Haptic Interface," *Proc. of the 10th Symposium on Haptic Interfaces for Virtual Environment and Teleoperator Systems (HAPTICS), 24–25 March 2002, Orlando, FL*, 255–262.

SPIEGEL (1979) — "Rest Unbehagen" [Discomfortable Guests], *Der Speigel*, 39: 46–51.

SRIHARI Sargur N. (2005) — "Authors' Response," *J. of Forensic Sciences*, (48) 4: 919–920.

——(2010) — *Computational Methods for Handwritten Questioned Document Examination*, technical report, Williamsville, NY: CedarTech.

——, Sung-Hyuk Cha, Hina Arora, Sangjik Lee (2002) — "Individuality of Handwriting," *J. of Forensic Sciences*, 47: 856–872.

——, Graham Leedham (2003) — "A Survey of Computer Methods in Forensic Document Examination," *Proc. of the 11th International Graphonomics Society Conference (IGS), 2–5 November 2003, Scottsdale, AZ*, 278–281.

——, C. Huang, H. Srinivasan (2008) — "On the Discriminability of the Handwriting of Twins," *J. of Forensic Sciences*, 53: 430–446.

SRIHARI Sargur N., Yong C. Shin, et al. (2009) — *Method and Apparatus for Analyzing and/or Comparing Handwritten and/or Biometric Samples*, Patent 7.580.551.

ST2AR (Skill-Task Training Assessment & Research) (2012) — *ST2AR*, online, accessed 2012.05.13, http://www.st2ar.org.

STAALDUINEN Mark van (2010) — *Content-Based Paper Retrieval. Towards Reconstruction of Art History*, Delft: Delft University of Technology.

STAUFER Eric, Beatrice Schiffer (2009) — "Training and Certification (in Criminalistics)," in Allan Jamieson, André Moenssens, eds., *Wiley Encyclopedia of Forensic Science*, Chichester: John Wiley & Sons, 5: 2545–2555.

STEENBERG Lindsay (2013) — *Forensic Science in Contemporary American Popular Culture: Gender, Crime, and Science*, New York: Routledge.

STEINKE Jocelyn (2003) — "Media Images of Women Engineers and Scientists and Adolescent Girls' Conceptions of Future Roles," *Proc. of the 2003 WEPAN National Conference [Women in Engineering ProActive Network], 8–11 June 2003, Chicago, IL*, accessed 2013.05.06, http://ojs.libraries.psu.edu/index.php/wepan/article/view/58329/58017.

——(2005) — "Cultural Representations of Gender and Science: Portrayals of Female Scientists and Engineers in Popular Films," *Science Communication*, 27 (1): 27–63.

SKAL David J. (1998) — *Screams of Reason: Mad Science and Modern Culture*, New York: W.W. Norton & Co.

STOEL Reinoud (2011) — "Towards a Context-Management Approach in Forensic Handwriting Examination," *ENFHEX Conference, 26–29 October 2011, Delft, Netherlands*, presented paper.

STONE Alan A. (1984) — *Law, Psychiatry and Morality: Essays and Analysis*, Washington, DC: American Psychiatric Press.

STONE Debbie, Caroline Jarrett, Wark Woodroffe, Shailey Minocha (2005) — *User Interface Design and Evaluation*, San Francisco: Morgan Kaufmann.

STRASSEL Stephanie M. (2009) — "Linguistic Resources for Arabic Handwriting Recognition," *Proc. of the 2nd International Conference on Arabic Language Resources & Tools, 22–23 April 2009, Cairo, Egypt*, 37–41.

STRUGALA Claire (2011) — "Développement de la biométrie et droit au respect de la vie privée : un droit lacunaire?" [Biometrics and Privacy: A Deficient Jurisprudence?], in Ceyhan and Piazza 2011: 275–302.

SWGDOC (Scientific Working Group for Forensic Document Examination) (2012a) — "Certification [of Forensic Document Examiners]," *SWGDOC*, online, accessed 2012.05.22, http://www.swgdoc.org/certification.htm.

——(2012b) — "Daubert Resources," *SWGDOC*, online, accessed 2012.05.12, http://www.swgdoc.org/daubert_resources.htm.

TAGOUGUI Najiba, Monji Kherallah, Adel M. Alimi (2012) — "Online Arabic Handwriting Recognition: A Survey," *International J. on Document Analysis and Recognition*, online pre-publication.

TARONI Franco, Christophe Champod, Pierre Margot (1999) — "Forerunners of Bayes-ianism in Early Forensic Science," *J. of Forensic Identification*, 49 (3): 285–305.

——, Colin G.G. Aitken, Paolo Garbolino, Alex Biedermann (2006) — *Bayesian Networks and Probabilistic Inference in Forensic Science*, Chichester: John Wiley & Sons.

——, Silvia Bozza, Alex Biedermann, Paolo Garbolino, Colin G.G. Aitken (2010) — *Data Analysis in Forensic Science. A Bayesian Decision Perspective*, Chichester: John Wiley & Sons.

TEULINGS Hans-Leo, G.E. Stelmach (1991) — "Control of Stroke Size, Peak Acceleration, and Stroke Duration in Parkinsonian Handwriting," *Human Movement Science*, 10: 315–334.

THOMPSON William C. (1997) — "A Sociological Perspective on the Science of Forensic DNA Testing," *UC Davis Law Review*, 30 (4): 1113–1136.

THORNTON Tamara Plakins (1998) — *Handwriting in America: A Cultural History*, New Haven, CT: Yale University Press.

TOTH Bori (2004) — *Biometric Security*, n.p.: Deloitte.

TIMES (London) (1999) — "Fear Raised by Euro Police Computer," *The Times*, 1999.01.02, online, accessed 2013.04.25, http://www.thetimes.co.uk, http://www.fitug.de/de bate/9901/msg00012.html.

TOGNAZZINI Bruce (1992) — *Tog on Interface*, Reading, MA: Addison-Wesley.

TREGAR Kirsten L., Gloria Proni (2010) — "A Review of Forensic Science Higher Education Programs in the United States: Bachelor's and Master's degrees," *J. of Forensic Science*, 55 (6): 1488–1493.

TRESSELTA M.E. (1946) — "A Study of the Factors in the Identification of Handwriting," *J. of Social Psychology*, 24 (1): 101–109.

TURNER Barry (2009) — "Expert Opinion in Court: A Comparison of Approaches," in Allan Jamieson, André Moenssens, eds., *Wiley Encyclopedia of Forensic Science*, Chichester: John Wiley & Sons, 2: 1004–1007.

TÜRK Alex (2011) — "La biométrie vue par le CNIL et le G29" [Biometrics as Seen by the CNIL and the G29], in Ceyhan and Piazza 2011: 259–274.

TYAN Émile (1945) — "Le notariat et le régime de la preuve par écrit dans la pratique du droit musulman" [The Notary and the Proof by Writing in the Practice of Islamic Law], *Annales de l'École française de Droit de Beyrouth*, 2: 3–99.

UCSB (University of California, Santa Barbara) (2013) — *The AlloShphere Research Facility*, online, accessed 2013.05.22, http://www.allosphere.ucsb.edu.

UIOWA (University of Iowa) (2012) — "Part V. Chapter 7: Facsimile Signatures and Signature Assignment," *University of Iowa Operations Manual*, Iowa City, IA: UIowa, accessed 2012.07.01, http://www.uiowa.edu/~our/opmanual/index.html.

UNICODE (The Unicode Consortium) (2012a) — *Codes for the Representation of Names of Scripts*, accessed 2012.06.05, http://www.unicode.org/iso15924/codelists.html.

UNICODE (The Unicode Consortium) (2012b) — *The Unicode Standard*, Mountain View, CA: The Unicode Consortium, accessed 2012.06.05, http://www.unicode.org.

UNODC (United Nations Office on Drugs and Crime) (2010) — *Guide for the Development of Forensic Document Examination Capacity*, New York / Vienna: UNODC.

——(2011) — *Staff Skill Requirements and Equipment Recommendations for Forensic Science Laboratories*, New York / Vienna: UNODC.

VAN PATTEN Isaac T., Paul Q. Delhauer (2007) — "Sexual Homicide: A Spatial Analysis of 25 Years of Deaths in Los Angeles," *J. of Forensic Sciences*, 52 (5): 1129–1141.

VUURPIJL G. Louis, Lambert R.B. Schomaker (1997) — "Finding Structure in Diversity: A Hierarchical Clustering Method for the Categorization of Allographs in Handwriting," *Proc. of the 4th International Conference on Document Analysis and Recognition (ICDAR), 18–20 August 1997, Ulm, Germany*, 387–393.

WAGGONER Kim (2007) — "The FBI Laboratory: 75 Years of Forensic Science Service," *Forensic Science Communications*, 9 (4): 4, accessed 2013.05.06, http://www.fbi.gov/about-us/lab/forensic-science-communications/fsc/oct2007/re search/2007_10_research01_test4.htm.

WALCH Mark A. (1993) — *Image Recognition System*, Patent 5.267.332.

——(2008) — *Systems and Methods for Biometric Identification Using Handwriting Recognition*, Patent 7.362.901 B2.

——(2010a) — *Systems and Methods for Identifying Characters and Words in a Document*, Patent 7.724.956 B2.

——(2010b) — *Systems and Methods for Biometric Identification Using Handwriting Recognition*, Patent 7.724.958 B2.

——, Donald T. Gantz (2004) — "Pictographic Matching: A Graph-Based Approach towards a Language Independent Document Exploitation Platform," *Proc. of the 1st ACM Workshop on Hardcopy Document Processing, 8–13 November 2004, Washington, DC*, 53–62.

WALLACH Wendell, Colin Allen (2009) — *Moral Machines: Teaching Robots Right from Wrong*, Oxford: Oxford University Press.

WALSH Simon J. (2009) — "Databases," in Allan Jamieson, André Moenssens, eds., *Wiley Encyclopedia of Forensic Science*, Chichester: John Wiley & Sons, 2: 677–684.

——, John S. Buckleton (2009) — "DNA Databases and Evidentiary Issues," in Allan Jamieson, André Moenssens, eds., *Wiley Encyclopedia of Forensic Science*, Chichester: John Wiley & Sons, 2: 831–839.

WAN Liang, Zhouchen Lin (2009) — "Signature Sample Synthesis," in Stan Z. Li, Anil K. Jain, eds., *Encyclopedia of Biometrics*, Berlin: Springer, 1205–1210.

WANG Jue, Chenyu Wu, Ying-Qing Xu, Heung-Yeung Shum (2004) — "Combining Shape and Physical Models for Online Cursive Handwriting Synthesis," *International J. on Document Analysis and Recognition*, 7 (4): 219–227.

WAYMAN James, Nicholas Orlans, eds. (2008) — *Technology Assessment for the State of the Art Biometrics Excellence Roadmap: Face, Iris, Ear, Voice, and Handwriter Recognition*, McLean, VA: MITRE Corporation, vol. 2.

WEBERLING Johannes, Giselher Spitzer, eds. (2007) — *Virtuelle Rekonstruktion „vorvernichteter" Stasi-Unterlagen. Technologische Machbarkeit und Finanzierbarkeit – Folgerungen für Wissenschaft, Kriminaltechnik und Publizistik* [Virtual Reconstruction of Pre-Destroyed Stasi Documents. Technical Feasibility and Financial Burden—Implications for Science, Forensics and Humanities], Berlin: Berliner Landesbeauftragten für die Unterlagen des Staatssicherheitsdienstes der ehemaligen DDR, 2nd ed.

WEINBERG Gerald M. (1971) — *The Psychology of Computer Programming*, Melbourne: Van Nostrand Reinhold.

WEINGART Peter (2008) — "The Ambivalence Towards New Knowledge: Science in Fiction Film," in Bernd Hüppauf, Peter Weingart, eds., *Science Images and Popular Images of the Sciences*, New York: Routledge, 267–281.

WEYERMANN Céline (2009) — "Dating: Document," in Allan Jamieson, André Moenssens, eds., *Wiley Encyclopedia of Forensic Science*, Chichester: John Wiley & Sons, 3: 684–692.

WIKIPEDIA (contributors) (2012a) — "Affaire Dreyfus," *Wikipedia: The Free Encyclopedia*, online, accessed 2012.05.17, http://fr.wikipedia.org/wiki/Affaire_Dreyfus.

——(2012b) — "Daubert Standard," *Wikipedia: The Free Encyclopedia*, online, accessed 2012.05.12, http://en.wikipedia.org/wiki/Daubert_standard.

——(2013a) — "Le Corbeau (Film, 1943)," *Wikipedia: The Free Encyclopedia*, online, accessed 2013.05.02, http://fr.wikipedia.org/wiki/Le_Corbeau_(film,_1943).

——(2013b) — "Edmond Locard," *Wikipedia: The Free Encyclopedia*, online, accessed 2013.05.02, http://fr.wikipedia.org/wiki/Edmond_Locard.

——(2013c) — "Semi-Automatic Ground Environment," *Wikipedia: The Free Encyclopedia*, online, accessed 2013.04.25, http://en.wikipedia.org/wiki/Semi-Automatic_Ground_Environment.

——(2013d) — "Tape Library," *Wikipedia: The Free Encyclopedia*, online, accessed 2013.05.01, http://en.wikipedia.org/wiki/Tape_library.

WILL Emily J. (2010) — "Progress in Digital Microscopy: A Technical Review of the Miscope Digital Microscope, *J. of Forensic Document Examination*, vol. 20.

WILLEMS Don, Ralph Niels (2008) — *Definitions for Features Used in Online Pen Gesture Recognition*, technical report, Nijmegen: Nijmegen Institute of Cognition and Information (NICI), Radboud University Nijmegen.

WILKINS Kelly (2011) — "The History of Handwriting Analysis in America," *Kelly Wilkins: Forensic Handwriting Analyst*, online, accessed 2012.05.26, http://www.thehandwritinganalyst.com/hwa_usa/.

WILKINSON R. Allen, Michael D. Garris, Jon Geist (1992a) — *Machine-Assisted Human Classification of Segmented Characters for OCR Testing and Training*, technical report, Gaithersburg, MD: National Institute of Standards and Technology.

——, Jon Geist, Stanley Janet, Patrick J. Grother, Christopher J.C. Burges, Robert Creecy, Bob Hammond, Jonathan J. Hull, Norman W. Larsen, Tomas P. Vogl, Charles L. Wilson (1992b) — *The First Census Optical Character Recognition Systems Conference*, technical report 4912, Gaithersburg, MD: National Institute of Standards and Technology.

WOLF Lior, Nachum Dershowitz, Liza Potikha, Tanya German, Roni Shweka, Yaacov Choueka (2011) — "Automatic Paleographic Exploration of Genizah Manuscripts," in Franz Fischer, Christiane Fritze, Georg Vogeler, eds., *Codicology and Palaeography in the Digital Age 2*, Norderstedt: Books on Demand, 157–179.

WOLMAN David (2012) — "Fraud U: Toppling a Bogus-Diploma Empire," *Wired*, online, accessed 2012.06.23, http://www.wired.com/magazine/2009/12/ff_fake_physics/all/.

WOODWARD John D. Jr., Nicholas M. Orlans, Peter T. Higgins (2003) — *Biometrics. Identity Assurance in the Information Age*, New York: McGraw-Hill / Osborne.

WYNNE M., ed. (2005) — *Developing Linguistic Corpora: A Guide to Good Practice*, Oxford: Oxbow Books, accessed 2012.04.13, http://www.ahds.ac.uk/creating/guides/linguistic-corpora/.

YAMASAKI Tosjinori, Tetsuo Hattori (1996) — "Forming Square-Styled Brush-Written Kanji through Calligraphic Skill Knowledge," *Proc. of the 3rd IEEE International Conference on Multimedia Computing and Systems (ICMCS), 17–23 June 1996, Hiroshima, Japan*, 501–504.

YAFFE Philip (2013) — "The Sixteen Character Traits of Science," Ubiquity Symposium "The Science In Computer Science," *Ubiquity*, March 2013, accessed 2013.04.30, http://ubiquity.acm.org/article.cfm?id=2447479.

YAO Fenghui, Guifeng Shao, Jianqiang Yi (2004) — "Trajectory Generation of the Writing–Brush for a Robot Arm to Inherit Block–Style Chinese Character Calligraphy Techniques," *Advanced Robotics*, 18 (3): 331–356.

YEUNG Dit-yan, Hong Chang, Yimin Xiong, Susan George, Ramanujan Kashi, Takashi Matsumoto, Gerhard Rigoll (2004) — "SVC2004: First International Signature Verification Competition," *Proc. of the International Conference on Biometric Authentication (ICBA), 15–17 July 2004, Hong Kong*, 16–22.

ZAJAC Rachel, Harlene Hayne (2009) — "Cross-Examination: Impact on Testimony," in Allan Jamieson, André Moenssens, eds., *Wiley Encyclopedia of Forensic Science*, Chichester: John Wiley & Sons, 2: 656–662.

ZEMON DAVIS Natalie (1983) — *The Return of Martin Guerre*, Cambridge, MA: Harvard University Press.

ZEZIMA Katie (2011) — "The Case for Cursive," *New York Times*, online, accessed 2012.06.21, http://www.nytimes.com/2011/04/28/us/28cursive.html.

ZWEIG Mark H., Gregory Campbell (1993) — "Receiver-Operating Characteristic (ROC) Plot: A Fundamental Evaluation Tool for Clinical Medicine," *Clinical Chemistry*, 39 (4): 561–577.

Index

3D (three-dimensional), 31, 33,
36, 50, 98, 99, 126, 128, 129
9/11 (September 11, 2001, terrorist
attacks), 29, 60, 87
See also cases

A

AAFS, *see* American Academy
of Forensic Sciences
accessibility, 46, 50, 100, 121
access, to resources, 14, 16, 17,
25, 31, 38, 39, 44, 47, 56, 81,
99, 113, 117, 120, 122, 125
acquisition, 15, 33, 50, 96, 110, 125, 126
AD751, 121, 127
See also software items
admissibility, 18, 57, 67–69, 76, 77
AFIS, *see* Automated Fingerprint
Information System
AKIM, 121, 122
See also databases and software items
allographs, 27, 34, 36, 48,
98, 99, 123, 125, 128
alterations, *see* charred; shredded
Americas, 132
See also regions
American Academy of Forensic
Sciences (AAFS), 12, 13, 31, 35, 94,
95, 101, 103, 106, 108, 109, 123
anthrax (attacks), 16, 58
See also cases
antiquity, 35, 62, 67, 122
anonymous letters, 17n7, 114, 134, 136
See also dataset types
anthropologists, 4, 19n1, 17, 78
See also management; police
Arabic (script | style), 16, 35n2, 35,
47, 60, 99, 116, 122, 123
See also script items

architecture, 66
archives, 16, 25, 28, 33, 35, 36, 45, 47,
49, 59, 100, 113, 114, 120, 124
Arkansas State Crime Laboratory, 122
art history, 93
Asia, 17, 79, 106, 132
See also regions
aspects (document), 11, 12, 14, 28,
45, 47, 49, 97–100, 102, 128, 129
ATF, *see* Bureau of Alcohol,
Tobacco and Firearms
Australia, 57, 59, 69n7, 103, 109, 118, 122
See also countries
Australian Police, 122
Austrian Federal Criminal Police
Office (BKA-AT), 114
authentication, of banknotes, 39n5
autoforgery 15, 99
See also disguise; forgery
autographs, 113, 114, 120
Automated Fingerprint Information
System (AFIS), 59, 73
See also biometrics: fingerprints

B

banks, banking, bankers, x,
12, 28, 29, 39, 50, 76
banknotes, 14, 17, 29n6, 37, 37n11,
38n1, 38n2, 96, 99, 117, 118
bank robbery notes, 10, 28, 58, 92, 114
See also dataset types
barcodes, 39, 96, 99
Basque (region; script | style), 47
See also regions
Bayes, Thomas, 63
See also people
Bayesian (theory), 63n1, 63n3, 80, 81
See also frequentist
benchmarking, *see* performance

— Out of the darkness of the unknown comes bright spark of light!

TRIBUTE

In *Charlie Chan's Chance* (2007 [1932]) the detective solves a murder mystery by discovering in an inkwell a pearl from a broken necklace—a most symbolic and poetic tribute to forensic documents by the cinema.

Credits

COVER

Front: *Bat Curry*. Bats (蝠 fú) are traditional Chinese symbols of good fortune (福 fú) because the two words sound alike. Picture by the author, from the doors of the imperial bedchamber in the Hall of Spiritual Cultivation, Forbidden City, Beijing, 2011; cover design by the author, with Nicolas Perrin (http://www.btws.ch), and Elisabeth Brügger; **Back, p. 198:** *Sartor*, Jean-Marc Ménadier; after a painting by Marco Giovanni (1576–?)

PICTURES

Pages vi, viii: *Computer Dreams*, Vlad Atanasiu; 7-bit punched paper tape for computers; **x:** © 1935, Twentieth Century Fox, All Rights Reserved; **1:** Metro-Goldwyn-Mayer & Stanley Kubrick; **2:** Talkback Thames; **6, 7:** Janus Film; **8:** Python (Monty) Pictures; American Broadcasting Company; **9:** Columbia Pictures; Nero-Film; **10:** Artisan Entertainment; **20:** Star Film; **21:** Anabase Production; **22:** Société française de production cinématographique; **23:** Warner Brothers Pictures; **24:** Constantin Film Produktion; **41:** Warner Brothers Pictures; **42:** Frères Lumière; Nero-Film; Warner Brothers Pictures; Warner Brothers Pictures; **43:** Universal Pictures; **44:** Twentieth Century Fox; **51:** Metro-Goldwyn Mayer & Stanley Kubrick; Twentieth Century Fox; **52:** Athos Films; Universal Pictures; HandMade Films; Paramount Pictures; **53:** Universum Film; Hyde Fundraisers; **54:** Embassy International Pictures; Escándalo Films; Lucasfilm; **65:** Office de Radiodiffusion-télévision française; **84:** Mapleton Films; Granada Television; **85:** Universal TV; **86:** Sveriges Television & Matador Film; **89:** Wiedemann & Berg Filmproduktion; **90:** Metro-Goldwyn-Mayer; Magnolia Filmproduktion; Globo Filmes; Cinema City; Dreamworks; **91:** Warner Brothers Pictures; **92:** Dog Run Pictures; **133:** Miramax Films; **134:** Warner Brothers Pictures; Comacico; Continental Films; **135, 136:** Warner Brothers Pictures; **196:** Twentieth Century Fox

FONTS

Text set in Adobe Egyptienne (created 1956) and Adobe Frutiger (1976), both by Adrian Frutiger (1928–); titles in Linotype Optima (1952) by Hermann Zapf (1918–), Linotype Eurostile (1962) by Aldo Novarese (1920–1995), and Nick Fonts Moonshine Script (2004) by Nick Curtis (1948–); small caps in FontShop Olsen (2001) by Morten Rostgaard Olsen (1964–); and Chinese characters in DynaLab BiaoKaiShu

Book layout by the author ⊕ a Kumagoro design
The bear appreciates paper and adores ink (Edmond Locard)

VLAD ATANASIU bid farewell to an engineering school on the fringes of Transylvania to study Oriental civilizations and linguistics in France and the Middle East. After much travel for fieldwork and a book on statistics of calligraphy later, he earned his PhD at the École pratique des Hautes Études in Paris with a thesis on Mamluk and Persian paleography and went on to study cognitive sciences at the Massachusetts Institute of Technology. As coordinator of the European project "Bernstein" at the Austrian Academy of Sciences he developed image processing and geographical information software for the analysis and history of paper. For ParisTech Telecom, Paris, he did research on writer identification. Presently he is teaching information visualization and studying for his second PhD, in the computer science field of document engineering, at the University of Fribourg, Switzerland. Vlad doesn't bite before midnight.

atanasiu@alum.mit.edu
http://alum.mit.edu/www/atanasiu/